"For many years, Bruce Perry's work has been deserving of our highest praise. This book is his crowning achievement, the ultimate combination of science and humanity."

—JOEL A. DVOSKIN, PH.D., ABPP, University of Arizona College of Medicine, and President, American Psychology-Law Society

"*The Boy Who Was Raised as a Dog* is Bruce Perry's finest achievement... It gives us the opportunity to unlock the deepest mystery of our species: why some children turn out to be heroes and others to be predatory sociopaths. Anyone who wants to understand childhood trauma and its heartbreaking consequences must read this book."

—ANDREW VACHSS, best-selling author of *Mask Market* and founder and national advisory board member of PROTECT: The National Association to Protect Children

"Filled with compassionate, caring stories by a wise healer and scientist, this book will appeal to all who are interested in understanding how children heal."

—LYNN PONTON, M.D., author of *The Romance of Risk*

"I have admired and respected Bruce Perry for over a decade. His commitment to helping young children raised in chaotic and abusive environments is nothing short of remarkable. This book is an important tool in helping us understand the critical impact of early experiences in children's lives, and it shows us how to help those who have been damaged by neglect. Anyone who deals with vulnerable or troubled youth—from social workers to judges, daycare workers to high school teachers, parents to politicians—can gain important perspectives from this book."

—ROB REINER

"In this harrowing but profoundly humane book, Perry and Szalavitz provide an all too timely, utterly engrossing account of traumatized children's lives... Once I opened it, I could not put it down."

—SARAH BLAFFER HRDY, author of *Mother Nature: Maternal Instincts and How They Shape the Human Species*

THE BOY
WHO WAS
RAISED
AS A DOG

THE BOY
WHO WAS
RAISED
AS A DOG

*And Other Stories from a Child
Psychiatrist's Notebook*

What Traumatized Children Can Teach Us
About Loss, Love, and Healing

BRUCE D. PERRY, MD, PhD,
and MAIA SZALAVITZ

BASIC BOOKS
New York

Basic Books
Hachette Book Group
1290 Avenue of the Americas, New York, NY 10104
www.basicbooks.com
@BasicBooks

Printed in the United States of America
Second Trade Paperback Edition: August 2017
Published by Basic Books, an imprint of Perseus Books, LLC, a subsidiary of Hachette Book Group, Inc.

The Hachette Speakers Bureau provides a wide range of authors for speaking events. To find out more, go to www.hachettespeakersbureau.com or call (866) 376-6591.

The publisher is not responsible for websites (or their content) that are not owned by the publisher.

Print book interior design by Tabitha Lahr.

The Library of Congress has catalogued the hardcover as follows
Perry, Bruce Duncan, 1955–
The boy who was raised as a dog : and other stories from a child psychiatrist's notebook : what traumatized children can teach us about loss, love, and healing / Bruce D. Perry, Maia Szalavitz
p. cm.
Includes bibliographical references and index.
ISBN-13: 978-0-465-05652-1 (alk. paper) ISBN-10: 0-465-05652-0 (alk. paper)
1.   Child psychiatry—Popular works. 2. Psychic trauma in children— Case studies.
I. Szalavitz, Maia. II. Title. [DNLM 1. Stress Disorders, Post-Traumatic—therapy—Case Reports. 2. Child Psychiatry—Case Reports. WM 170 P462b 2006] RJ499.34.P47   2006
618.92'89—dc22

ISBN: 978-0-465-09445-5 (2017 paperback)
ISBN: 978-0465-09446-2 (2017 e-book)

LSC-C

10   9   8   7   6

Contents

Author's Note

THE STORIES IN THIS BOOK are all true, but in order to ensure anonymity and protect privacy, we have altered identifying details. The children's names have been changed, as have the names of their adult family members if that information would identify the child. All other adult names are real names, except those identified with an asterisk. Despite these necessary changes, the essential elements of each case are reported as accurately as possible. Conversations, for example, are depicted as recalled and/or as recorded in notes, audio tapes, or video.

The sad reality is that these stories are but a tiny percentage of the many we could have told. Over the last ten years, our clinical group at The ChildTrauma Academy has treated more than a hundred children who have witnessed the murder of a parent. We have worked with hundreds of children who endured severe early neglect in institutions or at the hands of their parents or guardians. We hope that the strength and spirit of the children whose stories we tell in this book, and the many others who have suffered similar fates, come through on these pages.

Preface to the 2017 Edition

ONE LATE AFTERNOON IN THE SPRING of 2001, I was sitting in the Minneapolis-St. Paul Airport listening to my voicemail. I had spent the whole day talking; first to community leaders at a breakfast meeting, then at an all-day training session for clinicians working with maltreated children, and finally, at a meeting with academic colleagues who were hosting my visit. After fourteen hours of talking, the last thing I wanted to do was be on the phone there were dozens of messages waiting. I decided to return just one call and deal with the rest later.

Maia Szalavitz, a science writer and reporter, wanted to get my thoughts for a story she was writing. Maia and I had spoken before. I liked her; she was very curious, well prepared, asked great questions, and, to the degree possible in the popular press, was accurate with both the context and content of our conversations when she wrote her final story. Unlike most of the journalists I had run into, she always read the key scientific literature related to the stories she was writing—and was willing to read more. She also had a deadline.

I have no recollection of what we talked about, but at the end of the call she said, "You should write a book."

"I've thought about it, but I just don't have time. And the currency of academics is research articles and grants. Although I like to write—maybe someday—but I'm just too busy."

"I can help; we can write it together." And this started a series of conversations that led to our ongoing collaboration and *The Boy Who Was Raised as a Dog*.

When we started writing, we had no idea how the emerging field of traumatology was about to change, how many people hungered to understand the effects of trauma on the mind and brain, and the tremendous interest that would soon be generated in "trauma-informed" care. We didn't know that the book would be used as a textbook in undergraduate and graduate classes in sociology, neuroscience, psychology, criminology, and many other disciplines.

While we had hoped, of course, to have an impact, we did not expect the flood of responses we got from so many youth and adults who had been affected by trauma and neglect. Parents, teachers, social workers, police officers, military personnel, child welfare workers, juvenile justice officials, judges, coaches, psychiatrists, nurses, psychologists, pediatricians— and just about anyone else who lives or works with individuals experiencing trauma or maltreatment—have contacted us and written or spoken about having read and used concepts from the book in their work.

In the last ten years, awareness of the importance of developmental trauma and "adverse childhood experiences" (now widely known as "ACE's") in mental, physical, and even societal health has spread—almost explosively—from a relatively small group of clinicians and researchers into public systems and to the lay public. Public and private systems in education, child welfare, heath, mental health, juvenile justice, and more are implementing "trauma-informed," "trauma-aware," "trauma-focused," and "ACE aware" initiatives. *The Boy Who Was Raised as a Dog* has been a useful introduction to many of the core concepts, principles, and practice elements for a "trauma-informed" approach.

But when we started, I didn't really know what I was doing, at least as a writer. Unlike Maia, I had never written a book. We had several discussions about how to put everything together. We decided to use a series of clinical narratives—stories, basically—about patients whose experiences illustrated key concepts about the brain, development, or trauma. We sought a balance between these detailed, individual stories and the teaching of scientific material; we wanted the reader to be engaged and not overwhelmed by either the complexities of the brain or the emotional intensity of a child's painful history. It was a fine line, and, as it turns out, for some readers the intensity or complexity were too much. So please note: if you are reading this book for the first time and have a history of traumatic experience, be aware that it does contain some extremely disturbing material. Pace yourself accordingly.

For most, however, the balance worked. And if, for some moments, the reader was overwhelmed, she could put it down and come back to it later. We sought rhythm in our writing, both in the structure and the prose. I would like to say we were intentional about finding the right "doses" of emotional intensity, which can obviously be a stressor for the reader, and novelty, which can also cause stress. I'd also like to say that we intentionally had the proper pace to allow optimal learning to take place; that we were intentionally creating a resilience-building pattern of stress activation that included moderate, controllable and predictable stress for the reader. But we didn't know as much about those concepts then as we do now.

We both appreciated the beat of language and the power

of storytelling but we went by feel—and ultimately, I think we got the balance mostly right. In the new sections we've added to this edition, we will highlight just how crucial the rhythm, "dose," and spacing of experience is for building resilience. In the last ten years, we have come to much better understand these concepts as they apply to development, learning, therapy, parenting, and any other intentional process of changing the brain. But more on that later...

A second major choice in the book was the sequencing of the clinical vignettes.

We felt it was important to present these in roughly chronological order—to reflect the growth of the field and my personal growth as a clinician and researcher over time. My educational experiences in the neurosciences, medicine, and child and adolescent psychiatry occurred in parallel with the growth of the general field of traumatology. Being very developmentally focused, I knew it was always useful to understand "history"—how did this person come to be this way? How did this field come to be this way? Where did this idea come from? It has always been easier for me to understand the present if I knew what had happened in the past.

As we wrote *The Boy Who Was Raised as a Dog*, I had a rough outline of the key concepts that I felt were important in understanding trauma and maltreated children, as well as the sequence in which I first learned about these ideas and theories during my professional development. With this general structure in mind, we got to work.

Our process involved a set of hour-long interview style phone conversations; I lived in Houston and Maia lived in New York. Roughly once a week we would have an hour-long call in which I would either narrate the clinical work I had done with a client or elaborate on a concept or principle about development or the neurosciences. These interviews were recorded, transcribed and Maia would edit, arrange, and add to these and then send me a copy; then I would revise as well. Through this back and forth process our work together went remarkably smoothly.

After the publication of the book a trickle of positive feedback started. We received emails and letters from readers; many of these shared powerful personal experiences of childhood trauma, some were grateful that the book helped them "connect the dots" in their own lives. Over the years, as the popularity of the book has grown, it has been translated into twelve languages, and as noted above, has been adopted for use all types of classes that cover child development, trauma, and how they affect psychology and physiology.

In addition, the approach to clinical problem solving outlined in *The Boy Who Was Raised as a Dog*—the Neurosequential Model of Therapeutics (NMT)—has continued to generate strong interest. As we will discuss in more detail in the new final chapter (Chapter Twelve), "A Picture, Not a Label," the growth of this approach has been equally explosive. When we first published this book, my colleagues at The ChildTrauma Academy were the only people trained to use the approach. Today, over 10,000 clinicians are using some version of the Neurosequential Model in their work, directly affecting more than 200,000 clients. We estimate that more than 1,000,000 children, youth, and adults have been exposed to some aspect of the NMT.

We decided to write this updated and annotated version to ensure that *The Boy Who Was Raised as a Dog* continues to be a useful and accurate resource. In the last ten years, there have been advances in research, practice, program development, and policy related to trauma in childhood. This updated version will 1): correct and clarify content in the original book; 2) expand, elaborate, and update key concepts and principles described in the original and 3) present new and promising directions in these fields.

Again, we had some discussion on how best to accomplish this. The overwhelming feedback we had about the book was positive; the rhythm and balance of the narrative and the science worked well for most people. The science was overwhelmingly still accurate. We decided to leave each chapter fully intact (only making a few corrections in factual content where the data, in fact, has changed). At the end the book, a series of essays related to each chapter have been added to reflect and comment on the key elements in that chapter from our current perspective.

As we write these commentaries, we'd like to imagine sitting with our readers and having a short conversation about what you just read. Sometimes it might be updating you on the most current thinking about one of the key neuroscience concepts presented; in another instance, it may be elaborating on the clinical work or progress related to the issues of the particular case. In all cases, the intent is to enrich, update, and elaborate.

Of course, the process of creating these small sections required that I go back and actually read each chapter. As odd as this sounds, when the book was ultimately published, I never picked it up and read it. Obviously when we were writing—and doing the back and forth revisions—I read each chapter again and again. However, by the time we sent off the final draft for publication, I couldn't stand to even look at it. In some ways, now ten years later, I read each chapter with new eyes. Sometimes I was impressed with how well we explained something; other times, I cringed. I know more now; I have taught about these concepts more—I've learned more from my colleagues and my patients. And I think that we can use that to make the reader's experience more complete.

In keeping with our sequential presentation, we have also added one new chapter at the end of the book, as well as a study guide. This new chapter brings us to the present. We hope that here we can clarify the important core concepts and foreshadow future directions in this field.

The new study guide is adapted from a teacher's book study that I wrote with my colleague Steve Graner, a retired teacher and the Director of our Neurosequential Model in Education (NME) initiative. We hope it will be helpful for anyone who would like to have more structured discussion of the key concepts presented in *The Boy Who Was Raised as a Dog* and who would like to consider how to use the ideas in it for their interactions and work with children.

Taken together, the updates, the chapter addenda, the new chapter, and the book study guide are intended to ensure that *The Boy Who Was Raised as a Dog* remains an accessible and up-to-date source for anyone interested in—or affected by—childhood trauma.

Introduction

IT'S HARD TO IMAGINE TODAY, but when I was in medical school in the early 1980s researchers didn't pay much attention to the lasting damage that psychological trauma can produce. Even less consideration was given to how trauma might harm children. It wasn't considered relevant. Children were believed to be naturally "resilient," with an innate ability to "bounce back."

When I became a child psychiatrist and neuroscientist, it was not my goal to refute this misguided theory. But then, as a young researcher, I began to observe in the lab that stressful experience—particularly in early life—could change the brains of young animals. Numerous animal studies showed that even seemingly minor stress during infancy could have a permanent impact on the architecture and the chemistry of the brain and, therefore, on behavior. I thought: why wouldn't the same be true for humans?

That question became even more salient to me as I began my clinical work with troubled children. I soon found that the vast majority of my patients had lives filled with chaos, neglect, and/or violence. Clearly, these children weren't "bouncing back"—otherwise they wouldn't have been taken to a child psychiatry clinic! They'd suffered trauma—such as being raped or witnessing murder—that would have had most psychiatrists considering the diagnosis of post-traumatic stress disorder (PTSD), had they been adults with psychiatric problems. And yet these children were being treated as though their histories of trauma were irrelevant, and they'd "coincidentally" developed symptoms, such as depression or attention problems, that often required medication.

Of course, the diagnosis of PTSD was only itself introduced into psychiatry in 1980. At first, it was seen as something rare, a condition that only affected a minority of soldiers who had been devastated by combat experiences. But soon the same kinds of symptoms—intrusive thoughts about the traumatic event, flashbacks, disrupted sleep, a sense of unreality, a heightened startle response, extreme anxiety—began to be described in rape survivors, victims of natural disaster, and people who'd had or witnessed life-threatening accidents or injuries. Now the condition is believed to affect at least 7 percent of all Americans and most people are familiar with the idea that trauma can have profound and lasting effects. From the horrors of the 9/11 terrorist attacks to the aftermath of Hurricane Katrina, we recognize that catastrophic events can leave indelible marks on the mind. We know now—as my research and that of so many others has ultimately shown—that the impact is actually far greater on children than it is on adults.

I have made it my life's work to understand how trauma affects children and to develop innovative ways to help them cope with it. I have treated and studied children faced with some of the most horrendous experiences imaginable—from the surviving victims of the Branch Davidian cult conflagration in Waco, Texas, to neglected Eastern European orphans, to genocide survivors. I have also helped courts sort through the wreckage of misguided "Satanic Ritual Abuse" prosecutions based on coerced accusations from tortured, terrified children. I have done my best to help children who witnessed their parents' murders, and those who've spent years chained in cages or locked in closets.

While most children will never suffer anything as awful as what many of my patients have undergone, it is rare for a child to escape trauma entirely. By conservative estimates, about 40 percent of American children will have at least one potentially traumatizing experience by age eighteen: this includes the death of a parent or sibling, ongoing physical abuse and/or neglect, sexual abuse, or the experience of a serious accident, natural disaster, or domestic violence or other violent crime.

In 2004 alone, an estimated three million official reports of child abuse or neglect were made to government child protection agencies; around 872,000 of these cases were confirmed. Of course, the true number of abused and neglected children is far higher because most cases are never reported and some genuine cases cannot be sufficiently corroborated for official action to be taken. In one large survey, about one in eight children under the age of seventeen reported some form of serious maltreatment by adults within the past year, and about 27 percent of women and 16 percent of men reported as adults having been sexually victimized during childhood. In a national survey conducted in 1995, 6 percent of mothers and 3 percent of fathers even admitted to physically abusing their children at least once.

Furthermore, up to ten million American children are believed to be exposed to domestic violence annually, and 4 percent of American children under the age of fifteen lose a parent to death each year. Also, each year some 800,000 children will spend time in foster care and millions more are victims of natural disasters and devastating automobile accidents.

Although I do not mean to imply that all of these children will be severely "damaged" by these experiences, the most moderate estimates suggest that at any given time, more than eight million American children suffer from serious, diagnosable, trauma-related psychiatric problems. Millions more experience less serious but still distressing consequences.

Roughly one-third of children who are abused will have some clear psychological problems as a result—and research continues to show how even seemingly purely "physical" problems like heart disease, obesity, and cancer can be more likely to affect traumatized children later in their lives. Adults' responses to children during and after traumatic events can make an enormous difference in these eventual outcomes—both for good and for ill.

Over the years, research from my lab and many others has produced a much richer understanding of what trauma does to children and how we can help them heal from it. In 1996 I founded The ChildTrauma Academy, an interdisciplinary group of professionals dedicated to improving the lives of high-risk children and their families. We continue our clinical work and still have much to learn, but our primary goal is to bring treatments based on the best of our existing knowledge to others. We train people who work with children—whether they are parents or prosecutors, police officers or judges, social workers, physicians, policy makers, or politicians—to understand the most effective ways of minimizing the impact of trauma and maximizing recovery. We consult with government agencies and other groups to help them implement the best practices in dealing with these issues. My colleagues and I travel extensively around the world, speaking to parents, doctors, educators, child protection workers, and law enforcement officials, as well as high level stakeholders such as legislative bodies or committees and concerned corporate leaders. This book is part of our efforts.

In *The Boy Who Was Raised as a Dog* you'll meet some of the children who taught me the most important lessons about how trauma affects young people. And you'll learn what they need from us—their parents and guardians, their doctors, their government—if they are to build healthy lives. You'll see how traumatic experience marks children, how it affects their personalities and their capacity for physical and emotional growth. You'll meet my first patient, Tina, whose experience of abuse brought home to me the impact of trauma on children's brains. You'll meet a brave little girl named Sandy, who at the age of three had to be put in a witness protection program, and who taught me the importance of allowing a child to control aspects of her own therapy. You'll meet an astonishing boy called Justin, who showed me how children can recover from unspeakable deprivation. Each child I've worked with—the Branch Davidian children, who took comfort in caring for each other; Laura, whose body didn't grow until she felt safe and loved; Peter, a Russian orphan whose first grade classmates became his "therapists"— helped my colleagues and me place a new piece in the puzzle, allowing us to advance our treatment for traumatized children and their families.

Our work brings us into peoples' lives when they are most desperate, alone, sad, afraid, and wounded, but for the most part the stories you'll read here are success stories—stories of hope, survival, triumph. Surprisingly, it is often when wandering through the emotional carnage left by the worst of humankind that we find the best of humanity as well.

Ultimately, what determines how children survive trauma, physically, emotionally, or psychologically, is whether the people around them—particularly the adults they should be able to trust and rely upon—stand by them with love, support, and encouragement. Fire can warm or consume, water can quench or drown, wind can caress or cut. And so it is with human relationships: we can both create and destroy, nurture and terrorize, traumatize and heal each other.

In this book you will read about remarkable children whose stories can help us better understand the nature and power of human relationships. Although many of these boys and girls have had experiences far more extreme than most families will encounter (and thank goodness for that), their stories carry lessons for all parents that can help their children cope with the inevitable stresses and strains of life.

Working with traumatized and maltreated children has also made me think carefully about the nature of humankind and the difference between humankind and humanity. Not all humans are humane. A human being has to learn how to become humane. That process—and how it can sometimes go terribly wrong—is another aspect of what this book is about. The stories here explore the conditions necessary for the development of empathy—and those that are likely, instead, to produce cruelty and indifference. They reveal how children's brains grow and are molded by the people around them. They also expose how ignorance, poverty, violence, sexual abuse, chaos, and neglect can wreak havoc upon growing brains and nascent personalities.

I have long been interested in understanding human development, and especially in trying to figure out why some people grow up to be productive, responsible, and kind human beings, whereas others respond to abuse by inflicting more of it on others. My work has revealed to me a great deal about moral development, about the roots of evil and how genetic tendencies and environmental influences can shape critical decisions, which in turn affect later choices and, ultimately, who we turn out to be. I do not believe in "the abuse excuse" for violent or hurtful behavior, but I have found that there are complex interactions beginning in early childhood that affect our ability to envision choices and that may later limit our ability to make the best decisions.

My work has taken me to the intersection of mind and brain, to the place where we make choices and experience influences that determine whether or not we become humane and truly human. *The Boy Who Was Raised as a Dog* shares some of what I've learned there. Despite their pain and fear, the children in this book—and many others like them—have shown great courage and humanity, and they give me hope. From them I have learned much about loss, love, and healing.

The core lessons these children have taught me are relevant for us all. Because in order to understand trauma we need to understand memory. In order to appreciate how children heal we need to understand how they learn to love, how they cope with challenge, how stress affects them. And by recognizing the destructive impact that violence and threat can have on the capacity to love and work, we can come to better understand ourselves and to nurture the people in our lives, especially the children.

CHAPTER 1

Tina's World

TINA WAS MY FIRST CHILD PATIENT, just seven years old when I met her. She sat in the waiting room of the University of Chicago child psychiatry clinic: tiny and fragile, huddled with her mother and siblings, unsure what to expect from her new doctor. As I led her to my office and shut the door, it was hard to tell which one of us was more nervous: the three-foot-tall African-American girl with meticulously neat braids or the six-foot-two white guy with the long mane of unruly curls. Tina sat on my couch for a minute, checking me out, looking me up and down. Then, she walked across the room, crawled into my lap and snuggled in.

I was touched. Gosh, what a nice thing to do. What a sweet child. Stupid me. She shifted slightly and moved her hand to my crotch and tried to open my zipper. I was no longer anxious. Now, I was sad. I took her hand, moved it from my thighs, and carefully lifted her off my lap.

The morning before I first met with Tina I read through her "chart"—one small sheet of paper with minimal information

1

taken during a phone interview with our intake worker. Tina lived with her mother, Sara, and two younger siblings. Sara had called the child psychiatry clinic because her daughter's school had insisted that she get her evaluated. Tina had been "aggressive and inappropriate" with her classmates. She'd exposed herself, attacked other children, used sexual language, and tried to get them to engage in sex play. She didn't pay attention in class and often refused to follow directions.

The most relevant history the chart contained was that Tina had been abused for a two-year period that started when she was four and ended when she was six. The perpetrator was a sixteen-year-old boy, her babysitter's son. He had molested both Tina and her younger brother, Michael, while their mother was at work. Tina's mom was single. Poor, but no longer on public assistance, at the time Sara worked a minimum wage job at a convenience store to support her family. The only childcare she could afford was an informal arrangement with her next-door neighbor. That neighbor, unfortunately, often left the children with her son so she could run errands. And her son was sick. He tied the children up and raped them, sodomized them with foreign objects, and threatened to kill them if they told. Finally, his mother caught him and put a stop to the abuse.

Sara never let her neighbor care for her children again, but the damage had been done. (The boy was prosecuted; he went to therapy, not jail.) Here we were, one year later. The daughter had serious problems, the mother had no resources, and I didn't know squat about abused children.

"Here. Let's go color," I said gently as I took her from my lap. She seemed upset. Had she displeased me? Would I get angry? She anxiously studied my face with her dark brown eyes, watching my movements, listening to my voice for some nonverbal cue to help her make sense of this interaction. My behavior didn't fit with her internal catalog of previous experiences with men.

She had only known men as sexual predators: no loving father, no supportive grandfather, no kind uncle or protective older brother had touched her life. The only adult males she'd met were her mother's often inappropriate boyfriends and her own abuser. Experience had taught her that men wanted sex, either from her or her mother. So quite logically from her perspective, she assumed that's what I wanted as well.

What should I do? How do you change behaviors or beliefs, locked into place from years of experience, with one hour of therapy a week? None of my experience and training had prepared me for this little girl. I didn't understand her. Did she interact with everyone as though they wanted sex from her, even women and girls? Was this the only way she knew how to make friends? Was her aggressive and impulsive behavior at school related to this? Did she think I was rejecting her—and how might that affect her?

It was 1987. I was a fellow in Child and Adolescent Psychiatry at the University of Chicago, just starting the final two years of some of the best medical training in the country. I'd had almost a dozen years of postgraduate training. I was an MD, a PhD, and had finished three years as a medical and general psychiatry resident. I ran a basic neuroscience research laboratory that studied the stress response systems in the brain. I had learned all about brain cells and brain systems and their complex networks and chemistry. I had spent years trying to understand the human mind. And after all that time all I could think to do was this: I sat down with Tina at a small table set up in my office and handed her a set of crayons and a coloring book. She opened it up and paged through. "Can I color in this?" she asked softly, clearly unsure what to do in this strange situation.

"Sure," I told her.

"Should I make her dress blue or red?" I asked Tina.

"Red."

"OK." She held up her colored page for my approval, "Very nice," I said. She smiled. For the next forty minutes we sat on the floor, side by side, coloring quietly, reaching over to borrow crayons, showing our progress to each other and trying to get used to being in the same space with a stranger. When the session was over, I walked Tina back to the clinic waiting area. Her mother was holding a young infant and talking to her four-year-old son. Sara thanked me and we set up another appointment for the next week. As they left I knew I needed to talk to a supervisor with more experience, one who could help me figure out how to help this little girl.

Supervision in mental health training is a misleading term. When I was a medical intern learning to put in a central line, or run a code, or draw blood, there were older, more experienced physicians present to instruct, scold, assist, and teach me. I often received immediate—usually negative—feedback. And while it was true that we followed the model "watch one, do one, teach one," a more senior, experienced clinician was always close by to help during any interactions with patients.

Not so for psychiatry. As a trainee, when I was with a patient, or a patient and her family, I was almost always working alone. After meeting with the patient—sometimes multiple times—I discussed the case with my supervisor. During training, a child psychiatry fellow will typically have several supervisors for clinical work. Often I would present the same child or issue to multiple supervisors to gather their different impressions and gain from their multiple, hopefully complementary, insights. It is an interesting process that has some remarkable strengths but also has some clear deficiencies, which I was about to discover.

I presented Tina's case to my first supervisor, Dr. Robert Stine*. He was young, serious, intellectual, and in training to become a psychoanalyst. He maintained a full beard and wore

---

* Throughout this book an asterisk (*) after a name indicates that it is a pseudonym.

what seemed like the exact same outfit every day: a black suit, a black tie, and a white shirt. He seemed a lot smarter than me. He used psychiatric jargon with ease: "the maternal introject," "object relations," "counter-transference," "oral fixation." And whenever he did, I'd look him in the eyes and try to look appropriately serious and thoughtful, nodding as if what he was saying was clearing things up for me: "Ah, yes. OK. Well, I'll keep that in mind." But really I was thinking, "What the hell is he talking about?"

I gave a short but formal presentation, describing Tina's symptoms, history, family, and the complaints from her school, as well as detailing the key elements of my first visit with her. Dr. Stine took notes. When I finished he said, "Well, what do you think she has?"

I had no clue. "I'm not sure," I stalled. Medical training teaches a young physician to act much less ignorant than he or she really is. And I was ignorant. Dr. Stine sensed this and suggested we use the diagnostic guide for psychiatric disorders, the Diagnostic and Statistical Manual (DSM).

At that point, it was the DSM III. Every ten years or so it is revised to include updates in research and new ideas about disorders. This process is guided by objective principles but is very susceptible to sociopolitical and other nonscientific processes. For example, homosexuality was once considered a "disorder" in the DSM and now it is not. But the main problem with the DSM—to this day—is that it is a catalog of disorders based on lists of symptoms. It is kind of like a computer manual written by a committee with no knowledge of the machine's actual hardware or software, a manual that attempts to determine the cause of and cure for the computer's problems by asking you to consider the sounds it makes. As I knew from my own research and training, the systems in that "machine"—in this case, the human brain—are very complex. As a result it seemed to me that the same "output" might be caused by any number of different problems within it. But the DSM doesn't account for this.

"SO SHE IS INATTENTIVE, a discipline problem, impulsive, noncompliant, defiant, oppositional, and has problems with her peers. She meets diagnostic criteria for Attention Deficit Disorder and oppositional defiant disorder," Dr. Stine prompted.

"Yeah, I guess so," I said. But it didn't feel right to me. Tina was experiencing something more or something different than what was described by those diagnostic labels. I knew from my research on the brain that the systems involved in controlling and focusing our attention were especially complex. I also knew that there were many environmental and genetic factors that could influence them. Wasn't labeling Tina "defiant" misleading, given that her "noncompliance" was likely a result of her victimization? What about the confusion that made her think that sexual behavior with adults and peers in public is normal? What about her speech and language delays? And if she did have Attention Deficit Disorder (ADD), might the sexual abuse be important in understanding how to treat someone like her?

I didn't raise these questions, though. I just looked at Dr. Stine and nodded as if I was absorbing what he was teaching me.

"Go read up on psychopharmacology for ADD. We can talk more about this next week," he advised.

I left Dr. Stine feeling confused and disappointed. Is this what being a child psychiatrist was like? I had been trained as a general (adult) psychiatrist and was familiar with the limitations of supervision, and with the limitations of our diagnostic approach, but I was not at all familiar with the pervasive problems of the children I was seeing. They were socially marginalized, developmentally delayed, profoundly damaged, and sent to our clinic so we could "fix" things that to me didn't seem fixable with the tools we had at our disposal. How could a few hours a month and a prescription change Tina's outlook and behavior? Did Dr. Stine really believe that Ritalin or some other ADD drug would solve this girl's problems?

Fortunately, I had another supervisor as well: a wise and wonderful man, a true giant in the field of psychiatry, Dr. Jarl Dyrud. Like me, he was from North Dakota, and we hit it off immediately. Like Dr. Stine, Dr. Dyrud was trained in the analytic method. Yet he also had years of real-life experience trying to understand and help people. He had let that experience, not just Freud's theories, mold his perspective.

He listened carefully as I described Tina. When I finished, he smiled at me and said, "Did you enjoy coloring with her?"

I thought for a minute and said, "Yeah. I did."

Dr. Dyrud said, "Very nice start. So tell me more." I started to list Tina's symptoms, the complaints the adults had about her behaviors.

"No, no. Tell me about her. Not about her symptoms."

"What do you mean?"

"Where does she live? What is her apartment like, when does she go to sleep, what does she do during the day? Tell me about her."

I admitted that I didn't know any of that information. "Spend some time getting to know her—not her symptoms. Find out about her life," he advised.

For the next few sessions, Tina and I spent time coloring or playing simple games and talking about what she liked to do. When I ask children like Tina what they want to be when they grow up, they often respond with "If I grow up," because they've seen so much real-life death and violence at home and in their neighborhoods that reaching adulthood seems uncertain. In our conversations, sometimes Tina would tell me that she wanted to be a teacher, and other times she said she wanted to be a hair-dresser, all with the perfectly ordinary, rapidly changing desires of a girl of her age. But as we discussed specifics of these various goals, it took some time before I was able to help her recognize that the future can be something you plan for, something you can predict and even change, rather than a series of unforeseen events that just happen to you.

I also talked to her mother about her behavior in school and at home and found out more about her life. There was, of course, the daily routine of school. After school, unfortunately, there were often several hours between the time Tina and her younger brother came home and the time Sara got off from work. Sara had her children call her to check in, and there were neighbors nearby they could contact in an emergency, but she didn't want to risk more caregiver abuse. So the children stayed home alone, usually watching TV. And sometimes, Sara admitted, because of what they'd both been through, there was sexualized play.

Sara was far from a neglectful mother, but working to feed three young children often left her exhausted, overwhelmed, and demoralized. Any parent would have been hard-pressed to cope with the emotional needs of these traumatized children. The family had little time to play or just be together. As in many financially strapped homes, there was always some pressing need, an economic or medical or emotional emergency, that required immediate attention to avoid complete disaster, such as homelessness or job loss or overwhelming debt.

AS MY WORK WITH TINA CONTINUED, Sara always smiled when she first saw me. The hour that Tina had therapy was one time in her week when she didn't have to do anything more than be with her other children. Tina would run down to my office while I took a moment to goof with her little brother (he was in therapy as well, but with someone else at a different time) and smile at the baby. When I was sure they were settled in with something to occupy them in the waiting area, I'd rejoin Tina, who would be sitting at her little chair waiting for me.

"What should we do today?" she would ask, looking at the games, coloring books, and toys she had pulled from my shelves and put on the table. I would pretend to think hard while she'd look at me with anticipation.

My eyes would fix on a game on the table and I would say, "Mmm. How about let's play Operation?" She would laugh, "Yes!" She guided our play. I slowly introduced new concepts, like waiting and thinking before deciding what to do next. Occasionally she would spontaneously share some fact or some hope or some fear with me. I would ask questions to get some clarity. Then she would redirect the interaction back to play. And week by week, bit by bit, I got to know Tina.

Later that fall, however, Tina was late to therapy for several weeks in a row. Because appointments were only an hour, this sometimes meant we would only have twenty minutes for our sessions. I made the mistake of mentioning this to Dr. Stine during an update on the case. He raised his eyebrows and stared at me. He seemed disappointed.

"What do you think is going on here?"

"I'm not sure. I think the mom seems pretty overwhelmed."

"You must interpret the resistance."

"Ah. OK." What the hell is he talking about? Is he suggesting that Tina doesn't want to come to therapy and is somehow forcing her mother to be late? "You mean Tina's resistance or the mom's?" I asked.

"The mother left these children in harm's way. She may be resentful that this child is getting your attention. She may want her to remain damaged," he said.

9

"Oh," I responded, not sure what to think. I knew that analysts often interpreted lateness to therapy as a sign of "resistance" to change, but that was beginning to seem absurd, especially in this case. The idea left no room for genuine happenstance and seemed to go out of its way to blame people like Tina's mom, who, as far as I could tell, did everything possible to get help for Tina. It was clearly difficult for her to get to the clinic. To get to the medical center, she had to take three different buses, which often ran late during the brutal Chicago winter; she had no childcare so she had to bring all her children; sometimes she had to borrow money for the bus fare. It seemed to me she was doing the best she could in an extremely difficult situation.

Shortly thereafter, as I left the building one frozen night, I saw Tina and her family waiting for the bus home. They were standing in the dark and snow was slowly falling through the dim light of a nearby streetlight. Sara was holding the baby and Tina was sitting on the bench next to her brother under the heat lamp of the bus stop. The two siblings sat close to each other, holding hands and slowly rocking their legs back and forth. Their feet didn't reach the ground and they kept time with each other, in sync. It was 6:45. Icy cold. They would not be home for another hour at least. I pulled my car over, out of sight, and watched them, hoping the bus would come quickly.

I felt guilty watching them from my warm car. I thought I should give them a ride. But the field of psychiatry is very attentive to boundaries. There are supposed to be unbreachable walls between patient and doctor, strict borderlines that clearly define the relationship in lives that often otherwise lack such structure. The rule usually made sense to me, but like many therapeutic notions that had been developed in work with neurotic middle-class adults, it didn't seem to fit here.

Finally, the bus came. I felt relieved.

The next week, I waited a long time after our session before going to my car. I tried to tell myself that I was doing paperwork, but really I didn't want to see the family standing in the cold again. I couldn't stop wondering about what could be wrong with the simple humane act of giving someone a ride home when it was cold out. Could it really interfere with the therapeutic process? I went back and forth, but my heart kept coming down on the side of kindness. A sincere, kind act, it seemed to me, could have more therapeutic impact than any artificial, emotionally regulated stance that so often characterizes "therapy."

It was full winter in Chicago now and bitterly, bitterly cold. I ultimately told myself that if I saw the family again, I'd give them a ride. It was the right thing to do. And one night in December as I left work and drove by the bus stop, there they were. I offered them a ride. Sara declined at first, saying she had to stop at the grocery store on her way. In for a penny in for a pound, I thought. I offered to drive them to the store. After some more hesitation, she agreed and they all piled into my Toyota Corolla.

Miles away from the medical center, Sara pointed to a corner store and I stopped there. Holding her sleeping baby, she looked at me, unsure whether to take all the children into the store with her.

"Here. I'll hold the baby. We'll wait here," I said decisively.

She was in the store for about ten minutes. We listened to the radio. Tina sang along with the music. I was just praying the baby wouldn't wake up. I slowly rocked her, mimicking the rhythm that Tina's mother had used. Sara came out of the store with two heavy bags.

"Take these back there and don't touch anything," she said to Tina, putting the bags on the back seat.

When we arrived at her building, I watched as Sara struggled to get out of the car and walk through the unshoveled snow on the sidewalk, juggling the baby, her purse and a bag of groceries. Tina tried to carry the other bag of groceries, but it was too heavy for her and she slipped in the snow. I opened my door and got out, taking one bag from Tina and the other one from Sara.

"No. We can manage," she protested.

"I know you can. But tonight I can help." She looked at me, not sure how to deal with this. I sensed her trying to understand if this was kindness or something sinister. She seemed embarrassed. I felt embarrassed. But it still seemed right to help.

We all walked up three flights of stairs to their apartment. Tina's mother got out her keys and opened three locks all without disturbing her sleeping baby. How difficult this mother's life was, I thought, all alone caring for three children, no money, only episodic and often tedious work, no extended family nearby. I stood at the threshold of the door with the bags in my arms, not wanting to intrude.

"You can just put those on the table," Sara said as she walked to the back of the one-room apartment to put the baby down on a mattress against the wall. In two steps I was at the kitchen table. I put the bags down and glanced around the room. There was one couch facing a color television and a small coffee table with a few cups and dirty dishes on it. On a small table with three unmatched chairs near the kitchenette, there was a loaf of Wonderbread and a jar of peanut butter. One double mattress sat on the floor, with blankets and pillows neatly folded at one end. Clothes and newspapers were scattered around. A picture of Martin Luther King Jr. hung on the wall, and next to it on either side were brightly colored school portraits of Tina and her brother. On another wall hung a picture of Sara and the baby, slightly crooked. The apartment was warm.

Sara stood and awkwardly said, "Thanks again for the ride," and I assured her it had been no trouble. The moment was very uncomfortable. As I walked out the door and said, "See you all next week," Tina waved. She and her toddler brother were putting the groceries away.

They were better behaved than many children I'd seen in much better circumstances; it seemed to me that they had to be.

The drive home took me through some of the poorest neighborhoods in Chicago. I felt guilty. Guilty about the luck, the opportunities, the resources, and the gifts I had been given, guilty about all of the times I had complained about working too much, or not getting credit for something I had done. I also felt I knew much more about Tina. She had grown up in a world so very different from mine. And somehow that had to be related to the problems that brought her to see me. I didn't know exactly what it was, but I knew there was something important about how the world she grew up and lived in had shaped her emotional, behavioral, social, and physical health.

AFTERWARDS, OF COURSE, I WAS afraid to tell anyone what I'd done, that I'd driven a patient and her family home. Worse yet, that I had stopped at the store on the way and helped bring in some groceries. But part of me didn't care. I knew I'd done the right thing. You just don't let a young mother with two young children and a baby stand in the cold like that.

I waited two weeks and then, when I next met with Dr. Dyrud, I told him. "I saw them waiting for a bus and it was cold. So I gave them a ride home," I said nervously, scanning his face for his reaction, just like Tina had done with me. He laughed as I slowly told him about the extent of my transgression.

When I'd finished, he clapped his hands together, saying, "Great! We should do a home visit with all of our patients." He smiled and sat back. "Tell me all about it."

I was shocked. In an instant Dr. Dyrud's smile and the delight on his face released me from two weeks of nagging guilt. When he asked what I'd learned I told him that one moment in that tiny apartment had told me more about the challenges facing Tina and her family than I could ever have learned from any on-site session or interview.

Later in that first year of my child psychiatry fellowship, Sara and her family moved to an apartment closer to the medical center, one twenty-minute bus ride away. The lateness ceased. No more "resistance." We continued to meet once a week.

DR. DYRUD'S WISDOM AND MENTORSHIP continued to be liberating for me. Like other teachers, clinicians, and researchers who had inspired me, he encouraged exploration, curiosity, and reflection, but, most importantly, gave me the courage to challenge existing beliefs. Taking bits and pieces from each of my mentors, I began to develop a therapeutic approach that sought to explain emotional and behavioral problems as symptoms of dysfunction within the brain.

In 1987 child psychiatry had not yet embraced the neurosciences. In fact, the vast expansion of research on the brain and brain development that began in the 1980s and exploded in the 1990s ("the decade of the brain") had yet to occur, let alone influence clinical practice. Instead, there was active opposition by many psychologists and psychiatrists to taking a biological perspective on human behavior. Such an approach was considered mechanistic and dehumanizing, as though reducing behavior to biological correlates automatically meant that everything was caused by genes, leaving no room for free will and creativity, and no way to consider environmental factors like poverty. Evolutionary ideas were seen as even worse, as backwards racist and sexist theories that rationalized the status quo and reduced human action to animal drives.

Since I was just starting out within child psychiatry, I didn't yet trust my own capacity to think independently, to process and interpret accurately what I was seeing. How could my thoughts about this be right when none of the other established psychiatrists, the stars, my mentors, were talking about or teaching about these things?

Fortunately, Dr. Dyrud and several of my other mentors encouraged my tendency to fold neuroscience into my clinical thinking about Tina and other patients. What *was* going on in Tina's brain? What was different about her brain that made her more impulsive and inattentive than other girls her age? What had happened in her rapidly developing brain when she had suffered these abnormal, sexualized experiences as a toddler? Did the stress of poverty affect her? And why did she have speech and language delays? Dr. Dyrud used to point to his head as he said, "The answer is in there somewhere."

My introduction to neuroscience had started during my freshman year in college. My first college advisor, Dr. Seymour Levine, a world-famous neuroendocrinologist, had conducted pioneering work on the impact of stress during early life on the development of the brain, which had shaped all of my subsequent thinking. His work helped me see how early influences can literally leave imprints on the brain that last a lifetime.

Levine had done a series of experiments examining the development of important stress-related hormone systems in rats. His group's work demonstrated that the biology and function of these important systems could be altered dramatically by brief periods of stress during early life. Biology isn't just genes playing out some unalterable script. It is sensitive to the world around it, as evolutionary theories predicted. In some of the experiments the duration of the stress was only minutes long, involving just a few moments of human handling of rat pups (baby rats), which is highly stressful for them. But this very brief stressful experience, at a key time in the development of the brain, resulted in alterations in stress hormone systems that lasted into adulthood.

From the moment I started my formal education in the field, then, I was aware of the transformative impact of early life experiences. This became a template against which I compared all subsequent concepts.

Frequently, while at the lab, my thoughts would turn to Tina and the other children with whom I was working. I would force myself to work the problem: What do I know? What information is missing? Can I see any connections between what was known and what was not known? Was seeing me making any difference in the lives of these children? As I thought about my patients, I also considered their symptoms: Why these particular problems in this particular child? What could help change them? Could their behavior be explained by anything that I and other scientists in my field were learning about how the brain works? For example, could studying the neurobiology of attachment—the connection between parent and child—help solve problems between a mother and her son? Could Freudian ideas like transference—where a patient projects his feelings about his parents into other relationships, particularly the one he has with his therapist—be explained by examining the function of the brain?

There had to be some link, I thought. Just because we couldn't describe it or yet understand it, there just had to be a correlation between what went on in the brain and every human phenomenon and symptom. After all, the human brain is the organ that mediates all emotion, thought, and behavior. In contrast to other specialized organs in the human body, such as the heart, lungs, and pancreas, the brain is responsible for thousands of complex functions. When you have a good idea, fall in love, fall down the stairs, gasp when walking up stairs, melt at the smile of your child, laugh at a joke, get hungry, and feel full—all of those experiences and all your responses to these experiences are mediated by your brain. So it followed that Tina's struggles with speech and language, attention, impulsivity, and healthy relationships also had to involve her brain.

But what part of her brain? Could understanding this help me treat her more effectively? Which of Tina's brain regions, neural networks, neurotransmitter systems were poorly regulated, underdeveloped, or disorganized, and how could this information help me with Tina's therapy? To answer these questions I had to start with what I already knew.

THE BRAIN'S REMARKABLE FUNCTIONAL capabilities come from an equally remarkable set of structures. There are eighty-six billion neurons (brain cells), and for each neuron there are also equally important support cells, called glia. During development—from the first stirrings in the womb to early adulthood—all of these complicated cells (and there are many different types) must be organized into specialized networks. This results in countless intricately interconnected and highly specialized systems. These chains and webs of connected neurons create the varied architecture of the brain. For our purposes there are four major parts of the brain: the brainstem, the diencephalon, the limbic system, and the cortex.

The brain is organized from the inside out, like a house with increasingly complicated additions built on an old foundation. The lower and most central regions of the brainstem and the diencephalon are the simplest. They evolved first, and they develop first as a child grows. As you move upward and outward, things get increasingly more complex with the limbic system. The cortex is more intricate still, the crowning achievement of brain architecture. We share similar organization of our lowest brain regions with creatures as primitive as lizards, while the middle regions are similar to those found in mammals like cats and dogs. The outer areas we share only with other primates, like monkeys and the great apes. The most uniquely human part of the brain is the frontal cortex, but even this shares 96 percent of its organization with that of a chimpanzee!

Our four brain areas are organized in a hierarchical fashion: bottom to top, inside to outside. A good way to picture it is with a little stack of dollar bills—say five. Fold them in half, place them on your palm and make a hitchhiker's fist with your thumb pointing out. Now, turn your fist in a "thumbs down" orientation. Your thumb represents the brainstem, the tip of your thumb being where the spinal cord merges into the brainstem; the fatty part of your thumb would be the diencephalon; the folded dollars inside your fist, covered by your fingers and hand, would be the limbic system; and your fingers and hand, which surround the bills, represent the cortex. When you look at the human brain, the limbic system is completely internal; you cannot see it from the outside, just like those dollar bills. Your little finger, which is now oriented to be the top and front, represents the frontal cortex.

While interconnected, each of these four main areas controls a separate set of functions. The brainstem, for example, mediates our core regulatory functions such as body temperature, heart rate, respiration, and blood pressure. The diencephalon and the limbic system handle emotional responses that guide our behavior, like fear, hatred, love, and joy. The very top part of the brain, the cortex, regulates the most complex and highly human functions such as speech and language, abstract thinking, planning, and deliberate decision making. All of them work in concert, like a symphony orchestra, so while there are individualized capacities, no one system is wholly responsible for the sound of the "music" you actually hear.

Tina's symptoms suggested abnormalities in almost all of the parts of her brain. She had sleep and attention problems (brainstem), difficulties with fine motor control and coordination (diencephalon and cortex), clear social and relational delays and deficits (limbic and cortex), and speech and language problems (cortex).

This pervasive distribution of problems was a very important clue. My research—and the research of hundreds of others—indicated that all of Tina's problems could be related to one key set of neural systems, the ones involved in helping humans cope with stress and threat. Coincidentally, those were exactly the systems I was studying in the lab.

These systems were "suspect" to me for two main reasons. The first was that myriad studies in humans and animals had documented the role these systems play in arousal, sleep, attention, appetite, mood, impulse regulation—basically all of the areas in which Tina had major problems. The second reason was that these important networks originate in the lower parts of the brain and send direct connections to all of the other areas of the brain. This architecture allows a unique role for these systems. They are capable of integrating and orchestrating signals and information from all of our senses and throughout the brain. This capacity is necessary to effectively respond to threat: if, for example, a predator may be lurking, an animal needs to be able to respond just as quickly to his scent or sound as to actually seeing him.

Additionally, the stress response systems are among only a handful of neural systems in the brain that, if poorly regulated or abnormal, can cause dysfunction in all four of the main brain areas—just like what I was seeing with Tina.

The basic neuroscience work I'd been doing for years had involved examining the details of how these systems worked. In the brain, neurons transmit messages from one cell to the next by using chemical messengers called neurotransmitters that are released at specialized neuron-to-neuron connections called synapses. These chemical messengers fit only into certain, correctly shaped receptors on the next neuron, in the same way that only the right key will fit into the lock on your front door. Synaptic connections, at once astoundingly complex and yet elegantly simple, create chains of neuron-to-neuron-to-neuron networks that allow all of the many functions of the brain, including thought, feeling, motion, sensation, and perception. This also allows drugs to affect us, because most psychoactive medications work like copied keys, fitting into the locks meant to be opened by particular neurotransmitters and fooling the brain into opening or closing their doors.

I had done my doctoral research in neuropharmacology in the lab of Dr. David U'Prichard, who had trained with Dr. Solomon Snyder, a pioneering neuroscientist and psychiatrist. (Dr. Snyder's group was famous for, among many other things, finding the receptor at which opiate drugs like heroin and morphine act.) When I worked with Dr. U'Prichard, I did research on the norepinephrine (also known as noradrenaline) and epinephrine (also known as adrenaline) systems. These neurotransmitters are involved in stress. The classic "fight or flight" response begins in a central clump of norepinephrine neurons known as the locus coeruleus ("blue spot," named for its color). These neurons send signals to virtually every other important part of the brain and help it respond to stressful situations.

Some of my work with Dr. U'Prichard involved two different strains of rats, which were animals of the same species that had some slight genetic differences. These rats looked and acted exactly the same in ordinary situations, but even the most moderate stress would cause one type to break down. Under calm conditions, these rats could learn mazes, but give them the tiniest stress, and they would unravel and forget everything. The other rats were unaffected. When we examined their brains, we found that early in the development of the stress-reactive rats, there was over-activity in their adrenaline and noradrenaline systems. This small change led to a great cascade of abnormalities in receptor number, sensitivity, and function across many brain areas, and ultimately altered their ability to respond properly to stress for a lifetime.

I had no evidence that Tina was genetically "oversensitive" to stress. I did know, however, that the threat and the painful sexual assaults Tina experienced had, no doubt, resulted in repetitive and intense activation of her threat-mediating stress response neural systems. I recalled Levine's work that had shown that just a few minutes of stressful experience early in life could change a rat's stress response forever. Tina's abuse had gone on much longer—she'd been assaulted at least once a week for two years—and that had been compounded by the stress of living in a constant state of crisis with a family that was often on the economic edge. It occurred to me that if both genes and environment could produce similar dysfunctional symptoms, the effect of a stressful environment on a person already genetically sensitive to stress would probably be magnified.

And as I continued to work both with Tina and in the lab, I came to believe that in Tina's case the repeated activation of her stress response systems from a trauma endured at a young age, when her brain was still developing, had probably caused a cascade of altered receptors, sensitivity, and dysfunction throughout her brain, similar to the one I observed in animal models. Consequently, I started to think Tina's symptoms were the result of developmental trauma. Her attention and impulse problems might be due to a change in the organization of her stress response neural networks, a change that might have once helped her cope with her abuse, but was now causing her aggressive behavior and inattention to her class work in school.

It made sense: a person with an overactive stress system would pay close attention to the faces of people like teachers and classmates, where threat might lurk, but not to benign things like classroom lessons. A heightened awareness of potential threat might also make someone like Tina prone to fighting, as she would be looking everywhere for signs that someone might be about to attack her again, likely causing her to overreact to the smallest potential signals of aggression. This seemed a much more plausible explanation for Tina's problems than assuming that her attention problems were coincidental and unrelated to the abuse.

I looked back through her chart and saw that upon her first visit to the clinic her heart rate had been 112 beats per minute. A normal heart rate for a girl of that age should have been below 100. An elevated heart rate can be an indication of a persistently activated stress response, which was more evidence for my idea that her problems were a direct result of her brain's response to the abuse. If I had to give Tina a label now, it wouldn't be ADD, but rather post-traumatic stress disorder, PTSD.

OVER THE THREE YEARS I worked with Tina, I was delighted and relieved by her apparent progress. There were no more reports of "inappropriate" behavior at school. She was doing her homework, going to class, and no longer fighting with other children. Her speech had improved; most of her problems had been related to the fact that she was so soft spoken that teachers and even her mother often couldn't hear her well enough to understand her, let alone correct her pronunciation. As she learned to speak up and was spoken to more often, thereby receiving the repeated corrective feedback she needed, she caught up.

She had also rapidly become more attentive and less impulsive, so rapidly in fact that I didn't even discuss medication with my supervisors after that initial conversation with Dr. Stine.

Tina guided our play during our sessions, but I used every opportunity to teach her lessons that would help her feel more confident out in the world and help her behave more appropriately and rationally. We initially learn impulse control and decision making from those around us, sometimes from explicit lessons, sometimes by example. Tina, however, lived in an environment where neither explicit nor implicit lessons were taught. Everyone around her just reacted to what happened to them, and so that's what she did, too. Our meetings offered her the undivided attention she craved and our games taught her some of the lessons she had missed. For example, when I first began my work with Tina she hadn't understood the concept of taking turns. She couldn't wait to start things; she acted and reacted without thinking. In the simple games that we played, I modeled more appropriate behavior and repeatedly taught her to pause before doing the first thing that popped into her head. Based on her excellent progress in school, I truly believed I'd helped her.

UNFORTUNATELY, HOWEVER, TWO weeks before I left the clinic to start a new job, now ten-year-old Tina was caught performing fellatio on an older boy at school. What I'd taught her, it seemed, was not to change her behavior, but to better hide her sexualized activity and other problems from adults and to control her impulses in order to avoid getting in trouble. On the surface she could make others think she was behaving appropriately, but inside, she had not overcome her trauma.

I WAS DISAPPOINTED AND CONFUSED upon hearing this news. I had tried so hard, and she had really seemed to be getting better. It was difficult to accept that what seemed to be a positive therapeutic effort had been so hollow. What had happened? Or more importantly, what didn't happen in our work to help change her?

I kept thinking about the effects Tina's early childhood trauma and her unstable home life could have had on her brain. And soon I realized that I needed to expand my view of clinical mental health work. The answers to my failed, inefficient treatment for Tina—and to the big questions in child psychiatry—were in how the brain works, how the brain develops, how the brain makes sense of and organizes the world. Not in the brain as it has been caricatured as a rigid, genetically preset system that sometimes requires medication to adjust "imbalances," but in the brain in all its complexity. Not in the brain as a seething complex of unconscious "resistance" and "defiance," but in the brain as it evolved to respond to a complex social world. A brain, in short, that had genetic predispositions that were shaped by evolution to be exquisitely sensitive to the people who surrounded it.

Tina did learn to better regulate her stress system; her improved impulse control seemed to be good evidence of this. But Tina's most troubling problems had to do with her distorted and unhealthy sexual behaviors. I realized that some of her symptoms could be fixed by changing her overreactive stress response, yet that would not erase her memory. I began to think that memory was what I needed to understand before I could do better.

So, what is memory, really? Most of us think about it in relation to names, faces, phone numbers, but it is much more than that. It is a basic property of biological systems. Memory is the capacity to carry forward in time some element of an experience. Even muscles have memory, as you can see by the changes in them that result from exercise. Most importantly, however, memory is what the brain does, how it composes us and allows our past to help determine our future. In no small part memory makes us who we are and in Tina's case, her memories of sexual abuse were a large part of what stood in her way.

Tina's precocious and oversexualized interactions with males clearly stemmed from her abuse. I began considering memory and how the brain creates "associations" when two patterns of neural activity occur simultaneously and repetitively. For example, if the neural activity caused by the visual image of a fire truck and that caused by the sound of a siren co-occur repetitively, these once-separate neural chains (visual and sound related-neural networks) will create new synaptic connections and become a single, interconnected network. Once this new set of connections between visual and auditory networks is created, merely stimulating one part of the network (for example, hearing the siren) can actually activate the visual part of the chain and the person will almost automatically visualize a fire truck.

This powerful property of association is a universal feature of the brain. It is through association that we weave all of our incoming sensory signals together—sound, sight, touch, scent—to create the whole person, place, thing, and action. Association allows and underlies both language and memory.

Our conscious memory is full of gaps, of course, which is actually a good thing. Our brains filter out the ordinary and expected, which is utterly necessary to allow us to function. When you drive, for example, you rely automatically on your previous experiences with cars and roads; if you had to focus on every aspect of what your senses are taking in, you'd be overwhelmed and would probably crash. As you learn anything, in fact, your brain is constantly checking current experience against stored templates—essentially memory—of previous similar situations and sensations, asking "Is this new?" and "Is this something I need to attend to?"

So as you move down the road, your brain's motor vestibular system is telling you that you are in a certain position. But your brain is probably not making new memories about that. Your brain has stored in it previous sitting experiences in cars, and the pattern of neural activity associated with that doesn't need to change. There's nothing new. You've been there, done that, it's familiar. This is also why you can drive over large stretches of familiar highways without remembering almost anything at all that you did during the drive.

This is important because all of that previously stored experience has laid down the neural networks, the memory "template," that you now use to make sense out of any new incoming information. These templates are formed throughout the brain at many different levels, and because information comes in first to the lower, more primitive areas, many are not even accessible to conscious awareness. For example, young Tina almost certainly wasn't aware of the template that guided her interactions with men, and shaped her behavior with me when we first met. Further, all of us have probably had the experience of physically jumping up before we even figured out what it was that startled us in the first place. This happens because our brain's stress response systems carry information about potential threats and are primed to respond to them as quickly as possible, which often means before the cortex can consider what action to take. If, like Tina, we have had highly stressful experiences, reminders of those situations can be similarly powerful and provoke reactions that are similarly driven by unconscious processes.

What this also means is that early experiences will necessarily have a far greater impact than later ones. The brain tries to make sense of the world by looking for patterns. When it links coherent, consistently connected patterns together again, it tags them as "normal" or "expected" and stops paying conscious attention. So, for example, the very first time you were placed in a sitting position as an infant, you did pay attention to the novel sensations emanating from your buttocks. Your brain learned to sense the pressure associated with sitting normally, you began to sense how to balance your weight to sit upright via your motor vestibular system and, eventually, you learned to sit. Now, when you sit, unless it's uncomfortable or the seat is unusually textured or shaped or you have some kind of balance disorder, you pay little attention to staying upright or the pressure the seat puts on your rear. When you are driving, it's something you rarely attend to at all.

What you do scan the road for is novelty, things that are out of place, such as a truck barreling down the wrong side of the freeway. This is why we offload perceptions of things we consider normal: so that we can rapidly react to things that are aberrant and require immediate attention. Neural systems have evolved to be especially sensitive to novelty, since new experiences usually signal either danger or opportunity.

One of the most important characteristics of both memory, neural tissue, and of development, then, is that they all change with patterned, repetitive activity. So, the systems in your brain that get repeatedly activated will change, and the systems in your brain that don't get activated won't change. This "use-dependent" development is one of the most important properties of neural tissue. It seems like a simple concept, but it has enormous and wide-ranging implications.

And understanding this concept, I came to believe, was key to understanding children like Tina. She had developed a very unfortunate set of associations because she was sexually abused so early in life. Her first experiences with men and her teenage male abuser were what shaped her conception of what men are and how to act toward them; early experiences with those around us mold all of our worldviews. Because of the enormous amount of information the brain is confronted with daily, we must use these patterns to predict what the world is like. If early experiences are aberrant, these predictions may guide our behavior in dysfunctional ways. In Tina's world, males larger than she was were frightening, demanding creatures who forced her or her mother into sex. The scent, sight, and sounds associated with them came together to compose a set of "memory templates" that she used to make sense of the world.

And so, when she came into my office that first time and was alone in the company of an adult male, it was perfectly natural for her to assume that sex was what I wanted as well. When she went to school and exposed herself or tried to engage in sex play with other children, she was modeling what she knew about how to behave. She didn't consciously think about it. It was just a set of behaviors that were part of her toxic associations, her twisted template for sexuality.

Unfortunately, with only an hour a week of therapy, it was almost impossible to undo that set of associations. I could model the behavior of a different kind of adult male, I could show her that there were situations where sexual activity was inappropriate and help her learn to resist impulses, but I couldn't, in such a small amount of time, replace the template that had been forged in the fresh tissue of her young brain, that had been burned in with patterned, repetitive early experience. I would need to integrate a lot more about how the human brain works, how the brain changes, and the systems that interact in this learning into my treatments before I could even begin to do better for patients like Tina, patients whose lives and memories had been marred in multiple ways by early trauma.

CHAPTER 2

For Your Own Good

"I NEED YOUR HELP." THE CALLER, Stan Walker,* was an attorney for the Public Guardian's office in Cook County, Illinois. I had completed my training in child psychiatry and was now an assistant professor at the University of Chicago, still working at the clinic and running my lab. It was 1990.

"I just inherited a case scheduled to go to trial next week," he told me, explaining that it was a homicide. A three-year-old girl named Sandy had witnessed the murder of her own mother. Now, almost a year later, the prosecution wanted her to testify about it. "I'm concerned that this might be pretty overwhelming for her," Stan went on, asking if I might be able to help prepare her for court.

"Pretty overwhelming?" I thought sarcastically to myself, "You think so?"

Stan was a Guardian-ad-litem, an attorney appointed by the court to represent children in the legal system. In Cook County (where Chicago is located), the Public Guardian's Office has a full-time staff to represent children in the Child Protective

Services (CPS) system. In almost all other communities this role is played by an appointed attorney who may or may not have experience and training in child law. Cook County had created the full-time positions in the noble hope that if the attorneys worked their cases full time, they could develop experience with children, learn about maltreatment, and thus better serve those they represent. (Unfortunately, like all other components of the child protective system, the volume of cases was overwhelming and the office was underfunded.)

"Who is her therapist?" I asked, thinking that someone familiar to the child would be much better suited to help her prepare.

"She doesn't have one," he said. This was disturbing news.

"No therapist? Where is she living?" I asked.

"We don't really know. She is in foster care but the prosecutor and the Department of Child and Family Services are keeping her location undisclosed because there have been threats against her life. She knew the suspect and identified him for the police. He is in a gang and there is a contract out on her." This was sounding worse and worse.

"She gave a credible ID at age three?" I asked. I knew that eyewitness testimony is easily challenged in court because of the properties of narrative memory we noted earlier, especially its gaps and the way it tends to "fill in" the "expected." And from a four-year-old about an event that occurred when she was three? If the prosecutors didn't have some help, a good defense attorney would easily make Sandy's testimony appear completely unreliable.

"Well, she knew him," Stan explained. "She both spontaneously said he did it and later identified him from a photo array."

I asked if there was any additional evidence, thinking that maybe the little girl's testimony wouldn't even be necessary. If there was enough other evidence, perhaps I could help him convince the prosecutor that testifying posed too great a risk of further traumatizing the child.

Stan explained that there was indeed other evidence. In fact, numerous types of physical evidence placed the perpetrator at the scene. Investigators had found the girl's mother's blood all over his clothes. Despite having fled the country after committing the crime, the man still had blood on his shoes when he was arrested.

"So why does Sandy have to testify?" I asked. I was already starting to feel pulled to help this child.

"That is part of what we are trying to figure out. We are hoping to have the case postponed until we can either get her testimony by closed-circuit TV or make sure she is ready to testify in court." He went on to describe the details of the murder, the girl's hospitalization due to injuries she'd received during the crime, and her subsequent foster care placements.

As I listened, I debated whether or not to get involved. As usual I was overextended and extremely busy. Plus, I'm uncomfortable in court and I hate lawyers. But the more Stan talked, the more I couldn't believe what I was hearing. The people who were supposed to help this girl—from the Department of Children and Family Services (DCFS) to the justice system—seemed clueless about the effects of trauma on children. I began to feel that she deserved to have at least one person in her life who might not be.

"So, let me go over this again," I said, "A three-year-old girl witnesses her mother being raped and murdered. She has her own throat cut, twice, and is left for dead. She is alone with her dead mother's body for eleven hours in their apartment. Then, she's taken to the hospital and has the wounds on her neck treated. In the hospital, the physicians recommend ongoing mental health evaluation and treatment. But after she's released, she's placed in a foster home as a ward of the state.

Her CPS caseworker doesn't think she needs to see a mental health professional. So, despite the doctors' recommendations, he doesn't get her any help. For nine months, this child is moved from foster home to foster home with no counseling or psychiatric care whatsoever. And the details of the child's experiences are never shared with the foster families because she is in hiding. Right?"

"Yeah, I guess all of that is true," he said, hearing the unmistakable frustration in my voice and how terrible it all sounded when I described the situation so bluntly.

"And now, ten days before a murder trial is scheduled to start, you become aware of the situation?"

"Right," he admitted, sheepish now.

"When did your office get notified about this girl?" I demanded.

"Actually we opened the case right after this happened."

"No one in your office thought to ensure that she had some mental health support?"

"We tend to review cases when they come up for their hearings. We have hundreds of cases apiece." I wasn't surprised. The public systems working with high-risk families and children are overwhelmed. Oddly enough, during my years of clinical training in child mental health I had little introduction to the child protective system or to the special education and juvenile justice systems, despite the fact that more than 30 percent of the children coming to our clinics were in one or more of these systems. The compartmentalization of services, training, and points of view was staggering. And, I was learning, very destructive for children.

"When and where can I see her?" I asked. I couldn't help myself. I agreed to meet Sandy in an office at the court the next day.

I was somewhat surprised that Stan had called *me* for help. Earlier that year he had sent me a "cease and desist" letter. In four long paragraphs I was told that I must immediately provide justification for the use of a medication called clonidine to "control" children at a residential treatment center where I consulted. I provided the psychiatric services for the children at the center. The letter said that if I could not explain what I was up to, I must immediately stop this "experimental" treatment. It was signed by Stan Walker in his official capacity as attorney with the Public Guardian.

After receiving Stan's letter, I contacted him to explain why I was using this medication and why I believed it would be a mistake to stop. The children at this residential center were among the state's most difficult cases. More than one hundred boys had been placed in this program after "failing" in foster homes due to severe behavioral and psychiatric problems. Although the facility accepted boys from seven to seventeen, the average child in the facility was a ten-year-old who had lived in ten prior "homes," meaning that for most of them no fewer than ten parent substitutes had found them unmanageable. Easy to stir up and overwhelm but very difficult to calm down, these children had been a problem for every caregiver, therapist, and teacher they had encountered. Ultimately, they'd get kicked out of foster homes, child care settings, schools, and sometimes even therapy. The final stop was this center.

AFTER REVIEWING THE RECORDS of some 200 boys who were then living at the center or who had been there in the past, I found that every single one of these boys—without exception—had experienced severe trauma or abuse. The vast majority had had at least six major traumatic experiences. All of these children had been born into and raised with chaos, threat, and trauma. They were incubated in terror.

All of them had been evaluated multiple times both prior to

and during their stay at the center. Each had been given dozens of different DSM diagnostic labels, primarily attention deficit/hyperactivity disorder, oppositional-defiant disorder, and conduct disorder—just like Tina. But shockingly, very few of these children were viewed as "traumatized" or "stressed;" their trauma wasn't deemed relevant to diagnosis, much like in Tina's case. Despite lengthy histories of domestic violence, repeatedly interrupted familial relationships often including the loss of parents to violent death or disease, physical abuse, sexual abuse, and other overwhelmingly distressing events, few had been diagnosed with post-traumatic stress disorder (PTSD). PTSD did not even make it into the "differential diagnosis," a list included in the case report of possible alternative diagnoses with similar symptoms that each clinician considers, then rules out.

Post-traumatic stress disorder was a relatively new concept at the time, having been introduced into the DSM diagnostic system in 1980 to describe a syndrome found in Vietnam veterans who, upon returning from their tours of duty, often experienced anxiety, sleep problems, and intrusive and disturbing "flashback" memories of events that took place during the war. They were frequently jumpy and some responded aggressively to even the most minor signals of threat. Many had terrifying nightmares and reacted to loud noises as though they were gunshots and they were still back in the jungles of Southeast Asia.

During my general psychiatry training, I had worked with vets who suffered from PTSD. Many psychiatrists were, even then, beginning to recognize its prevalence in adults who'd suffered other kinds of traumatic experiences like rape and natural disasters. What struck me especially was that, although the experiences that had scarred adults with PTSD were often relatively brief (usually lasting for a few hours at most), their impact could still be seen in their behavior years—even decades—later. It reminded me of what Seymour Levine had found in those rat pups, where a few minutes of stress could change the brain for life. How much more powerful, I thought, must the impact of a genuinely traumatic experience be for a child!

Later, as a general resident in psychiatry, I studied aspects of the stress response systems in vets with PTSD. I and other researchers found that these veterans' stress response systems were overreactive, what scientists call "sensitized." This meant that when they were exposed to minor stressors their systems reacted as though they were facing great threat. In some cases the brain systems associated with the stress response had become so active that they eventually "burnt out" and lost their ability to regulate the other functions they would normally mediate. As a result the brain's capacity to regulate mood, social interactions, and abstract cognition was also compromised.

At the time I was working with the boys at the center, I was continuing to study the development of the stress-related neurotransmitter systems in the lab. I was looking not only at adrenaline and noradrenaline now, but exploring other related systems as well: those using serotonin, dopamine, and the endogenous opioids, which are known as enkephalins and endorphins. Serotonin is probably best known as the site of action for antidepressant medications like Prozac and Zoloft; dopamine is known as a chemical involved with pleasure and motivation involved in the "high" from drugs like cocaine and amphetamine; endogenous opioids are the brain's natural pain-killers and are affected by heroin, morphine, and similar drugs. All of these chemicals play important roles in the response to stress, with adrenaline and noradrenaline preparing the body for fight or flight, and dopamine providing a sense of competence and power to achieve one's goals. Serotonin's actions are less easy to characterize, but the opioids are known to soothe, relax, and reduce any pain that may be involved in responding to stress and threat.

After I'd recognized that Tina's attention and impulsivity-related symptoms were linked to a hyperaroused stress system, I had begun to think that medications that calmed the stress system might help others like her. Clonidine, an old and generally safe medication, had long been used to treat people whose blood pressure was usually normal, but skyrocketed into hypertension when they were under stress. Clonidine helped "quiet" this reactivity down. A preliminary study using this medication had shown that it also helped decrease PTSD-related hyperarousal symptoms in adult combat veterans. Knowing that the physical symptoms many of the boys at the residential treatment center exhibited were consistent with an overactive and overly reactive stress system, I'd decided to try clonidine on them with their guardian's permission.

And for many, it worked. Within a few weeks of beginning to take the medication, the boys' resting heart rates had normalized and their sleep improved. Their attention became more focused and their impulsivity was reduced. Even better, the boys' grades began to improve, as did their social interactions with each other. To me, of course, this was no surprise. By reducing the overactivity in their stress systems, the medication enabled the boys to be less distracted by signals of threat. This helped them become more attentive to both academic material and ordinary social cues, allowing them to improve their schoolwork and interpersonal skills (see Figure 3, Appendix, for additional details).

I'd explained all of this to Stan Walker after I'd gotten his letter. To my surprise, he withdrew his objections and asked me to send him some more information about trauma and children. Unfortunately, as I informed him, there was not much written on the topic at the time. I sent him some of these early reports and some writing I had done myself. Until this call I had not heard back from him.

THE NEXT DAY, AS I PREPARED to meet Sandy, I tried to imagine the crime she'd witnessed from her perspective. Nine months earlier she had been found covered in blood, lying over her murdered mother's naked body, whimpering incoherently. At the time she was not yet four. How could she go on, day after day, with those images in her mind? How could I possibly prepare her for testimony, and the confrontation of cross-examination, a threatening experience even for adults? What would she be like?

I also wondered how she had survived psychologically. How could her mind protect her from these traumatic experiences? And, how could any reasonable person, let alone someone trained to deal with troubled children, not realize that she needed help after what she'd been through?

Unfortunately, the prevailing view of children and trauma at the time—one that persists to a large degree to this day—is that "children are resilient." I recall visiting the scene of a murder around this time with a colleague who had started a trauma response team to help first responders to crime and accident scenes. Police, paramedics and fire fighters often see terrible panoramas of death, mutilation and devastation, and this, of course, can take an awful toll. My colleague was justifiably proud of the services he had put into place to help these professionals. As we walked through the house where the victim's blood still soaked the couch and splattered the walls, I saw three young children standing like zombies in the corner.

"What about the children?" I asked, as I nodded my head toward the three blood-speckled witnesses. He glanced at them, thought for a moment, and replied, "Children are resilient. They will be fine." Still young and respectful of my elders, I nodded my head as if to acknowledge his wisdom, but inside I was screaming.

If anything, children are more vulnerable to trauma than adults; I knew this from Seymour Levine's work and the work of dozens of others by then. Resilient children are made, not born. The developing brain is most malleable and most sensitive to experience—both good and bad—early in life. (This is why we so easily and rapidly learn language, social nuance, motor skills, and dozens of other things in childhood, and why we speak of "formative" experiences.) Children become resilient as a result of the patterns of stress and of nurturing that they experience early on in life, as we shall see in greater detail later in this book. Consequently, we are also rapidly and easily transformed by trauma when we are young. Though its effects may not always be visible to the untrained eye, when you know what trauma can do to children, sadly, you begin to see its aftermath everywhere.

At that time my laboratory was studying neurobiological mechanisms, which I knew were related to resilience and vulnerability to stress. We were examining a curious but very important effect of drugs that stimulate the systems I'd been studying in the brain. These effects are called sensitization and tolerance, and they have profound implications for understanding the human mind and its reaction to trauma.

In sensitization, a pattern of stimulus leads to increased sensitivity to future similar stimulus. This is what is seen in the Vietnam veterans and the rats that were genetically oversensitive to stress or became that way because of early exposure to it. When the brain becomes sensitized, even small stressors can provoke large responses. Tolerance, on the contrary, mutes one's response to an experience over time. Both factors are important for the functioning of memory: if we didn't get tolerant to familiar experiences, they would always appear new and potentially overwhelming. The brain would probably run out of storage capacity, like an old computer. Similarly, if we didn't become increasingly sensitive to certain things, we would not be able to improve how we respond to them.

Curiously, both effects can be achieved with the same amount of the same drug, but you get completely opposite results if the pattern of drug use is different. For example, if a rat, or a human, is given small, frequent doses of drugs like cocaine or heroin that act on the dopamine and opioid systems, the drugs lose their "strength." This is part of what happens during addiction: the addict becomes tolerant, and so more of the drug is needed to achieve the same "high." In contrast, if you give an animal the exact same daily quantity of drug, but in large, infrequent doses, the drug actually "gains" strength. In two weeks a dose that caused a mild reaction on day one can actually cause a profound and prolonged overreaction on day fourteen. Sensitization to a drug, in some cases, can lead to seizures and even death, a phenomenon that may be responsible for some otherwise inexplicable drug overdoses. Sadly for people with addiction, their drug craving tends to produce patterns of use that cause tolerance, not sensitization to the "high" that they desire, while simultaneously producing sensitization to certain undesirable effects, like the paranoia associated with cocaine use.

More importantly, for our purposes, resilience or vulnerability to stress depend upon a person's neural system's tolerance or sensitization following earlier experience. These effects can also help further explain the difference between stress and trauma, which is important to understand as we consider children like Tina and Sandy. For example, "use it or lose it" is something we hear at the gym with good reason. Inactive muscle gets weak, while active muscle gets stronger. This principle is referred to as "use-dependence." Similarly, the more a system in the brain is activated, the more that system will build—or maintain—synaptic connections.

The changes—memory of sorts—in muscle occur because patterned, repetitive activity sends a signal to muscle cells that "you will be working at this level" so they make the molecular changes required to do that work easily. In order to change the muscle, however, the repetitions must be patterned. Curling twenty-five pounds thirty times in three closely timed sets of ten curls leads to stronger muscle. If you curl twenty-five pounds thirty times at random intervals during the day, however, the signal to the muscle is inconsistent, chaotic and insufficient to cause the muscle cells to become stronger. Without the pattern the very same repetitions and very same total weight will produce a far less effective result. To create an effective "memory" and increase strength, experience has to be patterned and repetitive.

And so it is with the neurons, neural systems and the brain. Patterns of experience matter. On a cell-by-cell basis, no other tissue is more suited to change in response to patterned repetitive signals. Indeed, neurons are designed to do just that. It is this molecular gift that allows memory. It produces the synaptic connections that allow us to eat, type, make love, play basketball and do everything else a human being is capable of doing. It is these intricate webs of interconnection that make the brain work.

By forcing either your muscles or your brain to work, however, you do "stress" them. Biological systems exist in balance. In order to function they have to stay within a certain limited range appropriate to their current activity, and it is the brain that is charged with maintaining this essential equilibrium. The actual experience is a stressor; the impact on the system is stress. And so, if you get dehydrated during exercise, for example, that stress will make you thirsty because your brain is trying to drive you to replace the needed fluids. Similarly, when a child learns a new vocabulary word, there is a tiny stress applied to the cortex, which requires repetitive stimulation to create accurate recall. Without the stress, the system wouldn't know there is something new to attend to. In other words, stress is not always bad.

Indeed, if moderate, predictable and patterned, it is stress that makes a system stronger and more functionally capable.

Hence, the stronger muscle in the present is the one that has endured moderate stress in the past. And the same is true for the brain's stress response systems. Through moderate, predictable challenges our stress response systems are activated moderately. This makes for a resilient, flexible stress response capacity. The stronger stress response system in the present is the one that has had moderate, patterned stress in the past.

However, that is not the whole story. If you try to bench press 200 pounds on your first trip to the gym, if you do manage to lift the weight at all, you're not likely to build muscle, but tear it and hurt yourself. The pattern and intensity of experience matter. If a system is overloaded—worked beyond capacity—the result can be profound deterioration, disorganization, and dysfunction whether you are overworking your back muscles at the gym or your brain's stress networks when confronted with traumatic stress.

This also means that as a result of the strengthening effect of previous moderate and patterned experience, what may be traumatically stressful for one person may be trivial for another. Just as a body builder can carry weights that untrained people cannot even move, so too can some brains deal with traumatic events that would cripple others. The context, timing and response of others matters profoundly. The death of a parent is far more traumatic for the two-year-old child of a single mother than it is for a fifty-year-old married man with children of his own.

In Tina's case and that of the boys at the center, their experience of stress was far beyond their young systems' capacities to carry it. Rather than moderate, predictable and strengthening activation of their stress systems, they had suffered unpredictable, prolonged and extreme experiences that had marked their young lives profoundly. I couldn't see any way that this would not be true for Sandy as well.

BEFORE I MET HER I TRIED TO GET as much background and history on Sandy as I could. I talked with her current foster family, her new caseworker and, ultimately, with members of her extended family. I learned that she had profound sleep problems and was pervasively anxious. I was told that she had an increased startle response. Just like the traumatized Vietnam vets I'd worked with, she would jump at the slightest unexpected noise. She also had episodic periods of daydreaming, during which it was extremely difficult to get her to "snap out of it." A doctor who saw her without knowing her history might have diagnosed her with the "absence" or "petit mal" form of epilepsy: she was that hard to reach during these episodes.

I also learned that Sandy sometimes had aggressive, tantrum-like outbursts. Her foster family couldn't find any pattern to these behaviors, couldn't pinpoint what set them off. But they did report another set of "odd" behaviors: Sandy didn't want to use silverware. Unsurprisingly, she was especially afraid of knives; but she also refused to drink milk, or even look at milk bottles. When the doorbell rang, she would hide like a skittish cat, sometimes so effectively that it took twenty minutes for her foster parents to find her. She could also be found, on occasion, hiding underneath a bed, behind a couch, in a cabinet under the kitchen sink, rocking and crying.

So much for resilience. Sandy's startle reaction alone told me that her stress response systems had become sensitized. Testifying would immerse her in painful reminders of that terrible night. I had to get some sense of whether or not she could tolerate it. Though I didn't want to, at some point in my initial visit I was going to have to probe her memory a little to see how she would react. But I comforted myself with the knowledge that a little pain now could help protect her from a lot of pain later, and might even help her begin the healing process.

I FIRST MET SANDY IN A SMALL room housed in a typical, sterile government building. It had been set up to be "child-friendly" with some child-size furniture, toys, crayons, coloring books, and paper. A few cartoon figures had been painted on the walls, but "system" still screamed out from the tile floors and cinder-block construction. When I walked in, Sandy was sitting on the floor with some dolls around her. She was coloring. What first struck me, as it had when I first met Tina, was how small she was. I guessed she stood a bit less than four feet tall. She had huge, liquid brown eyes and long, thick, curly brown hair. On her neck were visible scars on both sides, from her ears to the middle of her throat. But they were much less noticeable than I had imagined they might be; the plastic surgeons had done a good job. As I walked in with Stan she stopped everything and stared at me, frozen.

Stan introduced me. "Sandy, this is the doctor I told you about. He is going to talk with you, OK?" he asked anxiously. She didn't move, not one millimeter. There was no change in her wary expression. In response Stan looked at me and back at her, gave a big smile and said in his best cheerful, kindergarten-teacher voice, "OK. Good. Well, I will leave you two together." As he walked out I looked at him like he was nuts, surprised by how he'd dismissed Sandy's lack of response to his question. When I looked back at Sandy her face wore the same expression that mine did. I shook my head, shrugged my shoulders, and gave a little smile. As if in a mirror, Sandy did the same.

Aha! A connection! This was a good start, I thought. Don't let it slip away. I knew if I walked toward this tiny girl—I'm pretty big—her sensitized alarm response would go crazy. Her surroundings were already unfamiliar enough—new adults, new place, new situation—I needed her to stay as calm as possible.

"I want to color some too." I said without looking at her. I wanted to be as predictable as possible and let her know what I was going to do step by step. No sudden moves. Make yourself smaller, I thought, get on the floor. Don't look at her, don't face her, use slow deliberate movements as you color. I sat down on the floor, a few feet away. I tried to make my voice as soothing and calm as possible.

"I really like red. This should be a red car," I said, pointing at a picture in my coloring book.

Sandy studied my face, my hands, and my slow movements. She was only partly attentive to my words. This little girl was justifiably suspicious. For a long time I colored alone, chattering about my choices of colors, being as casual and friendly as possible without being overly "bright" as Stan had been when he tried to mask his anxiety. Eventually, Sandy broke the rhythm by moving a bit closer toward me and silently directing me to use a specific color. I complied. Once she came over to me, I stopped talking. For many minutes more we colored together in silence.

I had yet to ask her about what had happened, but I could sense that she knew that was why I was there—and that she knew that I knew she knew. All of the adults in her "new" life had sooner or later, in some way, returned her to that night.

"What happened to your neck?" I asked, pointing to her two scars. She acted as if she did not hear me. She did not change her expression. She did not change the pace of her coloring.

I repeated the question. Now, she froze. Coloring stopped. Her eyes stared off into space, unblinking. I asked again. She took her crayon and scribbled over her well-formed, disciplined picture but gave no response.

Again, I asked. I hated this. I knew I was pushing her toward her painful memories.

Sandy stood up, grabbed a stuffed rabbit, held it by the ears and slashed at the neck of the animal with the crayon. As she slashed, she repeated, "It's for your own good, dude." Over and over—a stuck recording. She threw the animal to the floor, ran to the radiator, and climbed up and jumped off again and again. She did not respond to my warnings to be careful. Worried that she would hurt herself, I rose and caught her on one of her jumps. She melted into my arms. We sat together for a few more minutes. Her frenzied breathing slowed and then almost stopped.

And then, in a slow, robotic monotone she told me about that night.

An acquaintance of her mother had come to their apartment. He had rung the doorbell and her mother had let him in. "Mama was yelling, the bad guy was hurting her," she said. "I should have killed him."

"When I came out of my room and Mama was asleep, then he cut me," she continued, "He said, 'It's for your own good, dude.'"

The assailant had cut her throat—twice. Sandy immediately collapsed. Later, she regained consciousness and attempted to "wake up" her mother. She took milk from the refrigerator and gagged when she tried to drink some. It oozed through the slit in her throat. She tried to give some to her mother, but "she was not thirsty," Sandy told me. Sandy wandered that apartment for eleven hours before anyone came. A relative, worried that Sandy's mother had not answered the phone, had dropped by and discovered the horrifying crime scene.

BY THE END OF THAT INTERVIEW I was certain that testifying would be devastating for Sandy. She needed help and, if she did have to testify, more time to prepare. Stan would work successfully, as it turned out, to postpone the trial. "Could you do the therapy?" he asked me. Of course. I couldn't say no.

THE IMAGES OF SANDY BURNED into my mind during that interview were staggering: a three-year-old child, her throat cut, weeping, trying to comfort and also seeking comfort from her naked mother's hog-tied, bloody, and ultimately cold body. How helpless, confused, and terrified she must have felt! Her symptoms—her "absences," her avoidant responses to my questions, her hiding, her specific fears—were defenses constructed by her brain to keep the trauma at bay. Understanding those defenses would be critical to helping her and other children like her.

Even *in utero* and after birth, for every moment of every day, our brain is processing the nonstop set of incoming signals from our senses. Sight, sound, touch, smell, taste—all of the raw sensory data that will result in these sensations enter the lower parts of the brain and begin a multistage process of being categorized, compared to previously stored patterns, and ultimately, if necessary, acted upon.

In many cases the pattern of incoming signals is so repetitive, so familiar, so safe, and the memory template that this pattern matches is so deeply engrained, that your brain essentially ignores them. This is a form of tolerance called habituation.

We ignore familiar patterns in ordinary contexts, so much so that we forget large portions of our days, which are spent doing routine things like brushing our teeth or getting dressed.

We'll remember if a familiar pattern occurs out of context, however. For example, you might be on a camping trip, brushing your teeth as the sun comes up. The beauty of the moment is so powerful that you will remember this one time as unique. Emotions are powerful markers of context. The pleasure and joy of the sunrise in this instance is unusual in the "brushing teeth" memory template, so it makes it more vivid and memorable.

Similarly, if you happen to be brushing your teeth when an earthquake destroys your home, those events may become forever connected in your mind and recalled together. Negative emotions often make things even more memorable than positive ones because recalling things that are threatening—and avoiding those situations in the future if possible—is often critical to survival. A mouse that didn't learn to avoid the scent of cats after one bad experience, for example, would not be a mouse likely to produce many offspring. As a result, however, such associations can become the source of trauma-related symptoms. For an earthquake survivor who was brushing her teeth when the house collapsed around her, simply seeing a toothbrush might be enough to provoke a full-fledged fear response.

In Sandy's case, milk, once associated with nurturing and nutrition, now became the stuff that spilled from her throat, that her mother "refused" as she lay dead. Silverware was now no longer something used to eat your food, but rather something that killed and maimed and horrified. And doorbells— well, that was what had started the whole thing: the ringing of the doorbell had announced the arrival of the killer.

For her these mundane and ordinary things had become evocative cues that kept her in a state of continual fear. This, of course, confused her foster parents and her teachers, who didn't know the details of what had happened to her and therefore often couldn't recognize what might be prompting her strange behavior. They couldn't understand why she would be so sweet one moment and then impulsive, defiant, and aggressive the next. The outbursts seemed disconnected from any event or interaction that the adults could identify. But both the seeming unpredictability and the nature of her behaviors made complete sense. Her brain was trying to protect her based upon what it had previously learned about the world.

The brain is always comparing current incoming patterns with previously stored templates and associations. This matching process takes place initially in the lowest, simplest parts of the brain, where, as you may recall, the neural systems involved in responding to threat originate. As the information moves upward from this first stage of processing, the brain has opportunities to take a second look at the data for more complex consideration and integration. But at first all it wants to know is: Does this incoming data potentially suggest danger?

If the experience is familiar and known as safe, the brain's stress system will not be activated. However, if the incoming information is initially unfamiliar, new, or strange, the brain instantly begins a stress response. How extensively these stress systems are activated is related to how threatening the situation appears. It's important to understand that our default is set at suspicion, not acceptance. At a minimum, when faced with a new and unknown pattern of activity, we become more alert. The brain's goal at this point is to get more information, to examine the situation and determine just how dangerous it might be. Since humans have always been the deadliest animal encountered by other humans, we closely monitor nonverbal signals of human menace, such as tone of voice, facial expression, and body language.

Upon further evaluation, our brain may recognize that the new pattern of activation has been caused by something familiar, but out of context. For example, if you are in the library reading and someone drops a heavy book on a table, the loud noise will immediately make you stop reading. You will activate your arousal response, focus on the source of the noise, categorize it as a safe, familiar accident—perhaps annoying, but nothing to worry about. If, on the other hand, you hear a loud noise in the library, turn and discover that other people around you seem alarmed, then look up and see a man with a gun, your brain would move from arousal to alarm and probably then into full-blown fear. If in a few minutes, you learn that this was a bad student prank, your brain would slowly move back down this arousal continuum toward a state of calm.

The fear response is graded, calibrated by the brain's per-ceived level of threat (see Figure 3, Appendix). As you become increasingly frightened, the threat systems in your brain con-tinue to integrate incoming information and orchestrate a total body response aimed at keeping you alive. To that end an impressive set of interacting neural and hormonal systems work together to make sure your brain and the rest of your body do the right things. First, your brain makes you stop thinking about irrelevant things by shutting down the chatter of the frontal cortex. Then, it focuses on cues from others around you to help you determine who might protect or threaten you, by letting the limbic system's "social cue reading" systems take over. Your heart rate increases to get blood to your muscles in case you need to fight or flee. Your muscle tone also increases and sensations like hunger are put aside. In thousands of differ-ent ways your brain prepares to protect you.

When we are calm it is easy to live in our cortex, using the highest capacities of our brains to contemplate abstractions, make plans, dream of the future, read. But if something attracts our attention and intrudes on our thoughts, we become more vigilant and concrete, shifting the balance of our brain activity to subcortical areas to heighten our senses in order to detect threats. As we move up the arousal continuum toward fear, then, we necessarily rely on lower and faster brain regions. In complete panic, for example, our responses are reflexive and under virtually no conscious control. Fear quite literally makes us dumber, a property that allows faster reactions in short peri-ods of time and helps immediate survival. But fear can become maladaptive if it is sustained; the threat system becomes sen-sitized to keep us in this state constantly. This "hyperarousal" response accounted for many of Sandy's symptoms.

But not all of them. The brain doesn't have just one set of adaptations for threat. In the situation Sandy faced she was so small and so powerless and the threat she experienced so overwhelming, that she was unable to fight or flee. If her brain had responded by raising her heart rate and preparing her muscles for action, that would only have made her more likely to bleed to death when she was injured. Amazingly, our brains have a set of adaptations for these kinds of situations as well, which accounts for another important set of trauma-related symptoms, known as "dissociative" responses.

Dissociation is a very primitive reaction: the earliest life forms (and the youngest members of higher species) can rarely escape dire situations under their own steam. Their only possible response to being attacked or hurt, then, is essentially to curl up, to make themselves as small as possible, to cry for help and hope for a miracle. This response appears to be driven by the most primitive brain systems, located in the brainstem and immediately surrounding it. For infants and young children, incapable of or ineffective at fighting or fleeing, a dissociative response to extreme stressors is common. It is also more common in females than males and, if prolonged, dissociation is connected with increased odds for post-traumatic stress symptoms.

During dissociation, the brain prepares the body for injury. Blood is shunted away from the limbs and the heart rate slows to reduce blood loss from wounds. A flood of endogenous opioids—the brain's natural heroin-like substances—is released, killing pain, producing calm and a sense of psychological distance from what is happening.

Like the hyperarousal response, the dissociative response is graded and occurs on a continuum. Ordinary states like daydreaming and transitions between sleep and wakefulness are mild forms of dissociation. Hypnotic trance is another example. In extreme dissociative experiences, however, the person becomes completely focused inward and disconnected from reality. Brain regions that dominate thinking shift from planning action to concerning themselves with brute survival. There is a sense that time has slowed and what's happening isn't "real." Breathing slows. Pain and even fear shut down. People often report feeling emotionless and numb, as though they are watching what's happening to them affect a character in a movie.

In most traumatic experiences, however, not one but a combination of these two major responses occurs. Indeed, in many cases a moderate dissociation during a traumatic event can modulate the intensity and duration of the hyperarousal response. The capacity to become "numb" and partially robotic during combat, for example, allows the soldier to continue to function effectively without panic. But in some cases one pattern or the other predominates. And if these patterns are activated repeatedly long enough, due to the intensity, duration, or pattern of the trauma, there will be "use-dependent" changes in the neural systems that mediate these responses. The result is that these systems can become overactive and sensitized, leading to a host of emotional, behavioral, and cognitive problems long after the traumatic event is over.

We have come to understand that many post-traumatic psychiatric symptoms, in fact, are related to either dissociative or hyperarousal responses to memories of the trauma. These responses can help people survive immediate trauma, but if they persist, they can cause serious problems in other areas of life down the road.

There are few better examples of trauma-related problems than what I saw in those boys at the residential center. The impact of trauma—and the frequent misinterpretation of its symptoms—revealed itself in the fact that nearly every one of them had some kind of diagnosis related to attention and conduct problems. In a classroom setting, unfortunately, both dissociation and hyperarousal responses look remarkably like attention deficit disorder, hyperactivity, or oppositional-defiant disorder. Dissociated children quite obviously are not paying attention: they seem to be daydreaming or "spacing out," rather than focusing on schoolwork, and indeed, they have tuned out the world around them. Hyperaroused youth can look hyperactive or inattentive because what they are attending to is the teacher's tone of voice or the other children's body language, not the content of their lessons.

The aggression and impulsivity that the fight or flight response provokes can also appear as defiance or opposition, when in fact it is the remnants of a response to some prior traumatic situation that the child has somehow been prompted to recall. The "freezing" response that the body makes when stressed—sudden immobility, like a deer caught in the headlights—is also often misinterpreted as defiant refusal by teachers because, when it occurs, the child literally cannot respond to commands. While not all ADD, hyperactivity, and oppositional-defiant disorder are trauma-related, it is likely that the symptoms that lead to these diagnoses are trauma-related more often than anyone has begun to suspect.

THE FIRST TIME I MET SANDY FOR therapy it was in the foyer of a church. Still in a form of witness protection, she had to be protected from the killer's fellow gang members, who could not be arrested because they hadn't directly taken part in the crime. So we met in unusual places at atypical times. Often, this turned out to be Sundays at a church. She was there with her foster parents. I greeted them. Sandy recognized me, but did not smile.

I brought her foster mother into the room where we were to hold the session, a preschool classroom. Then, I took some crayons and paper and lay down on the carpet to color. In a minute or two Sandy came over and joined me on the floor. I looked over to the foster mother and said, "Sandy, Mrs. Sally* is going to go to church while we play. Is that OK?"

She didn't look up, but said, "OK."

We sat on the floor and colored in silence. For ten minutes our play was just like the initial visit in the court. Then, it changed. Sandy stopped coloring. She took the crayon from my hand, pulled at my arm and tugged at my shoulder to make me lay face down on the floor.

"What game is this?" I asked playfully.

"No. Don't talk," she said. She was deadly serious and forceful. She had me bend my knees and put my arms behind my back, as if I was hog-tied. And then, the reenactment took place. For the next forty minutes, she wandered the classroom, muttering things, only some of which I heard.

"This is good. You can eat this," she said, coming over to me with plastic vegetables and opening my mouth to try to feed me. Then, she brought a blanket over to cover me. During that initial therapy session she would approach me, lay on me, shake me, open my mouth and my eyes, and then leave again to find something in the room, almost always returning with a toy or another object. She did not reenact her own assault, and for the rest of the time I worked with her she never did fully reenact it, but she frequently said, "For your own good, dude," as she walked around.

While she did this, I had to do exactly what she wanted: don't talk, don't move, don't interfere, don't stop. She needed to have total control while she performed this reenactment. And that control, I began to recognize, would be critical to helping her heal.

AFTER ALL, ONE OF THE DEFINING elements of a traumatic experience—particularly one that is so traumatic that one dissociates because there is no other way to escape from it—is a complete loss of control and a sense of utter power-lessness. As a result, regaining control is an important aspect of coping with traumatic stress. This can be seen vividly in the classic research on a phenomenon that has come to be known as "learned helplessness." Martin Seligman and his colleagues at the University of Pennsylvania created this experimental paradigm in which two animals (in this case, rats) are housed in separate but adjacent cages. In one of these cages, each time the rat presses a lever to obtain food, it is first given an electric shock. This is, of course, stressful for the rat, but over time, rec-ognizing that it will receive food after the shock, it adjusts and becomes tolerant. The rat knows that the only time it will be shocked is when it presses the lever, so it has some level of control over the situation. As we've discussed, over time, a predictable and controllable stressor actually causes less "stress" on the sys-tem while tolerance increases.

But in the second cage, while the rat can press the bar to receive food just like the rat in the first cage does, this one gets shocked when the *other* rat presses the lever. In other words, the second rat has no idea when it will be shocked and no control over the situation. This rat becomes sensitized to the stress, not habituated to it. In both rats major changes can be seen in the stress systems of their brains: healthy changes in the case of the rats with control over the stress, and deterioration and dysregulation in the others. The animals that don't have control over the shock often develop ulcers, lose weight, and have compromised immune systems that actually make them more susceptible to disease. Sadly, even when the situation is changed so that they can control the shock, animals that have been placed in a situation without control for long enough become too frightened to explore the cage to figure out how to help themselves. The same kind of demoralization and res-ignation can often be seen in humans who become depressed, and research increasingly links the risk of depression to the number of uncontrollable stressful events people experience during their childhood. Unsurprisingly, PTSD is frequently accompanied by depression.

As a result of the link between control and habituation, and between lack of control and sensitization, recovery from trauma requires that the victim return to a situation that is predictable and safe. Our brains are naturally pulled to make sense of trauma in a way that allows us to become tolerant to it, to mentally shift the traumatic experience from one in which we are completely helpless to one in which we have some mastery.

That's what Sandy was doing in her reenactment behavior. She controlled our interactions in a way that allowed her to "titrate" the degree of stress during the sessions. Like a doctor balancing desired effects and side effects of a drug by choosing the right dose, Sandy regulated her exposure to the stress of her reenactment play. Her brain was pulling her to create a more tolerable pattern of stress, a more predictable experience that she could put in its place and leave behind. Her brain was trying, through reenactment, to make the trauma into something predictable, and, hopefully, ultimately boring. Pattern and repetition are the key to this. Patterned, repetitive stimuli lead to tolerance, while chaotic, infrequent signals produce sensitization.

To restore its equilibrium, the brain tries to quiet our sensitized, trauma-related memories by pushing us to have repetitive, small "doses" of recall. It seeks to make a sensitized system develop tolerance. And, in many cases, this works. In the immediate aftermath of a distressing or traumatic event we have intrusive thoughts: we keep thinking about what happened, we dream about it, we find ourselves thinking about it when we don't want to, we often tell and retell the event to trusted friends or loved ones. Children will reenact the events in play, drawings, and their daily interactions. The more intense and overwhelming the experience, however, the harder it becomes to "desensitize" all of the trauma-related memories.

In her reenactments with me, Sandy was attempting to develop tolerance to her terrible traumatic memories. She had control of these reenactments; this control let her modulate her own level of distress. If it became too intense she could redirect our play, and that's what she often did. I did not try to interfere with the process or push her to recall anything after that first time, when I had to do it for the evaluation.

In the first months of our work together each session would start the same way: silently. She would reach up for my hand and lead me to the middle of the room, pull me down and gesture. I would lay down and curl myself into the hog-tied position. She would explore the room, coming back and forth to me. Finally she would come and lay on my back. She would start to hum quietly and rock. I knew better by then not to talk or change position. I let her have the total control she needed. It was heartbreaking.

The responses of traumatized children are often misinterpreted. This even happened to Sandy at some points in foster care. Because new situations are inherently stressful, and because youth who have been through trauma often come from homes in which chaos and unpredictability appear "normal" to them, they may respond with fear to what is actually a calm and safe situation. Attempting to take control of what they believe is the inevitable return of chaos, they appear to "provoke" it in order to make things feel more comfortable and predictable. Thus, the "honeymoon" period in foster care will end as the child behaves defiantly and destructively in order to prompt familiar screaming and harsh discipline. Like everyone else, they feel more comfortable with what is "familiar." As one family therapist famously put it, we tend to prefer the "certainty of misery to the misery of uncertainty." This response to trauma can often cause serious problems for children when it is misunderstood by their caretakers.

Fortunately, in this case I was able to educate those who worked with Sandy about what to expect and how to respond to it. But still, outside of therapy, at first her sleep, anxiety, and behavioral problems persisted. Her resting heart rate was over 120, extremely high for a girl her age. Despite occasional profound dissociative behaviors, she was likely to appear "tuned up" and hypervigilant—similar, in some ways, to the boys I was seeing in the residential center. I discussed the potential positive effects of clonidine with her foster family, her caseworker, and with Stan. They agreed that we should try it and, indeed, her sleep soon improved and the frequency, intensity, and duration of her meltdowns decreased. She started to be easier to live with and to teach, at home as well as in her preschool classroom.

Our therapy continued as well. After about a dozen sessions she started to change the position in which she wanted me to lie. No more being hog-tied; now I would lie on my side. The same ritual took place. She explored the room, always coming back to my body lying in the middle of the floor and bringing me the things she collected. She would still hold my head to try to feed me. And then she'd lie down on me, rocking, humming fragments of tunes, sometimes stopping as if frozen. Sometimes, she would cry. Throughout this part of the session, usually about forty minutes, I would remain silent.

But over time, little by little, she transformed her reenactment. She did less muttering and exploring and spent more time rocking and humming. Finally, after many months of having me lie on the floor, as I started to walk to the middle of the room to lay down, she took my hand and led me to a rocking chair instead. She had me sit. She walked over to the bookcase, pulled down a book, and crawled into my lap. "Read me a story," she said. And as I started she said, "Rock." Thereafter, Sandy sat in my lap and we rocked and read books.

It was not a cure, but it was a good start. And even though

she had to go through an awful custody battle as her biological father, her maternal grandmother, and her foster family fought for custody of her, I'm pleased to say that ultimately, Sandy did all right. Her progress was slow but steady, especially after the custody case was resolved in favor of the foster family, with whom she spent the rest of her childhood. Sometimes, she struggled, but mostly she did amazingly well. She made friends, got good grades, and was notably kind and nurturing in her interactions with others. Often, years would go by and I wouldn't hear anything about her. But frequently, I thought about Sandy and what she had taught me in our work together. As I write this I am pleased to say that only months ago I received an update. She is doing well. Because of the circumstances of her case I cannot reveal any further details. Suffice it to say, she's having the kind of satisfying and productive life we had all wanted for her. Nothing could make me happier.

CHAPTER 3

Stairway to Heaven

INSIDE THE BRANCH DAVIDIAN compound in Waco, Texas, children lived in a world of fear. Even babies weren't immune: cult leader David Koresh believed that the wills of infants—some just eight months old—needed to be broken with strict physical discipline if they were to stay "in the light." Koresh was mercurial: one moment kind, attentive, and nurturing, and the next, a prophet of rage. His wrath was inescapable and unpredictable. The Davidians, as the members of the Mount Carmel religious community were called, became exquisitely sensitive to his moods as they attempted to curry his favor and tried, often in vain, to stave off his vengeance.

With his volatile temper and fearsome anger, Koresh excelled at using irregular doses of extreme threat—alternating with kind, focused attention—to keep his followers off balance. He maintained an iron grip, controlling every aspect of life in the compound. He separated husband from wife, child from parent, friend from friend, undermining any relationship that could challenge his position as the most dominant, powerful force in each person's life. Everyone's love converged upon him, like spokes connecting to the hub of a wheel. Koresh was the source of all insight, wisdom, love, and power; he was the conduit to God, if not God himself on earth.

And he was a god who ruled by fear. Children (and sometimes even adults) were in constant fear of the physical attacks and public humiliation that could result from the tiniest error, like spilling milk. Punishment often involved being beaten bloody with a wooden paddle called "the helper." Davidian children also feared hunger: those who "misbehaved" could be deprived of food for days or put on a bland diet of only potatoes or bread. Sometimes, they would be isolated overnight. And, for the girls, there was knowledge that they would ultimately become a "Bride of David." In a unique form of sanctioned sexual abuse girls as young as ten were groomed to become Koresh's sexual partners. A former member said Koresh once excitedly compared the heartbeats of the prepubescent girls he violated to those of hunted animals.

But perhaps the most pervasive fear that Koresh instilled was the fear of the "Babylonians": outsiders, government agents, nonbelievers. Koresh preached about and constantly prepared his community for the "final battle." The Branch Davidians, including children, were being readied for the imminent end of the world (hence Koresh's nickname for the compound, Ranch Apocalypse). This preparation involved military drills, interrupted sleep, and one-on-one fighting. If the children didn't want to participate or weren't vicious enough in battle training, they were humiliated and sometimes beaten. Even the youngest members were taught how to handle guns. They were instructed in the most lethal suicide techniques with firearms, being told to aim for the "soft spot" in the back of the mouth if they faced capture by the "Babylonians." The rationale was that "unbelievers" would ultimately come to kill everyone. After this apocalyptic battle, however, members were promised that they would be reunited with their families in heaven and Koresh— God—would return to earth to smite his enemies.

I CAME TO TEXAS IN 1992 TO become the vice chairman for research in the department of psychiatry at Baylor College of Medicine (BCM) in Houston. I also served as chief of psychiatry at Texas Children's Hospital (TCH) and director of the Trauma Recovery Program at the Houston Veterans Administration Medical Center (VAMC). My experiences with Tina, Sandy, the boys at the residential center, and others like them had convinced me that we didn't know enough about trauma and its effects on children's mental health. We didn't know how trauma during development produced particular problems in particular children. No one could say why some came away from trauma seemingly unscathed while others developed serious mental illnesses and behavioral problems. No one knew where the devastating symptoms of conditions like posttraumatic stress disorder came from, and why some children would develop, say, primarily dissociative symptoms, while others would mainly be hypervigilant. The only way to figure this out, it seemed, was to closely study groups of children immediately after a traumatic event. Unfortunately, children were usually brought to us for help only years after they'd suffered trauma, not right away.

It was to attempt to solve this problem that I, in coordination with BCM, TCH, and VAMC, put together a "rapid response" Trauma Assessment Team. It was our hope that while helping children cope with acute traumas like shootings, car accidents, natural disasters, and other life threatening situations, we could learn what to expect from children in the immediate aftermath of a traumatic experience and how this related to any symptoms they might ultimately suffer. The children of Waco would provide one unfortunately apt sample to study.

ON FEBRUARY 28, 1993, THE "Babylonians" in the form of the Bureau of Alcohol, Tobacco and Firearms (BATF) came to the Branch Davidian compound to arrest David Koresh for firearms violations. He would not allow himself to be taken alive. Four BATF agents and at least six Branch Davidians were killed in the ensuing raid. The FBI and its hostage negotiation team managed to secure the release of twenty-one children over the following three days. It was at this point that my team was brought in to help with what we thought would be the first wave of children from the compound. What none of us knew at the time was that we would never meet more Davidian children. The siege would end with a second and far more catastrophic raid on April 19, which left eighty members (including twenty-three children) dead in a horrific conflagration.

I heard about the first raid on the Branch Davidian compound like most people did: from the news on television. Almost immediately, reporters began calling to ask me how the raid might affect the children. When I was questioned about what was being done to help those who'd been removed from the compound, I replied almost off-handedly that I was sure the state was making sure they were properly cared for.

But just as soon as the words left my mouth, I realized that this was probably not true. Government agencies—especially the chronically underfunded and overburdened Child Protective Service (CPS) systems—rarely have concrete plans to deal with sudden influxes of large groups of children. Furthermore, chains of command between the federal, state and local agencies involved in law enforcement and CPS are often unclear in unusual, fast-moving crises like the Waco standoff.

As I thought more about this I felt pulled to see whether the expertise on childhood trauma that our Trauma Assessment Team had been developing could be helpful. I figured we could provide the people working with these children some basic information, consult by phone to help them solve particular problems, and play a supportive role in helping them better understand the situation. I contacted several agencies but no one could tell me who was "in charge." Finally I reached the governor's office. Within a few hours I was called by the state office of CPS and was asked to come to Waco for what I thought would be a one-time consultation. That afternoon meeting turned into six weeks of one of the most difficult cases I have ever had.

WHEN I ARRIVED IN WACO I FOUND disarray, both in the official agencies responding to the crisis and in the care of the children. During the first few days, when the children were released, they were driven away from the compound in large tank-like vehicles. No matter what time of day or night it was when they came out, they were immediately interrogated by the FBI and the Texas Rangers, often for hours. The FBI had the best intentions; they wanted information quickly so that they could help defuse the situation at the Ranch and get more people out safely. Witnesses' statements were needed, and the Texas Rangers were charged with gathering evidence for future criminal trials in order to prosecute those involved in the shooting deaths of the BATF agents. But neither group had thought through how overwhelming it would be for a child to be taken from his parents, put in a tank after witnessing a deadly raid on his home, driven to an armory, and questioned at length by numerous armed, strange men.

It was only dumb luck that kept the Davidian children together after the first raid. Originally, Texas CPS had planned to place them in individual foster homes, but they couldn't find enough homes fast enough to take all of them. Keeping them together turned out to be one of the most therapeutic decisions made in their case: these children would need each other. After what they had just experienced, ripping them from their peers and/or siblings would only have increased their distress.

Instead of foster homes the children were brought to a pleasant, campus-like setting, the Methodist Children's Home in Waco. There, they lived in a large cottage, initially guarded by two armed Texas Rangers. They were cared for by two rotating live-in couples, the "house mothers" and "house fathers." While the state's efforts to provide mental health care were well intentioned, unfortunately, they were not especially effective. Texas had pulled in professionals from its busy public systems, basically utilizing anyone who could spare an hour. As a result, the timing and consistency of these mental health visits was random, and the children were further confused by meeting with yet more strangers.

In those early days the atmosphere of the cottage was also chaotic. Officers from various law enforcement agencies would show up at any time, day or night, and pull aside particular girls or boys for interviews. There was no schedule to their daily life and no regularity to the people that they would see. One of the few things I knew for sure by then about traumatized children was that they need predictability, routine, a sense of control and stable relationships with supportive people. This was even more important than usual for the Davidian children: they were coming from a place where they had for years been kept in a state of alarm, led to expect catastrophe at any minute.

During my initial afternoon meeting with the key agencies involved, my advice boiled down to this: create consistency, routine, and familiarity. That meant establishing order, setting up clear boundaries, improving cross-organizational communication, and limiting the mental health staff to those who could regularly be there for the children. I also suggested that only those who had training in interviewing children be allowed to conduct the forensic interviews for the Rangers and the FBI. At the end of the meeting CPS asked me if I would be willing to lead in the coordination of these efforts. Later that day, after meeting with FBI agents, I was also asked to do the forensic interviews myself. At that point we still thought that the crisis would be over in days, so I agreed. I figured it would be an interesting opportunity to learn while simultaneously helping these children. I drove to the cottage to meet a remarkable group of young people.

WHEN I ARRIVED ONE OF THE Rangers stopped me at the door. He was tall, imposing in his hat, the archetype of Texas law enforcement. He was not impressed by this long-haired man in jeans claiming to be a psychiatrist who had come to help the children. Even after I'd established that I was indeed Dr. Perry, he told me that I didn't look like a doctor, and further, "Those kids don't need a shrink. All they need is a little love and to get as far away from here as possible."

Ultimately, this Ranger would turn out to be one of the most positive and healing figures in the children's lives for the weeks they stayed at the cottage. He was calm, good with children, and intuitively seemed to know how to provide a supportive but not intrusive presence. But right then, he was in my way. I said to him, "OK, I'll tell you what. Do you know how to take a pulse?" I directed his attention to a young girl who was fast asleep on a nearby couch. I told him that if her pulse was less than 100, I would turn around and go home. The normal heart rate range for a child her age at rest is 70–90 beats per minute (bpm).

He bent down gently to pick up the girl's wrist, and within moments his face filled with anxiety. "Get a doctor," he said.

"I am a doctor," I replied.

"No, a real doctor," he said. "This child's pulse is 160."

After reassuring him that psychiatrists are physicians with standard medical training, I began to describe the physiological effects of trauma on children. In this case an elevated heart rate was likely a reflection of the girl's persistently activated stress-response system. The ranger understood the basics of the fight or flight response; almost all law enforcement officers have some direct experience with this. I noted that the same hormones and neurotransmitters that flood the brain during a stressful event—adrenaline and noradrenaline—are also involved in regulating heart rate, which makes sense since changes in heart rate are needed to react to stress. From my work with other traumatized children, I knew that even months and years after trauma many would still exhibit an overactive stress response. It was a safe bet then that being so close to an overwhelming experience, this little girl's heart would still be racing.

The Ranger let me in.

THE DAVIDIAN CHILDREN HAD been released in small groups—two to four at a time—in the first three days following the February raid. They ranged in age from five months to twelve years old. Most were between four and eleven. They came from ten different families and seventeen of the twenty-one were released with at least one sibling. Although some former members have disputed accounts of child abuse among the Davidians (and although I was misquoted in the press to suggest that I didn't believe that the children were living in an abusive situation), there was never any doubt that the children had been traumatized, certainly by the raid on the compound, but also by their life beforehand.

One little girl had been released with a note pinned to her clothing that said her mother would be dead by the time the relatives to whom it was addressed got to read it. Another was given a kiss by her mother, handed to an FBI agent, and told, "Here are the people who will kill us. I will see you in heaven." Long before the compound burned, the Davidian children released to us acted as though their parents (at least one of whom they knew to be alive at the time they left) had already died. When I first met the children, in fact, they were sitting and eating lunch. As I walked into the room one of the younger children looked up and calmly asked, "Are you here to kill us?"

These children did not feel as though they had just been liberated. Instead, because of what they'd been taught about outsiders and because of the violence they'd survived, they felt like hostages. They were more frightened of us now than they had been at home, not only because they were suddenly deprived of family and familiarity, but also because Koresh's predictions about an attack had come true. If he was right that the "unbelievers" had come for them, they figured, his assertion that we intended to kill them and their families was probably correct as well.

WE IMMEDIATELY RECOGNIZED THAT WE had a group of children that had essentially been marinated in fear. The only way we could get them the help they needed was to apply our understanding of how fear affects the brain and then consequently changes behavior.

Fear is our most primal emotion, and with good evolutionary reason. Without it few of our ancestors would have survived. Fear literally arises from the core of the brain, affecting all brain areas and their functions in rapidly expanding waves of neurochemical activity. Some of the critical chemicals involved include those we've already discussed, such as adrenaline and noradrenaline, but also important is a stress hormone called cortisol. Two of the key brain regions involved with fear are the locus coeruleus, the origin of the majority of noradrenaline neurons in the brain, and an almond-shaped part of the limbic system called the amygdala.

As noted earlier, the brain evolved from the inside out, and it develops in much the same order. The lowest, most primitive region—the brainstem—completes much of its development in utero and in early infancy. The midbrain and limbic systems develop next, elaborating themselves exuberantly over the first three years of life. Parents of teenagers won't be surprised to learn that the frontal lobes of the cortex, which regulate planning, self-control, and abstract thought, do not complete their development until late in adolescence, showing significant reorganization well into the early twenties.

The fact that the brain develops sequentially—and also so rapidly in the first years of life—explains why extremely young children are at such great risk of suffering lasting effects of trauma: their brains are still developing. The same miraculous plasticity that allows young brains to quickly learn love and language, unfortunately, also makes them highly susceptible to negative experiences as well. Just as fetuses are especially vulnerable to particular toxins depending on the trimester of pregnancy in which they are exposed, so are children vulnerable to the lasting effects of trauma, depending on when it occurs. As a result different symptoms may result from trauma experienced at different times. For example, a toddler with no language to describe the painful and repetitive sexual abuse he experiences may develop a complete aversion to being touched, wide-ranging problems with intimacy and relationships, and pervasive anxiety. But a ten-year-old who is subjected to virtually identical abuse is more likely to develop specific, event-related fears and to work deliberately to avoid particular cues associated with the place, person, and manner of abuse. Her anxiety will wax and wane with exposure to reminders of the molestation. Further, an older child will probably have associated feelings of shame and guilt—complex emotions mediated by the cortex. That region is far less developed in a toddler, therefore, related symptoms are less likely if abuse begins and ends earlier in life.

At any age, however, when people are faced with a frightening situation their brains begin to shut down their highest cortical regions first. We lose the capacity to plan, or to feel hunger, because neither is of any use to our immediate survival. Often we lose the ability to "think" or even speak during an acute threat. We just react. And with prolonged fear there can be chronic or near-permanent changes in the brain. The brain alterations that result from lingering terror, especially early in life, may cause an enduring shift to a more impulsive, more aggressive, less thoughtful, and less compassionate way of responding to the world.

This is because systems in the brain change in a "use-dependent" way, as we noted earlier. Just like a muscle, the more a brain system like the stress response network gets "exercised," the more it changes and the more risk there is of altered functioning. At the same time, the less the cortical regions, which usually control and modulate stress, are used, the smaller and weaker they get. Exposing a person to chronic fear and stress is like weakening the braking power of a car while adding a more powerful engine: you're altering the safety mechanisms that keep the "machine" from going dangerously out of control. Such use-dependent changes in the relative power of different brain systems—just like the use-dependent templates one forms in one's memory about what the world is like—are critical determinants of human behavior. Understanding the importance of use-dependent development was vital to our work in treating traumatized children like those we saw in the immediate aftermath of the first raid on Ranch Apocalypse.

BY THIS POINT IN MY WORK, AS ODD as that may seem now, I'd only just begun to discover how important relationships are to the healing process. Our group and others had observed that the nature of a child's relationships—both before and after trauma—seemed to play a critical role in shaping their response to it. If safe, familiar, and capable caregivers were available to children, they tended to recover more easily, often showing no enduring negative effects of the traumatic event. We knew that the "trauma-buffering" effect of relationships had to be mediated, somehow, by the brain.

But how? In order for an animal to be biologically successful, its brain must guide it to meet three prime directives: first, it must stay alive, second, it must procreate, and third, if it bears dependent young as humans do, it must protect and nurture these offspring until they are able to fend for themselves. Even in humans, all of the thousands of complex capacities of the brain are connected, in one way or another, to systems originally evolved to drive these three functions.

In a social species like ours, however, all three essential functions are deeply dependent upon the brain's capacity to form and maintain relationships. Individual humans are slow, weak, and incapable of surviving for long in nature without the aid of others. In the world in which our ancestors evolved a lone human would soon be a dead one. Only through cooperation, sharing with members of our extended family, living in groups, and hunting and gathering together could we survive. That's why, as children, we come to associate the presence of people we know with safety and comfort; in safe and familiar settings our heart rates and blood pressure are lower, our stress response systems are quiet.

But throughout history, while some humans have been our best friends and kept us safe, others have been our worst enemies. The major predators of human beings are other human beings. Our stress response systems, therefore, are closely interconnected with the systems that read and respond to human social cues. As a result we are very sensitive to expressions, gestures, and the moods of others. As we shall see, we interpret threat and learn to handle stress by watching those around us. We even have special cells in our brains that fire, not when we move or express emotions, but when we see others do so. Human social life is built on this ability to "reflect" each other and respond to those reflections, with both positive and negative results. For example, if you are feeling great and go to work where your supervisor is in a vile mood, soon you will probably feel lousy, too. If a teacher becomes angry or frustrated, the children in her classroom may begin to misbehave, reflecting the powerful emotion being expressed by the teacher. To calm a frightened child, you must first calm yourself.

Recognizing the power of relationships and relational cues is essential to effective therapeutic work and, indeed, to effective parenting, caregiving, teaching, and just about any other human endeavor. This would turn out to be a major challenge as we started working with the Davidian children. Because, as I soon discovered, the CPS workers, law enforcement officers, and mental health workers involved in trying to help the children were all overwhelmed, stressed out, and in a state of alarm themselves.

Furthermore, the more I learned about Koresh and the Davidians, the more I knew that we would have to approach the Davidian children as if they were from a completely alien culture; certainly their worldview was going to be very different from those shared by their new caretakers. Unfortunately, the very same capacity that allows us to bond with each other also allows us to collaborate to defeat a common enemy; what permits us to perform great acts of love also enables us to marginalize and dehumanize others who are not "like" us, not part of our "clan." This tribalism can result in the most extreme forms of hatred and violence. Additionally, after their indoctrination from Koresh, I knew that these children viewed us as outsiders, nonbelievers—and as a threat. What I didn't know was what to do about that.

DURING MY FIRST TWO DAYS IN WACO, I began the delicate task of individually interviewing each child to try to get useful information to help the FBI negotiators defuse the standoff. In any situation where child abuse is suspected, such interviews are difficult because children, quite reasonably, worry about getting their parents in trouble. In this case, it was further complicated by the fact that the Davidians had been brought up to believe that it was OK to deceive "Babylonians" because we were the enemies of God. I knew they might fear that being honest with us was not only a possible betrayal of their parents, but a grievous sin as well.

To my horror, every child gave me the distinct sense that they had a big, terrible secret. When I asked what was going to happen at the Ranch, they'd say ominous things like, "You'll see." Every child, when asked explicitly where his or her parents were, replied, "They're dead," or, "They are all going to die." They told me that they would not see their parents again until David came back to earth to kill the unbelievers. But they wouldn't be more specific.

It is not unusual for children to be deceptive or withholding or to purposefully lie in order to avoid things they don't want to share, especially when they have been instructed to do so by their families. However, it is far more difficult for them to hide their true thoughts and feelings in their artwork. And so, with each child old enough to color, I sat with him and colored as we talked. I asked one ten-year-old boy named Michael, who was one of the first children interviewed, to draw me a picture of whatever he wanted. He went to work quickly, producing a fine unicorn surrounded by a lush, earthly landscape of forested hills. In the sky were clouds, a castle and a rainbow. I praised his drawing skills and he told me that David loved it when he drew horses. He'd also received kudos from the group and its leader for his renditions of heavenly castles and the incorporation of the group's symbol into his drawings: the star of David.

Then I asked him to draw a self-portrait. What he drew was virtually a stick figure, something that a four-year-old could produce. Even more shockingly, when I asked him to draw his family, he paused and seemed confused. Finally, he created a page that was blank but for a tiny picture of himself, squeezed into the far right hand corner. His drawings reflected what he'd learned in the group: the elaboration of things that Koresh valued, the dominance of its supreme leader, a confused, impoverished sense of family, and an immature, dependent picture of himself.

As I got to know the Davidian children, I saw similar contrasts again and again: islands of talent, knowledge, and connection surrounded by vast empty spaces of neglect. For example, they could read well for their ages, as they had to study the Bible regularly. But they knew virtually no math. The talents were linked to brain regions that had been exercised and behaviors that had been rewarded. The lacunae resulted from lack of opportunities for development, in Michael's case, lack of opportunities to make choices for himself, lack of exposure to the basic choices that most children get to make as they begin to discover what they like and who they are.

Inside the compound almost every decision—from what to eat and wear to how to think and pray—had been made for them. And, just like every other area in the brain, the regions involved in developing a sense of self grow or stagnate depending upon how often they are exercised. To develop a self, one must exercise choice and learn from the consequences of those choices; if the only thing you are taught is to comply, you have little way of knowing what you like and want.

One of my next interviews was with a little girl, almost six years old. I asked her to draw a picture of her home. She drew a picture of the compound. Then I asked her what she thought was going to happen at home. She redrew the same compound building with flames everywhere. Atop it was a stairway to heaven. I knew then—just days after the first raid—that the siege was headed for a potentially cataclysmic conclusion. During that time other children drew pictures of fires and explosions as well; some even said things like "We're going to blow you all up," and "Everyone is going to die." I knew that this was important information to convey to the FBI's hostage negotiation team and to the FBI's leadership team.

Earlier, we had created a group to facilitate communication between the various law enforcement agencies and our team. We'd made a deal with the FBI: if they'd respect the boundaries that we'd created to help these children heal, we'd share any information our work revealed that might help them negotiate an end to the standoff. After I saw these drawings and heard these remarks I immediately communicated my concerns that any further attack on the compound had the potential to precipitate some kind of apocalypse. I didn't know the exact form it would take, but it seemed it would be an explosive, fiery end. The words, the drawings, and the behaviors of the children all pointed to a shared belief that the siege would end in death. What they were describing was essentially a group-precipitated suicide.

I was afraid they wanted to provoke the FBI to start this final battle. I met repeatedly with my FBI liaison and members of the behavioral science team, who, I later learned, agreed with me that further escalation by law enforcement would more likely provoke disaster, not surrender. But they were not in charge. The tactical team was, and they would listen but not hear. They believed that they were dealing with a fraud and a criminal. They didn't understand that Koresh's followers truly believed that their leader was a messenger of God, possibly even Christ returned, with the self-sacrificing devotion and commitment such a belief implies. This clash of group worldviews shaped the escalating actions that contributed to the final catastrophe.

AFTER I'D COMPLETED MY INITIAL interviews more than a dozen people from my home institutions in Houston joined me in Waco to form the core of our clinical team. Along with the guards, CPS workers, and Methodist Home staff, we worked to end the unstructured chaos in the cottage. We scheduled a regular bedtime and regular meal times, created time for school, for free play, and for the children to be given information about what was happening at the Ranch. Since the outcome of the siege was unpredictable, we did not allow them to watch TV or expose them to any other media coverage.

In the beginning there was a push by some in our group to start "therapy" with the children. I felt it was more important at this time to restore order and be available to support, interact with, nurture, respect, listen to, play with, and generally "be present." The children's experience was so recent and so raw, it seemed to me that a conventional therapeutic session with a stranger, particularly a "Babylonian," would potentially be distressing.

Incidentally, since Waco, research has demonstrated that rushing to "debrief" people with a new therapist or counselor after a traumatic event is often intrusive, unwanted, and may actually be counterproductive. Some studies, in fact, find a doubling of the odds of post-traumatic stress disorder following such "treatment." In some of our own work we've also found that the most effective interventions involve educating and supporting the existing social support network, particularly the family, about the known and predictable effects of acute trauma and offering access to more therapeutic support if—and only if—the family sees extreme or prolonged post-traumatic symptoms.

I thought these children needed the opportunity to process what had happened at their own pace and in their own ways. If they wanted to talk, they could come to a staff member that they felt comfortable with; if not, they could play safely and develop new childhood memories and experiences to begin offsetting their earlier, fearful ones. We wanted to offer structure, but not rigidity; nurturance, but not forced affection.

Each night after the children went to bed our team would meet to review the day and discuss each child. This "staffing" process began to reveal patterns that suggested therapeutic experiences were taking place in short, minutes-long interactions. As we charted these contacts we found that, despite having no formal "therapy" sessions, each child was actually getting hours of intimate, nurturing, therapeutic connections each day. The child controlled when, with whom, and how she interacted with the child-sensitive adults around her. Because our staff had a variety of strengths—some were very touchy-feely and nurturing, others were humorous, still others good listeners or sources of information—the children could seek out what they needed, when they needed it. This created a powerful therapeutic web.

And so children would gravitate toward particular staffers who matched their specific personality, stage of development, or mood. Because I like to joke around and roughhouse, when children wanted that kind of play, they would seek me out. With some, I would color or play a game and answer questions or respond to fears. With others, I played a different role. There was one boy, for example, who liked to sneak up on me. I played along, sometimes acting startled, sometimes letting him know I saw him coming, other times genuinely surprised. This form of peek-a-boo—hide-and-seek—was engaging and playful. These short interactions helped create a sense of connection for him and, I believe, safety. Because I'd interviewed all of the children and because they could see that the other staff deferred to me, they knew that I was somehow "in charge." Because of how they'd been raised, they were acutely sensitive to signs of dominance and cues related to who currently had the most power. These cues were, due to the patriarchal system Koresh had imposed, explicitly gendered.

For this boy, then, the idea that "the dominant male in the group is being playful with me" conveyed a real sense of security. Knowing that he could interact and predictably get this dominant male to be friendly gave him a sense of control—a stark contrast to the powerlessness and fear he'd previously lived with. Similarly, a little girl who was worried about her mother might go to a female staffer to talk about it. But when the conversation got too intense, too intimate, too threatening, she could walk away and do something else or simply stay alongside the woman and play with her toys. In staff meetings we would chart each child's daily contacts so that everyone would know the full story of what was going on with each child and be able to guide their next engagement with him or her appropriately.

But these children needed more than just the ability to choose whom to talk to and what to discuss. They also needed the stability that comes from routine. In the first days following the assault with no external organization imposed upon them, they immediately replicated the authoritarian, sexually segregated culture of the Davidian compound, where men and boys over twelve were segregated from women and girls, and where David Koresh and his representatives ruled with absolute power.

Two of the oldest children, siblings, a boy and a girl, declared themselves "scribes." The female scribe dominated and made decisions for the girls, and the boy led the boys and also held sway over the female scribe, with the other children falling into line and complying without complaint. The girls and boys sat at separate tables for meals; they played separately and deliberately avoided interaction if at all possible. The oldest girls, who had been in the process of preparing to be David's "Brides," would draw stars of David on yellow Post-it notes or write "David is God" on them and put them up around the cottage.

But none of the children knew what to do when faced with the simplest of choices: when offered a plain peanut butter sandwich as opposed to one with jelly, they became confused, even angry. Inside the compound almost every decision had been made for them. Having never been allowed the basic choices that most children get to make as they begin to discover what they like and who they are, they had no sense of self. The idea of self-determination was, like all new things for them, unfamiliar and, therefore, anxiety provoking. So the children turned to the scribes for guidance and let them make these decisions.

We weren't sure how to deal with this issue. We wanted them to have a sense of the familiar and to feel "at home," and we thought that allowing them these rituals might help them feel safe. On the other hand we knew that they would need to learn what would soon be expected of them in the outside world.

We had only trial and error to guide us. My first attempt to break the segregation between the boys and the girls was a disaster. One day I sat down at the girls' table for lunch. Immediately, all of the children seemed to tense up. A three- or four-year-old girl challenged me, saying, "You can't sit here." I asked why. She said, "Because you're a boy."

"How do you know?" I asked, trying to use humor to defuse the situation, but she stuck with her challenge and looked to the female scribe, who confirmed to her that I was male. When I continued to sit there almost all of the children became angry and the air became so charged and hostile that I was afraid they would riot. Some of them stood up, taking an aggressive stance. I backed off. After that, we allowed them to maintain their separate tables and the bizarre dietary restrictions that Koresh had imposed, such as not eating fruit and vegetables at the same meal.

We decided that all we could do was to allow them to see how we adults lived and interacted with each other, and hope that over time they would see that there would not be negative consequences if they chose to live as we did.

Discipline was an especially charged issue, of course. We intentionally avoided imposing rigid restrictions, corporal punishment, isolation, or physical restraint—any of the disciplinary techniques that had been used at the compound. On the rare occasions when children did become physically aggressive or said something hurtful, we gently redirected their behavior until they calmed down and had them apologize if necessary. Because the post-traumatic response can keep a child in a persistently aroused, fearful state, we knew that fear might prompt them to act impulsively or aggressively and that they might not immediately be able to control these reactions. We didn't want to punish them for these natural responses.

And we began to see that as children cope with the aftermath of terrifying experiences like the first raid on Ranch Apocalypse, they respond to reminders of what happened similarly to the way they responded at the time. So, for example, if they were able to flee, they may respond with avoidance; if they fought back, they might respond aggressively; if they dissociated—that phenomenon in which a person's mind and body feel disconnected from the reality of the event—they do that again. When the Davidian children were upset, or when they had to confront things they were not yet ready to think about—for example, in interviews with law enforcement—we would see these reactions.

During an interview with one of the girls, Susie, a six-year-old, I saw one of the most extreme dissociative responses I'd ever witnessed. I had asked Susie where she thought her mother was. She responded as though she had not heard the question. She crawled under a table, tucked herself into a fetal position, and did not move or talk. Even when I tried to touch her to comfort her, she was so nonresponsive that she didn't notice when I walked out of the room six minutes later. I watched her through a two-way mirror from another room for another three minutes before she slowly began to move and become aware of outside stimuli again. The children, usually boys but sometimes girls as well, would sometimes behave aggressively, throwing things when asked a question that made them recall what had happened, or responding verbally with anger. Some would break crayons or get up and walk away.

Our questions, of course, were not the only reminders of what they'd witnessed. One day a press helicopter flew over the cottage when the children were playing outside. They had been told by Koresh that the FBI would fly over them with helicopters, douse them with gasoline, and light them on fire. Within seconds, the children had disappeared and taken cover, like a platoon in a combat movie. When the helicopter had passed, they formed two single file lines, one of boys, one of girls, and marched into the building chanting a song about being soldiers of God. It was one of the eeriest things I have ever seen.

Similarly, upon seeing a white delivery van that looked like one of the ATF vehicles they'd seen near the compound before the raid, the children once again fled and hid. As we had hypothesized and other researchers have also confirmed since, post-traumatic stress disorder is not signaled by a constellation of new symptoms that develop long after a stressful event but is, in many regards, the maladaptive persistence of the once adaptive responses that began as coping mechanisms in response to the event itself.

DURING THE STANDOFF AT WACO our team literally lived with the Branch Davidian children. I would make the hours-long drive to Houston now and then to take care of the bare minimum of my administrative duties and family responsibilities. I spent hours in meetings with partner organizations dealing with the crisis, trying to ensure that when they left us, these children would go to safe, healthy families, and also trying to see to it that those who needed it received continuing mental health care. I also spent many frustrating hours trying to get the information we'd learned about the high probability of a mass suicide or suicidal terror attack on the officers surrounding the compound to someone who would listen and who could change the tactics being used. I told the FBI about the fiery drawings and the threats the children had repeated; I described how, when they came into the interview room, which was filled with toys, every boy and girl immediately gravitated to a very realistic-looking toy rifle and looked down the barrel to see if it was loaded. One four-year-old girl picked it up, pulled the toy bolt action mechanism, then said with disgust, "This isn't real."

Unfortunately, however, the tactical team in charge of operations continued to see Koresh as a con man, not a religious leader. Just as the group dynamics within the cult pushed them toward their horrific conclusion, so too did the group dynamics within law enforcement. Both groups tragically disregarded input that did not fit their world view, their templates. The law enforcement echo chamber magnified rumors about Koresh beyond belief; at one point, there was actually concern that he'd developed a nuclear weapon and was planning to deploy it at the compound. Both groups listened primarily to people who simply confirmed what they already believed.

Working with the Davidian children—and seeing the unfolding crisis in Waco from the inside—repeatedly reiterated to me how powerful group influences are in human life and how the human brain cannot really be understood outside of its context as the brain of a member of a highly social species.

EARLY IN THE MORNING OF APRIL 19, while in Houston, I received a call from an FBI agent I didn't know. He said that I needed to come to Waco immediately: the government had begun a raid on the compound intended to end the siege and free the young people who remained inside. As I drove I listened to the radio. When I crested the hill at the boundary of the city, I saw a massive pillar of thick gray smoke and orange fire. I continued immediately to the Methodist Children's Home. The adults looked stricken, but they had managed so far to avoid betraying their distress to the children. They'd been preparing to care for the twenty-three children still inside the compound, getting to know them through their siblings and through videotapes made of the children inside the compound by Koresh and released to the FBI. Now they felt their loss, and were all too aware of how their deaths would affect the children they were already treating.

Adding to our pain was the fact that we knew that much of the trust we'd developed with these children would probably now evaporate. We'd told them that we were not their enemies and that their parents, siblings, and friends would not be killed. But events would now further confirm the accuracy of Koresh's prophecies: just as he'd told them that the "bad guys" would attack the compound, he'd also accurately foreseen the fiery end of the group. That would add to their ongoing trauma. And, of course, the next part of the prophecy was that Koresh would return to earth to slay all the "unbelievers," a group that the children who had been moving away from his teachings would now quite logically fear included them.

We had to carefully decide the best way to break the news. Due to the unfolding of events, we waited until the next day because we didn't have information about survivors until then.

We set up a meeting in the living room of the cottage. Each child there had developed a close relationship with at least one or more of the staff in our team. Our plan was that I would tell the group what happened in as factual and clear a manner as possible. We would ask them if they had any questions. After that, each child or sibling group would spend time with the two or three staff members they were close to.

It was one of the most difficult moments of my clinical life. How do you tell a dozen children that their fathers, brothers, mothers, sisters, and friends are dead? And yes, they died just as Koresh foretold. And yes, we assured you that this wouldn't happen. At first, some simply refused to believe me. "It's not true," they said over and over, as many people do when faced with the death of loved ones, "It can't be." Others said, "I knew this would happen," or, "I told you so."

The worst part of all was knowing that things didn't have to end this way. The response of the Davidians to the final assault was predictable, and the loss of life could have certainly been mitigated if not entirely prevented. Nonetheless, the federal government had taken the action most likely to result in a disaster, and eighty people, virtually everyone these children knew, had died.

BY THE TIME OF THE FIRE MANY of the children had already gone to live with relatives outside the group; only about eleven girls and boys remained at the cottage. The raid was, unsurprisingly, a setback for most of them. Their traumatic symptoms returned, as did their observance of Koresh's dietary rules and sexual segregation.

By this time we'd learned how careful we had to be. There was a big debate, for example, as to what to do about the fact that the girls and boys still took their meals at two separate tables. I finally suggested that we remove one of the tables and see what happened. When one of the girls asked why we were taking it away, I told her that we didn't need it any more. She accepted my reply without further inquiry; it was clear that there were far fewer children living at the cottage by then. At first the girls sat at one end and the boys at the other. Then slowly and naturally, they began to interact and mix. Over time their traumatic symptoms and their observance of Koresh's rules began to recede again.

NOW, TWENTY-FOUR YEARS LATER, WE have had various opportunities to follow the Davidian children—all informal. We know that all of them have been permanently and profoundly affected by what occurred. About half left to live with relatives who still believed in Koresh's message, and some still follow the religion in which they were raised. Some have gone on to college and careers, and have had their own families; others have led troubled and chaotic lives.

There were inquiries, Congressional hearings, books, exposés and documentaries. However, despite all this attention, it was still only a few short months before interest in these children dropped away. There were criminal trials, civil trials, lots of sound and fury. All of the systems—CPS, the FBI, the Rangers, our group in Houston—returned, in most ways, to our old models and our ways of doing things. But while little changed in our practice, a lot had changed in our thinking.

We learned that some of the most therapeutic experiences do not take place in "therapy," but in naturally occurring healthy relationships, whether between a professional like myself and a child, between an aunt and a scared little girl, or between a calm Texas Ranger and an excitable boy. The children who did best after the Davidian apocalypse were not those who experienced the least stress or those who participated most enthusiastically in talking with us at the cottage. They were the ones who were released afterwards into the healthiest and most loving worlds, whether it was with family who still believed in the Davidian ways or with loved ones who rejected Koresh entirely. In fact, the research on the most effective treatments to help child trauma victims might be accurately summed up this way: what works best is anything that increases the quality and number of relationships in the child's life.

I also saw how bringing disparate groups together—even those with conflicting missions—could often be effective. Dozens of state, federal, and local agencies had worked together to care for these children. The power of proximity—spending time side-by-side—had pulled us all to compromise in our efforts to help these children. Relationships matter: the currency for systemic change was trust, and trust comes through forming healthy working relationships. People, not programs, change people. The cooperation, respect and collaboration we experienced gave us hope that we could make a difference, even though the raids themselves had ended in such catastrophe. The seeds of a new way of working with traumatized children were sown in the ashes of Waco.

CHAPTER 4

Skin Hunger

LIKE EVERYONE ELSE, DOCTORS ENJOY being recognized for their achievements. One sure way of attaining medical fame is to discover a new disease or to solve a particularly daunting medical puzzle. And the physicians at one Texas hospital where I consulted saw the little girl in room 723E as such a challenge. At four years old, Laura weighed just twenty-six pounds, despite having been fed a high-calorie diet via a tube inserted through her nose for weeks. The stack of her medical files that confronted me at the nurses' station was about four feet high, taller than the shrunken little girl herself. Laura's story, like that of the children of Waco, helped us learn more about how children respond to early experience. It illustrates how the mind and body cannot be treated separately, reveals what infants and young children need for healthy brain development and demonstrates how neglecting those needs can have a profound impact on every aspect of a child's growth.

Laura's files contained literally thousands of pages of documents, detailing visits with endocrinologists, gastroenterologists, nutritionists, and other medical specialists. There were endless lab reports of blood work, chromosome tests, hormone levels, biopsies. The documents included results from even more invasive tests, which had used scopes inserted into her throat to examine her stomach, and scopes inserted rectally to examine her bowels. There were dozens of reports from consulting physicians. The poor girl had even had an exploratory laparoscopy, in which doctors inserted a tube into her abdomen to scrutinize her internal organs; a snippet of her small intestine had been clipped off and sent to the National Institutes of Health for analysis.

Finally, after being on the special gastrointestinal research unit for a month, a social worker pressured Laura's physicians to get a psychiatry consult. Just as the gastroenterology fellows thought they'd discovered a case of "intestinal epilepsy" when they first saw Laura years before, the shrinks, too, had a novel theory about Laura's case. The psychologist who came for the initial consultation specialized in eating disorders, and he believed he was seeing the first documented instance of "infantile anorexia." Fascinated and excited, he discussed the case with his mental health colleagues. Ultimately, he requested a consultation from me because I had more experience with academic publishing and he was sure that this would be a reportable case. He told me that the child had to be purging secretly, or perhaps getting up at night to exercise furiously. Otherwise, how could she be fed so many calories but still not grow? He wanted my insight on this disturbing new problem, seen for the first time in a young child.

I was curious. I had never heard of infantile anorexia. I went to the hospital planning to start the consult like I always do, by reviewing the chart to learn as much about the child's history as possible. But when I discovered the four-year, twenty-previous-admission, six-specialty-clinic, four-foot-tall pile of documents, I just scanned the admission intake report and went in to introduce myself to the patient and her mother.

In the girl's hospital room I found a distressing scene. Laura's twenty-two-year-old mom, Virginia*, was watching television, seated about five feet away from her child. Mother and daughter were not interacting. Tiny, emaciated Laura was sitting quietly, her eyes big, staring at a plate of food. She also had a feeding tube, which pumped nutrients into her stomach. I would later learn that Virginia had been discouraged from interacting with Laura during mealtimes by the eating disorders psychologist. This was supposed to stop Laura—the alleged cunning, infantile anorectic—from manipulating her mother around food and meals. The theory then was that people with anorexia enjoy the attention they get when they don't eat, and use it to control other family members; denying them this "reward" was supposed to aid recovery. But all I could see here was a despondent, skinny little girl and a disengaged mother.

The brain is an historical organ. It stores our personal narrative. Our life experiences shape who we become by creating our brain's catalog of template memories, which guide our behavior, sometimes in ways we can consciously recognize, more often via processes beyond our awareness. A crucial element in figuring out any brain-related clinical problem, therefore, is getting an accurate history of the patient's experiences. Since much of the brain develops early in life, the way we are parented has a dramatic influence on brain development. And so, since we tend to care for our children the way we were cared for ourselves during our own childhoods, a good "brain" history of a child begins with a history of the caregiver's childhood and early experience. To understand Laura I would need to know about her family, which in her case consisted of her mom.

I started by asking Virginia innocuous, basic questions. Almost immediately I began to suspect that the source of Laura's problems lay in her young, well-intentioned, but inexperienced mother's past.

"Where are you from?" I asked her.

"I guess, Austin," she said.

"Where are your parents from?"

"I don't know."

Within minutes I discovered that Virginia was a child of the foster care system. Abandoned at birth by a drug-addicted mother, father unknown, Virginia had grown up at a time when it was common for the child welfare system to move infants and toddlers to a new foster home every six months; the rationale was that this way they wouldn't become too attached to any particular caregiver. Now, of course, we know that an infant's early attachment to a small number of consistent caregivers is critical to emotional health and even to physical development. But at that time this knowledge hadn't even begun to penetrate the child welfare bureaucracy.

More than in any other species, human young are born vulnerable and dependent. Pregnancy and early childhood are tremendous energy drains on the mother and, indirectly, on the larger family group. But despite the severe pain of childbirth, the numerous discomforts of pregnancy and breast-feeding, and the loud, continuous demands of a newborn, human mothers overwhelmingly tend to devote themselves to comforting, feeding, and protecting their young. Indeed, most do so happily; we find it pathological when one does not.

To a Martian—or even to many nonparents—this behavior might seem like a mystery. What could prompt parents to give up sleep, sex, friends, personal time, and virtually every other pleasure in life to meet the demands of a small, often irritatingly noisy, incontinent, needy being? The secret is that caring for children is, in many ways, indescribably pleasurable. Our brains reward us for interacting with our children, especially infants: their scent, the cooing sounds they make when they are calm, their smooth skin, and especially, their faces are designed to fill us with joy. What we call "cuteness" is actually an evolutionary adaptation that helps ensure that parents will care for their children, that babies will get their needs met, and that parents will take on this seemingly thankless task with pleasure.

So during our development, in the ordinary course of things we will receive attentive, attuned, and loving care. When we are cold, hungry, thirsty, frightened, or distressed in any way, our cries will bring the comforting caregivers who meet our needs and dissolve our distress in their loving attention. With this loving care two major neural networks are stimulated simultaneously in our developing brains. The first is the complex set of sensory perceptions associated with human relational interactions: the caregiver's face, smile, voice, touch, and scent. The second is stimulation of the neural networks mediating "pleasure." This "reward system" can be activated in a number of ways, one of which is the relief of distress. Quenching thirst, satisfying hunger, calming anxiety—all result in a sense of pleasure and comfort. And as we have discussed earlier, when two patterns of neural activity occur simultaneously with sufficient repetition, an association is made between the two patterns.

In the case of responsive parenting, pleasure and human interactions become inextricably woven together. This interconnection, the association of pleasure with human interaction, is the important neurobiological "glue" that bonds and creates healthy relationships. Consequently, the most powerful rewards we can receive are the attention, approval, and affection of people we love and respect. Similarly, the most powerful pain we experience is the loss of that attention, approval, and affection—the most obvious example being, of course, the death of a loved one. This is why even our greatest intellectual, athletic, or professional triumphs seem empty if we have no one with whom to share them.

If you are one of the majority of infants born to a loving home, a consistent, nurturing caregiver—say a mother or father—will be present and repeatedly meet your needs. Time and again, one or both parents will come when you cry and soothe you when you are hungry, cold, or scared. As your brain develops these loving caregivers provide the template that you use for human relationships. Attachment, then, is a memory template for human-to-human bonds. This template serves as your primary "world view" on human relationships. It is profoundly influenced by whether you experience kind, attuned parenting or whether you receive inconsistent, frequently disrupted, abusive, or neglectful "care."

As noted earlier, the brain develops in a use-dependent manner. Neural systems that are used become more dominant; those that are not grow less so. As a child grows, many systems of the brain require stimulation if they are to develop. Furthermore, this use-dependent development must occur at specific times in order for these systems to function at their best. If this "sensitive period" is missed, some systems may never be able to reach their full potential. In some cases the neglect-related deficit may be permanent. For example, if one of a kitten's eyes is kept closed during the first few weeks of its life, it will be blind in that eye, even though the eye is completely normal. The visual circuitry of the brain requires normal experience of sight in order to wire itself; lacking visual stimuli, the neurons in the closed eye fail to make crucial connections and the opportunity for sight and depth perception is lost. Similarly, if a child is not exposed to language during his early life, he may never be able to speak or understand speech normally. If a child doesn't become fluent in a second language before puberty, he will almost always speak any new language he does learn with an accent.

While we don't know whether there is a fixed "sensitive period" for the development of normal attachment the way there appears to be for language and sight, research does suggest that experiences like Virginia's, in which children are not allowed the chance to develop permanent relationships with one or two primary caregivers during their first three years of life have lasting effects on people's ability to relate normally and affectionately to each other. Children who don't get consistent, physical affection or the chance to build loving bonds simply don't receive the patterned, repetitive stimulation necessary to properly build the systems in the brain that connect reward, pleasure, and human-to-human interactions. This is what had happened to Virginia. As a result of transient and fragmented caregiving during childhood she just didn't get the same degree of reward—pleasure, if you will—from holding, smelling, and interacting with her baby that most mothers would.

At the age of five Virginia had finally settled into what would be her most permanent childhood home. Her foster parents were loving, highly moral Christian people, and good parents. They taught her manners. They taught her to "do unto others." They provided a basic, humane, script for normal behavior. They taught her that stealing was wrong, so she didn't take things from others without permission. They taught her that drugs were bad for you, so she didn't use drugs. They taught her to work hard and go to school, so she did that, too. They wanted to adopt her and she wanted to be adopted by them, but the state never terminated the parental rights of her biological parents and there was occasional talk by her caseworkers of the potential for reuniting her with her biological mother, so the adoption never went through. Unfortunately, this meant that when she turned eighteen, the state was no longer legally "responsible" for Virginia. As a result she had to leave her foster home and the foster parents were told to have no further contact with her. Their future as foster parents for other children was linked to their compliance with the wishes of the caseworkers. Because of yet another inhumane child welfare policy—one aimed at reducing the system's legal liabilities, not protecting children—Virginia lost the only parents she'd ever really known.

By then she had graduated high school. She was placed in a halfway house for children "aging out" of foster care in a low-income community. Cut off from her loved ones, with no clear-cut rules to follow and seeking affection, Virginia rapidly became pregnant. The father of her child left her, but she wanted a baby to love and she wanted to do the right thing, as her foster parents had taught her. She sought prenatal care and was quickly enrolled in a good program for high-risk mothers. Unfortunately, as soon as the baby was born, she no longer qualified for that program because she wasn't pregnant anymore. After she gave birth, she was on her own.

But Virginia had no idea what to do with her baby after she left the hospital. Having had her own early attachments abruptly and brutally terminated, she didn't have what some might call the "maternal instinct." Cognitively, she knew what basic acts needed to be performed: feed Laura, dress her, bathe her. Emotionally, however, she was lost. No one had thought to specifically instruct her to provide the loving, physical interactions that infants need, and she didn't feel compelled to do them on her own. Simply, Virginia got no pleasure from these things and she had not been taught that she should do them.

Not pulled by her limbic, emotional systems and not pushed by her cognitive, information-carrying cortex, Virginia parented in an emotionally disconnected way. She didn't spend much time holding her baby; she fed the little one propped up with a bottle, not nuzzled close to her bosom. She didn't rock her, didn't sing to her, didn't coo or stare into her eyes or count her perfect tiny toes over and over or do any of the other silly but hugely important things that people with ordinary childhoods instinctively do when caring for a baby. And without these physical and emotional signals that all mammals need to stimulate growth, Laura stopped gaining weight. Virginia did what she thought was the right thing, not because she felt it in her heart, but because her mind told her that's what a mother "should" do. When she got frustrated, she either harshly disciplined the child or ignored her. She simply didn't feel the contentment and joy from the positive caregiving interactions that normally help parents overcome the difficult emotional and physical challenges of child-rearing.

The term used to describe babies who are born normal and healthy but don't grow, or even lose weight following this form of emotional neglect, is "failure to thrive." Even back in the eighties, when Laura was an infant, "failure to thrive" was a well-known syndrome in abused and neglected children, especially those raised without enough individualized nurturing and attention. The condition has been documented for centuries, most commonly in orphanages and other institutions where there is not enough attention and care to go around. If not addressed early, it can be deadly. One study in the forties found that more than a third of children raised in an institution without receiving individual attention died by age two—an extraordinarily high death rate. The children who survive such emotional deprivation—like the recent Eastern European orphans, one of whom we'll meet later—often have severe behavioral problems, hoard food, and may be overly affectionate with strangers while having difficulty maintaining relationships with those who should be closest to them.

When Virginia first sought medical attention for her baby eight weeks after she was born, Laura was correctly diagnosed with "failure to thrive" and was admitted to the hospital for nutritional stabilization. But the diagnosis wasn't explained to Virginia. Upon being discharged she was only given nutritional advice, not advice on mothering. A social work consult had been suggested yet it was never ordered. The issue of neglect was ignored by the medical team in large part because many physicians find "psychological" or social aspects of medical problems less interesting and less important than the primary "physiological" issues. Further, Virginia didn't seem like a neglectful mother. After all, would an uncaring mother seek out early intervention for her newborn?

And so, Laura still didn't grow. Several months later Virginia brought her back to the emergency room seeking help. Unaware of Virginia's history of disrupted early attachment, the doctors who saw her child next thought Laura's problems had to be related to her gastrointestinal system, not her brain. And so began Laura's four-year medical odyssey of tests, procedures, special diets, surgeries and tube feeding. Virginia still didn't realize that her baby needed to be held, rocked, played with and physically nurtured.

Babies are born with the core elements of the stress response already intact and centered in the lower, most primitive parts of their developing brains. When the infant's brain gets signals from inside the body—or from her external senses—that something is not right, these register as distress. This distress can be "hunger" if she needs calories, "thirst" if she is dehydrated, or "anxiety" if she perceives external threat. When this distress is relieved, the infant feels pleasure. This is because our stress response neurobiology is interconnected with the "pleasure/reward" areas in the brain, and with other areas that represent pain, discomfort and anxiety. Experiences that decrease distress and enhance our survival tend to give us pleasure; experiences that increase our risk usually give us a sensation of distress.

Babies immediately find nursing, being held, touched, and rocked soothing and pleasurable. If they are parented lovingly, and someone consistently comes when they are stressed by hunger or fear, the joy and relief of being fed and soothed becomes associated with human contact. Thus, in normal childhood, as described above, nurturing human interactions become intimately and powerfully connected with pleasure. It is through the thousands of times we respond to our crying infant that we help create her healthy capacity to get pleasure from future human connection.

Because both the brain's relational and pleasure-mediating neural systems are linked with our stress response systems, interactions with loved ones are our major stress-modulating mechanism. At first babies must rely upon those around them not only to ease their hunger, but also to soothe the anxiety and fear that come from not being able to obtain food and otherwise care for themselves. From their caregivers they learn how to respond to these feelings and needs. If their parents feed them when they are hungry, calm them when they are frightened, and are generally responsive to their emotional and physical needs, they ultimately build the baby's capacity to soothe and comfort themselves, a skill that serves them well later when they face life's ordinary ups and downs.

We've all seen toddlers look to Mom after scraping a knee: if she doesn't look worried, the child doesn't cry; but if the baby sees a look of concern, the loud wailing begins. This is only the most obvious example of the complex dance that occurs between caregiver and child that teaches emotional self-regulation. Of course some children may be genetically more or less sensitive to stressors and stimulation, but genetic strengths or vulnerabilities are magnified or blunted in the context of the child's first relationships. For most of us, including adults, the mere presence of familiar people, the sound of a loved one's voice, or the sight of their figure approaching can actually modulate the activity of the stress-response neural systems, shut off the flood of stress hormones, and reduce our sense of distress. Just holding a loved one's hand is powerful stress-reducing medicine.

There is also a class of nerve cells in the brain known as "mirror" neurons, which respond in synchrony with the behavior of others. This capacity for mutual regulation provides another basis for attachment. For example, when a baby smiles, the mirror neurons in his mother's brain usually respond with a set of patterns that are almost identical to those that occur when Mom herself smiles. This mirroring ordinarily leads the mother to respond with a smile of her own. It's not hard to see how empathy and the capacity to respond to relationships would originate here as mother and child synchronize and reinforce each other, with both sets of mirror neurons reflecting back each other's joy and sense of connectedness.

However, if a baby's smiles are ignored, if she's left repeatedly to cry alone, if she's not fed, or fed roughly without tenderness or without being held, the positive associations between human contact and safety, predictability, and pleasure may not develop. If, as happened in Virginia's case, she begins to bond with one person, but is abandoned as soon as she feels comfortable with her particular smell, rhythm, and smile, and then abandoned again once she acclimates to a new caregiver, these associations may never gel. Not enough repetition occurs to clinch the connection; people are not interchangeable. The price of love is the agony of loss, from infancy onward. The attachment between a baby and his first primary caregivers is not trivial: the love a baby feels for his caregivers is every bit as profound as the deepest romantic connection. Indeed, it is the template memory of this primary attachment that will allow the baby to have healthy intimate relationships as an adult.

As a baby Virginia never really got the chance to learn that she was loved; as soon as she grew used to one caretaker, she was whisked off to another one. Without one or two consistent caregivers in her life she never experienced the particular relational repetitions a child needs to associate human contact with pleasure. She did not develop the basic neurobiological capacity to empathize with her own baby's need for physical love. However, because she did live in a stable, loving home when the higher, cognitive regions of her brain were most actively developing, she was able to learn what she "should" do as a parent. Still, she didn't have the emotional underpinnings that would make those nurturing behaviors feel natural.

So when Laura was born, Virginia knew that she should "love" her baby. But she didn't feel that love the way most people do, and so she failed to express it through physical contact.

For Laura, this lack of stimulation was devastating. Her body responded with a hormonal dysregulation that impeded normal growth, despite receiving more than adequate nutrition. The problem is similar to what in other mammals is called "runt syndrome." In litters of rats and mice and even in puppies and kittens, without outside intervention, the smallest, weakest animal often dies in the few weeks following birth. The runt doesn't have the strength to stimulate the mother's nipple to produce adequate milk (in many species, each baby prefers and suckles exclusively from a particular nipple) or to elicit adequate grooming behaviors from the mother. The mother neglects the runt physically, not licking or grooming him as much as she does the others. This, in turn, further limits his growth. Without this grooming his own growth hormones turn off, so even if he does somehow get enough to eat, he still doesn't grow properly. The mechanism, rather cruelly for the runt, directs resources to those animals best able to utilize them. Conserving her resources, the mother feeds the healthier animals preferentially, since they have the best chance of surviving and passing on her genes.

Infants diagnosed with "failure to thrive," are often found to have reduced levels of growth hormone, which explains Laura's inability to gain weight. Without the physical stimulation needed to release these hormones, Laura's body treated her food as waste. She didn't need to purge or exercise to avoid gaining weight: the lack of physical stimulation had programmed her body to do so. Without love, children literally don't grow. Laura wasn't anorexic; like the scrawny runt in a litter of puppies, she just wasn't receiving the physical nurturing her body needed to know that she was "wanted," and that it was safe to grow.

WHEN I'D FIRST ARRIVED IN HOUSTON, I'd gotten to know a foster mother who often brought children to our clinic. A warm, welcoming person who didn't stand on ceremony and always spoke her mind, Mama P.* seemed to know intuitively what the maltreated and often traumatized children she took in needed.

As I considered how to help Virginia help Laura, I thought back on what I'd learned from Mama P. The first time I met her I was relatively new to Texas. I had set up a teaching clinic where we had a dozen or more psychiatrists, psychologists, pediatric and psychiatry residents, medical students, and other staff and trainees. This was a teaching clinic designed, in part, to allow trainees to observe senior clinicians and "experts" doing clinical work. I was introduced to Mama P. during the feedback part of an initial evaluation visit for one of her foster children.

Mama P. was a large, powerful woman. She moved with confidence and strength. She wore a large brightly colored muumuu and had a scarf around her neck. She'd come for a consultation about Robert, a seven-year-old child she was fostering. Three years before our visit, this boy had been removed from his mother's custody. Robert's mom was a prostitute who'd been addicted to cocaine and alcohol for her son's whole life. She had neglected and beaten him; the boy had also seen her beaten by customers and pimps and had himself been terrorized and abused by her partners.

Since being removed from his home Robert had been in six foster homes and in three shelters. He had been hospitalized for out-of-control behaviors three times. He had been given a dozen diagnoses including attention deficit hyperactivity disorder (ADHD), oppositional deficit disorder (ODD), bipolar disorder, schizoaffective disorder, and various learning disorders. He was often a loving and affectionate child, but he had episodic "rages" and aggression that scared peers, teachers, and foster parents enough for them to reject him and have him removed from whatever setting he was in after he went on one of his rampages. Mama P. had brought him to us because once again, his inattentiveness and aggression had gotten him into trouble at school and the school had demanded that something be done. He reminded me of many of the boys I had worked with in Chicago at the residential treatment center.

As I began talking I tried to engage Mama P. and make her feel comfortable. I knew that people can "hear" and process information much more effectively if they feel calm. I wanted her to feel safe and respected. Thinking back now, I must have seemed very patronizing to her. I was too confident; I thought I knew what was going on with her foster child and the implicit message was, "I understand this child, and you don't." She looked at me defiantly, her face unsmiling, her arms folded. I went into a long-winded and very likely unintelligible explanation of the biology of the stress response and how it could account for the boy's aggression and hypervigilance symptoms. I had not yet learned how to clearly explain the impact of trauma on a child.

"So what can you do to help my baby?" she asked. Her language struck me: why was she calling this seven-year-old child a baby? I wasn't sure what to make of it.

I suggested clonidine, the medication I'd used with Sandy and the boys at the center. She interrupted quietly but firmly, "You will not use drugs on my baby."

I tried to explain that we were quite conservative with medications, but she wouldn't hear it. "No doctor is going to drug up my baby," she said. At this point the child psychiatry fellow, Robert's primary clinician, who was sitting next to me, started to fidget. This was awkward. Mr. Bigshot Vice-Chairman and Chief of Psychiatry was making an ass of himself. I was alienating this mother and getting nowhere. I again tried to explain the biology of the stress response system, but she cut me off.

"Explain what you just told me to the school," she said pointedly. "My baby does not need drugs. He needs people to be loving and kind to him. That school and all those teachers don't understand him."

"OK. We can talk to the school." I retreated.

And then I surrendered. "Mama P., how do you help him?" I asked, curious about why she didn't have the problems with his "rages" that had gotten him expelled from prior foster homes and schools.

"I just hold him and rock him. I just love him. At night when he wakes up scared and wanders the house, I just put him in bed next to me, rub his back, and sing a little and he falls asleep." The fellow was now stealing looks at me, clearly concerned: seven-year-olds should not sleep in bed with their caregivers. But I was intrigued and continued to listen.

"What seems to calm him down when he gets upset during the day?" I asked.

"Same thing. I just put everything down and hold him and rock in the chair. Doesn't take too long, poor thing."

As she said this I recalled a recurring pattern in Robert's records. In every one of them, including the latest referral from the school, angry staff reported frustration with the boy's non-compliance and immature "baby-like" behaviors, and complained about his neediness and clinginess. I asked Mama P., "So when he acts like that, don't you ever get frustrated and angry?"

"Do you get angry with a baby when a baby fusses?" she asked. "No. That is what babies do. Babies do the best they can and we always forgive them if they mess, if they cry, if they spit up on us."

"And Robert is your baby?"

"They are all my babies. It's just that Robert has been a baby for seven years."

We ended the session and made another appointment for a week later. I promised to call the school. Mama P. looked at me as I walked with Robert down the clinic hall. I joked that Robert needed to come back to teach us more. At that, she finally smiled.

Over the years Mama P. continued to bring her foster children to our clinic. And we continued to learn from her. Mama P. discovered, long before we did, that many young victims of abuse and neglect need physical stimulation, like being rocked and gently held, comfort seemingly appropriate to far younger children. She knew that you don't interact with these children based on their age, but based on what they need, what they may have missed during "sensitive periods" of development. Almost all of the children sent to her had a tremendous need to be held and touched. Whenever my staff saw her in the waiting room holding and rocking these children, they expressed concern that she was infantilizing them.

But I came to understand why her overwhelmingly affectionate, physically nurturing style, which I'd initially worried might be stifling for older children, was often just what the doctor should order. These children had never received the repeated, patterned physical nurturing needed to develop a well-regulated and responsive stress response system. They had never learned that they were loved and safe; they didn't have the internal security needed to safely explore the world and grow without fear. They were starving for touch—and Mama P. gave it to them.

NOW AS I SAT WITH LAURA AND HER mother, I knew that they both could benefit, not only from Mama P.'s wisdom about childrearing, but also from her own incredibly maternal and affectionate nature. I went back to the nurses' station, dug out her phone number, and called. I asked her if she'd be willing to have a mother and her child move in with her, so that Virginia could learn how to raise Laura. She immediately agreed. Fortunately, both families were involved in a privately funded program that allowed us to pay for this kind of care, which the foster care system is usually too inflexible to permit.

Now, I had to convince Virginia—and my colleagues. When I returned to the room where she was waiting, Virginia seemed anxious. My psychiatry colleague had given her one of the papers I had written that focused on our clinical work with abused children. Virginia assumed that I had deemed her an incompetent parent. Before I could even speak, she said, "If it will help make my baby better, please take her." Virginia did love her baby—so much that she was willing to let her go if that's what it took for her to recover.

I explained what I wanted to do instead, that I wanted her to live with Mama P. She, too, assented right away, saying she would do anything to help Laura.

My pediatric colleagues, however, were still extremely concerned about Laura's nutritional needs. She was so underweight that they were afraid that she would not take in enough calories without medical support. After all, she was currently being fed through a tube. I told the other doctors that we would strictly monitor her diet to be sure she was getting enough calories, and it turned out to be a good thing that we did. We could then document her remarkable progress. For the first month with Mama P., Laura consumed the exact same number of calories she had in the prior month in the hospital, during which her weight had barely been maintained at twenty-six pounds. In Mama P's nurturing environment, however, Laura gained ten pounds in one month, growing from twenty-six to thirty-six pounds! Her weight increased by 35 percent on the same number of calories that had previously not been enough to prevent weight loss, because she was now receiving the physical nurturing her brain needed to release the appropriate hormones required for growth.

By observing Mama P. and by receiving the physical affection Mama showered on everyone around her, Virginia began to learn what Laura needed and how to provide it for her. Before Mama P., meals had been robotic or filled with conflict: the constantly changing dietary instructions and advice given by various doctors and hospitals who were trying to help just added to the confused hollow experience of eating for Laura. Also, because of Virginia's lack of understanding of her child's needs, she'd swing from being affectionate to being tough and punitive to simply ignoring her daughter. Without the rewards that nurturing normally provides both mother and child, Virginia had been especially prone to frustration. Parenting is difficult. Without the neurobiological capacity to feel the joys of parenting, irritations and annoyances loom especially large.

Mama P.'s sense of humor, her warmth, and her hugs allowed Virginia to get some of the mothering she'd missed. And by watching how Mama P. responded to her other children and to Laura, Virginia began to pick up on Laura's cues. Now she could better read when Laura was hungry, when she wanted to play, when she needed a nap. The four-year-old had seemed stuck in the defiant stage of the "terrible twos," but now she began to mature, both emotionally and physically. As Laura grew, the tension between mother and daughter during mealtimes ended. Virginia relaxed and was able to discipline with more patience and consistency.

Virginia and Laura lived with Mama P. for about a year. Afterwards, the two women remained tight friends, and Virginia moved into Mama's neighborhood so that she could remain in close touch. Laura became a bright little girl, similar to her mother in that she tended to be emotionally distant, but

with a powerful moral compass; they both had strong positive values. When Virginia had a second child, she knew how
to care for him appropriately, right from the start, and he suffered no growth problems. Virginia went on to college and both
of her children are doing well in school. They have friends, an
invested church community and, of course, Mama P. just down
the street.

Both Laura and Virginia still bear scars from their early
childhoods, however. If you were to secretly observe either
mother or daughter, you might find her facial expression vacant,
or even sad. Once she became aware of your presence, she would
put on her social persona and respond appropriately to you,
but if you paid close attention to your "gut" you would sense
something awkward or unnatural in your interactions. Both can
mimic many of the normal social interactive cues, but neither
feels naturally pulled to be social, to spontaneously smile or to
express warm nurturing physical behaviors such as a hug.

Though we all "perform" for others to some extent, the
mask slips easily for those who have suffered early neglect. On
a "higher" more cognitive level both mother and daughter are
very good people. They have learned to use moral rules and a
strong belief system to tame their fears and desires. But in the
relational and social communication systems of their brain, the
source of emotional connections to others, there are shadows of
the disrupted nurturing of their early childhoods. The nature
and timing of our developmental experiences shape us. Like
people who learn a foreign language late in life, Virginia and
Laura will never speak the language of love without an accent.

CHAPTER 5

The Coldest Heart

ENTERING A MAXIMUM-SECURITY prison is always daunting: after the extensive identity check at the gate, you have to hand over your keys, wallet, phone, and anything else that could possibly be stolen or used as a weapon. Everything that identifies you, except your clothing, is confiscated. One of the first locked doors you pass through is marked by a sign saying, in effect, that if you are taken hostage past this point, you're on your own. The policy is ostensibly to prevent visitors from pretending to be held captive by prisoners and enabling their escape, but it also immediately instills an unsettling feeling. There are at least three or four double sets of thick metal doors, with many layers of human and electronic security between them, which slam solidly behind you before you can meet with the kind of prisoner I had been brought in to examine. Leon, at age sixteen, had sadistically murdered two teenage girls, and then raped their dead bodies.

Virginia and Laura demonstrated one way that neglect in early childhood can disrupt the development of the areas in the brain that control empathy and the ability to engage in healthy relationships—a loss that often leaves people awkward, lonely, and socially inept. Emotional deprivation in the first years of life, however, can also predispose people to malice or misanthropy. In the mother's and the daughter's cases, fortunately, despite their underdeveloped capacity for empathy, both became highly moral people; their early childhood experiences had left them emotionally crippled and often oblivious to social cues, but not filled with rage and hatred. Leon's story illustrates a much more dangerous—and fortunately, less common—potential outcome. Leon would teach me more about how much damage parental neglect—even unintentional neglect—can inflict, and how modern Western culture can erode the extended family networks that have traditionally protected many children from it.

Leon had been convicted of a capital offense and faced the death penalty. His defense had hired me to testify during the sentencing phase of his trial. This hearing determines whether there are "mitigating" factors, such as a history of mental health problems or abuse, that should be weighed when sentencing decisions are made. My testimony would help the court decide between life without parole and the ultimate punishment.

I VISITED THE PRISON ON A PERFECT Spring day, the kind of clear day that makes most people happy to be alive. The cheery sound of chirping birds and the warmth of the sun seemed almost inappropriate as I stood in front of the massive gray building. It was five stories tall and made of cement block. It had too-few barred windows and a tiny green one-room guardhouse with a red door attached to one wall, which looked incongruously small compared to the imposing bulk of the prison. The grounds were surrounded by a twenty-foot wire fence with three coils of barbwire at the top. I was the only person outside. A few old cars were parked in the lot.

I approached the red door, my heart beating fast, my palms sweating. I had to tell myself to calm down. The whole place seemed fenced by tension. I walked in through a double door, passed through a metal detector, was summarily frisked and then taken into the compound by a guard who seemed as caged and resentful as a prisoner.

"You a psychologist?" she asked, looking me over disapprovingly.

"No. I'm a psychiatrist."

"OK, whatever. You could spend a lifetime here." She laughed disdainfully. I forced a smile. "Here's the rules. You must read this." She handed me a one-page document and continued, "No contraband. No weapons. You may not bring gifts or take anything out of the prison." Her tone and attitude told me she had no use for me. Maybe she was angry that she had to spend this perfect day in prison. Maybe she was resentful because she thought that mental health professionals working with the justice system mainly help criminals escape responsibility for their actions.

"OK," I said, trying to be respectful. But I could tell she had already made up her mind about me. It's no wonder that she was hostile, though. Our brains adapt to our environments, and this place wasn't likely to elicit kindness or trust.

THE INTERVIEW ROOM WAS SMALL with a single metal table and two chairs. The floor was a tiled institutional gray with green speckles and the walls were painted cinderblock. Leon was brought in by two male guards. He looked small and childlike as he faced me, wearing an orange jumpsuit, his arms and legs shackled and chained to each other. He was thin and short for his age. He didn't look lethal. Sure, his stance was aggressive, and I could see that he already had jailhouse tattoos, his forearm branded with a crooked "X." But the toughness came across as phony and artificial, like an undersized tomcat with his hair on end, trying to appear larger than he actually was. It was almost impossible to believe that this now eighteen-year-old boy/man had brutally murdered two people.

He'd seen his two young victims in an elevator in the high-rise building where he lived. Although it was only three or four in the afternoon, he'd already been drinking beer. He had crudely propositioned the teenagers. When the girls—not surprisingly—rejected him, he'd followed them into an apartment and, apparently after a physical confrontation, stabbed both of them to death with a table knife. Cherise was twelve and her friend Lucy was thirteen. Both were barely pubescent. The attack had happened so fast and Leon was so much larger than his victims that neither girl had been able to defend herself. He'd managed to quickly restrain Cherise with a belt. After that, while Lucy tried to fight him off, he killed her and then, either to avoid leaving a witness, or still in a rage, slaughtered the bound girl as well. He then raped both bodies. His anger still not sated, he'd kicked and stomped them.

Though he had often been in trouble with the law, Leon's records didn't indicate that he was capable of anything like this level of violence. His parents were hard-working, married legal immigrants, solid citizens without criminal histories. His family had never been involved with child protective services; there was no history of abuse, nor foster care placements, nor any other obvious red flags for attachment problems. Yet all of his records suggested that he was a master at manipulating people around him and, more ominously, that he was completely devoid of emotional connection to others. He was often described as having little to no empathy: remorseless, callous, indifferent to most of the "consequences" set up in school or in juvenile justice programs.

Seeing him now, looking so small in his shackles in this terrible prison, I almost felt sorry for him. But then we began to talk.

"You the doctor?" he asked, looking me over, clearly disappointed.

"Yep."

"I told her I wanted a lady shrink," he sneered. He pushed his chair away from the table and kicked it. I asked him whether he'd discussed my visit with his lawyer and understood its purpose.

He nodded, trying to act tough and indifferent, but I knew he had to be scared. He probably would never admit it or even understand it, but inside he was always on guard, always vigilant and always studying the people around him. Trying to work out who could help him and who could hurt him. What is this person's weak point, what does he want, what does he fear?

From the moment I came in I could see that he was studying me, too. Probing for weakness, seeking ways to manipulate me. He was smart enough to know the stereotype of the liberal, bleeding-heart shrink. He had successfully read his lead attorney. She felt sorry for him now; he had convinced her he was the one who'd been wronged. Those girls had invited him into the apartment. They promised to have sex with him. Things got rough and it was an accident. He tripped over their bodies; that's how he got blood on his boots. He never intended to hurt them. And now he set out to persuade me, too, that he was a misunderstood victim of two teen vixens who had teased and tempted him.

"Tell me about yourself." I started with open questions, trying to see where he would go.

"What do you mean? Is that some kind of shrink trick?" he asked, suspicious.

"No. I just figured you are the best person to tell me about you. I've read a whole lot of other people's opinions. Teachers, therapists, probation officers, the press. They all have opinions. So I want to know yours."

"What do you want to know?"

"What do you want to tell me?" The dance continued. We circled around each other. It was a game I knew well. He was pretty good. But I was used to this.

"Well. Let's start with right now. What it is like living in prison?"

"It's boring. It's not so bad. Not too much to do."

"Tell me your schedule." And so it started. He slowly began to loosen up as he described the routines of the prison and his earlier experiences in the juvenile justice system. I let him talk and then after a few hours, we took a break so he could smoke a cigarette. When I came back, it was time to get to the point. "Tell me what happened with those girls."

"It was no big deal really. I was just hanging out and these two girls came by. We started talking and they invited me up to their apartment to fool around. Then when they got me up there, they changed their minds. It pissed me off." This was different from his original statement and from other accounts he'd given. It seemed that the more time that passed since the crime, the less violent he made the story. Each time he told it, he was less and less responsible for what had happened; he, rather than the girls, increasingly became the victim.

"It was an accident. I just wanted to scare them. Stupid bitches wouldn't shut up," he went on. My stomach churned. Don't react. Be still. If he senses how horrified and disgusted you feel, he won't be honest. He will edit. Stay calm. I nodded.

"They were loud?" I asked as neutrally as I could manage.

"Yes. I told them I wouldn't hurt them if they would just shut up." He was giving me a short, sanitized version of the murders. He left out the rape. He left out how he'd brutally kicked the girls.

I asked whether their screams had enraged him, if that was why he'd kicked the bodies. The autopsy report showed that the thirteen-year-old had been kicked in the face and stomped on the neck and chest.

"Well, I didn't really kick them. I just tripped. I had been drinking some. So, you know," he said, hoping I would fill in the blanks. He looked up to see if I had bought his lies. There was little emotion on his face or in his voice. He described the murders as if he were giving a geography report in school. The only trace of emotion was the disdain he expressed that his victims had "made him" kill them, furious with them for fighting back, for resisting.

His coldness was breathtaking. This was a predator, someone whose only concern for other people was what he could get from them, what he could make them do, and how they could serve his selfish ends. He could not even put on a compassionate performance for a shrink hired by his defense, someone looking for the smallest glimmer of goodness or promise in him.

It wasn't that he didn't know that he should try to appear remorseful. He simply wasn't capable of taking into account the feelings of others in any way other than to take advantage of them. He could not feel compassion for others, so he couldn't fake it very well, either. Leon was not unintelligent. In fact, his IQ was significantly above average in some ways. However, it was uneven. While his verbal IQ was in the low to normal range, his performance score, which measures things like the ability to properly sequence a series of pictures and manipulate objects in space, was quite high. He scored especially well in his ability to read social situations and understand other people's intentions.

This split between verbal and performance scores is often seen in abused or traumatized children and can indicate that the developmental needs of certain brain regions, particularly those cortical areas involved in modulating the lower, more reactive regions have been not been met. In the general population about 5 percent of people show this pattern, but in prisons and juvenile treatment centers that proportion rises to over 35 percent. It reflects the use-dependent development of the brain: with more developmental chaos and threat the brain's stress response systems and those areas of the brain responsible for reading threat-related social cues will grow, while less affection and nurturing will result in underdevelopment of the systems that code for compassion and self-control. These test results were the first clues that something had probably gone wrong in his early childhood.

I tried to figure out what might have happened from our interview, but didn't get very far. Most people don't remember much from the developmentally critical years of birth through kindergarten, anyway. There was evidence indicating he had been troubled from very early on, however. His records showed reports of aggressive behavior dating back to his preschool years. From our conversation I could also tell that he'd had few friends or lasting relationships with anyone outside his family. His charts showed a history of bullying and of petty crimes like shoplifting and other thefts, but he had never been to an adult prison before now. His run-ins with the law as an adolescent had mainly resulted in probation; he hadn't even spent much time in juvenile detention, despite having committed some serious assaults.

I did discover, however, that he'd committed, or been suspected of committing, several major offenses for which he had not been charged or convicted because there was not enough evidence to make the charges stick. For example, he'd once been found in possession of a stolen bicycle. The bike's teenage owner had been beaten so severely that he'd wound up in the hospital with life-threatening injuries. But there were no witnesses to the assault—or none that would come forward—so Leon was only charged with possession of stolen property. Over the course of several evaluation visits he eventually bragged about previous sexual assaults to me, with the same cold disdain with which he'd discussed the murders.

Looking for any sign of remorse, I finally asked what should have been an easy question.

"Now that you look back on all this, what would you have done differently?" I said, expecting him to at least mouth some platitudes about controlling his anger, about not harming people.

He seemed to think for a minute, then responded, "I don't know. Maybe throw away those boots?"

"Throw away the boots?"

"Yeah. It was the boot prints and the blood on the boots that got me."

MANY PSYCHIATRISTS WOULD HAVE left the prison believing that Leon was the archetypal "bad seed," a genetic freak of nature, a demonic child incapable of empathy. And there are genetic predispositions that appear to affect the brain's systems involved in empathy. My research, however, has led me to believe that behavior as extreme as Leon's is rare among people who have not suffered certain forms of early emotional and/or physical deprivation.

Furthermore, if Leon had the genetic makeup that increased the risk of sociopathic behavior—if such genes even exist—his family history should have revealed other relatives, such as a parent, a grandparent, maybe an uncle, with similar, even if less extreme, problems. Perhaps a history of multiple arrests, for example. But there was none. Also, Leon had been turned in to the police by his own brother, a brother who seemed to be everything that Leon was not.

Frank,* Leon's brother, like his parents and other relatives, was gainfully employed. He was a successful plumber, married, a dutiful father of two who was respected in the community.

The day of the crime, he'd come home to find Leon, still wear-ing his blood-encrusted boots, watching TV in his living room. On the news was an urgent bulletin about the recent discovery of the violated bodies of two young girls in Leon's building. Sneaking occasional glances at the boots, Frank waited until Leon left, then called the police to report his suspicions about his brother's connection to the crime.

Siblings share at least 50 percent of their genes. While Frank could have been genetically blessed with a far greater capacity for empathy than Leon, it was unlikely that this alone accounted for their very different temperaments and life paths. Yet as far as I knew, Leon and Frank had shared the same home and parents, so Leon's environment didn't appear to be a likely culprit either. I would only discover what I now believe to be at the root of Leon's problems after I met with Frank and his parents, Maria* and Alan.* In our first meeting they were all in obvious distress over the situation.

MARIA WAS SMALL AND CONSERVATIVELY dressed, wearing a cardigan buttoned all the way up. She sat erect, knees together, with both hands on the handbag in her lap. Alan wore dark green work clothes; his name was sewn into a white oval over his pocket. Frank was wearing a button-down, collared blue shirt and khaki pants. Maria looked sad and fragile, Alan seemed ashamed, and Frank seemed angry. I greeted each of them with a handshake and tried to establish eye contact.

"I'm sorry we have to meet under these circumstances," I said, carefully watching them. I wanted to see how they related to others, whether they showed an ability to empathize, whether there were any hints of pathological or odd behavior that might not have shown up in Leon's medical records and family his-tory. But they responded appropriately. They were distressed, guilty, concerned, everything you would expect from family members who'd discovered that one of their own had committed an unspeakable crime.

"As you know, your son's attorney has asked me to evaluate him for the sentencing phase of the trial. I've met with Leon now twice. I wanted to spend some time with you to get a better understanding of how he was when he was younger." The parents listened, but neither would look me in the eye. Frank stared at me, however, defensive and protective of his parents. "We are all trying to understand why he did this," I concluded. The parents looked at me and nodded; the father's eyes filled with tears. Their grief filled the room; Frank finally looked away from me, blinking back tears of his own.

I could see that these parents had spent hours wracked with sadness, confusion, and guilt as they searched for the "why." *Why had our son done this? Why had he turned out this way? What did we do wrong? Are we bad parents? Was he born bad?* They spoke with total bewilderment about Leon, telling me that they'd done their best, worked hard, given him what they could. They'd taken him to church, they told me, they'd done everything the teachers and schools and counselors had asked. I heard their recriminations: *Maybe we should have been stricter. Maybe we should have been less strict. Maybe I should have sent him to live with my mother when he first got in trouble.* They struggled to get through every day, tired from their grief, from sleepless nights, and from pretending that they didn't see the stares and disapproving looks from their neighbors and coworkers.

"Let's start at the beginning. Tell me about how you two met," I said. Alan spoke first, beginning to smile slightly as he thought of his own childhood and his courtship. Alan and Maria had met as young children. They both lived in large extended families in the same small, rural community. They attended the same school, prayed in the same church, and lived in the same neighborhood. They were economically poor, but wealthy in family. They grew up surrounded by cousins, aunties, uncles, and grandparents. Everyone knew everyone else's business, but that meant everyone cared, too. In Alan and Maria's hometown children were never far from the watchful eyes of one relative or another.

Maria dropped out of high school at fifteen, becoming a maid at a local hotel. Alan stayed on until graduation, then started work at a nearby factory. They got married when he was twenty and she was eighteen. He did well at the factory and made a good living. Soon Maria got pregnant.

This pregnancy was a joyous event for both extended families. Maria was pampered, and she was able to quit work to stay home with their child. The young family lived in the basement apartment of a building owned by an uncle. Her parents lived next door; his family, one block over. As they discussed this time in their lives, they smiled at each other. Alan did most of the talking, while Maria nodded her agreement. Frank listened intently as if he had never heard about his parents' early life. At moments the family almost seemed to forget what had brought them here.

As Alan dominated the conversation, I would occasionally try to direct a question to Maria, but most of the time she would just smile at me politely and then look to her husband who would then answer instead. In time it became clear that Maria, though kindhearted and polite, was mentally impaired. She didn't seem to understand many of my questions. Finally, I asked her, "Did you like school?" Alan looked at me and said quietly, "She is not good at those things. She is maybe a little slow in that way." She looked at me sheepishly and I nodded and smiled back. Both her husband and her son were clearly protective of her.

Alan went on, describing the birth of their first son, Frank. After Maria came home from the hospital, the grandmothers, aunties, and older cousins spent hours with the young mother and her new child. Both mother and baby were immersed in the attention and love of their extended families. When Maria felt overwhelmed by the responsibility of caring for this dependent little being, there was always an aunt or a cousin or her own mother around to help. When his cries drove her crazy, she could always get a break by asking a family member to babysit. But then Alan lost his job. He looked diligently for new work, but the factory had closed and decent jobs for people without a college education became nearly impossible to find. After six months of unemployment he managed to get another factory job, but it was in a city, one hundred miles away. He felt he had no choice but to take it.

The family, with now three-year-old Frank, relocated to an apartment complex in the city. The only place they could afford was in a devastated inner-city neighborhood plagued with high rates of violent crime and drug use. Few people worked and few had roots in the area. As is often the case in this country, extended families were scattered, not living close together as they had back home. Most of the households with children were headed by single mothers.

Soon Maria became pregnant with Leon. This pregnancy, however, was very different from her first one. Maria was now alone all day long in a small apartment with a toddler as her only companion. She was bewildered by her new life—and lonely. She didn't know anyone and didn't know how to reach out to her neighbors. Alan worked long hours, and when he came home he was exhausted. Maria's three-year-old son became her best friend. They spent hours together. They would walk to a nearby park, take the bus to the free museums in the city, and participate in a mother's drop-in program at a church. Maria developed a routine in which she would leave the apartment early in the morning and stay out all day, picking up groceries just before she returned home. The routine was comforting. She created a repetitive pattern of activity and the familiar faces she saw each day were some tiny connection to others, reminding her of the familiarity of the world she left behind. Still, she missed her family. She missed her neighborhood. She missed the group of experienced women who had helped her raise her first baby.

Then, Leon was born. Maria was now overwhelmed by the inevitable neediness of a newborn. She never had to raise a baby alone before. It became clear to me that the family had understood Maria's limitations and, when needed, had stepped in to provide a loving, predictable, and safe environment for Frank. But when Leon was born this relational safety net was absent. I was starting to see why Leon and Frank had turned out so differently.

"He was such a fussy baby. He cried," Maria told me, describing Leon.

She smiled. I smiled back.

"And how would you calm him down?"

"I tried to feed him. Sometimes he would take the bottle and stop."

"Anything else?"

"Sometimes he would not stop. So we would go on our walk."

"We?"

"Me and Frank."

"Ah."

"Did anyone ever come to help you take care of Leon?"

"No. We would wake up and feed him and then go for our walk."

"Was this like the walks you took before Leon was born?"

"Yes. We go to the park. Play for a while. Take the bus to the church and have lunch. Then go to the children's museum. Take the bus to the market to buy food for dinner. And then go home."

"So you were gone most of the day."

"Yes."

Little by little it became clear that from the time Leon was four weeks old, the mother had resumed her "walks" with her oldest son, by then a four-year-old. She left baby Leon alone in a dark apartment. My heart sank as I listened to the mother—innocent, yet ignorant of the crucial needs of an infant—describe her systematic neglect of her youngest son. It was hard to be critical: she had given her four-year-old loving and attentive care. But at the same time she had deprived her newborn of the experiences necessary for him to form and maintain healthy relationships.

"He stopped crying so much," she said, indicating that she thought that her solution to the problem had worked.

But as he grew older, both parents related, Leon never responded to their parenting the same way that Frank did. Whenever they reprimanded Frank, he felt bad that he had disappointed his parents and he corrected his behaviors. When Frank was told that he'd done well, he smiled and it was easy to see that he found pleasing his parents to be rewarding. The little boy was always hugging someone, running up to Mom or Dad and wrapping his little arms around them.

When Leon was scolded or punished, however, he showed no emotion. He didn't seem to care that he'd let his parents down or hurt someone else emotionally or physically. He didn't correct his behavior. When his parents or teachers were pleased with him and gave him positive attention, he seemed equally unaffected. He actively avoided being touched, or touching others.

Over time he learned to use flattery, flirtation, and other forms of manipulation to get what he wanted. If that did not work, he did what he wanted when he wanted anyway, and if he wasn't given what he asked for, then he took it. If he got caught doing something wrong, he would lie, and if he got caught in a lie, he was indifferent to lectures and punishment. All he seemed to learn from punishment was how to improve his deception and better hide his bad behavior. Teachers, counselors, youth ministers, and coaches all said the same thing: Leon didn't seem to care about anyone or anything but himself. The normal relational rewards and consequences—making your parents proud, making a friend happy, feeling upset if you hurt a loved one—did not matter to him.

So he started to get in trouble, first at preschool, then kindergarten, then elementary school. At first it was little things: stealing candy, minor bullying, poking classmates with pencils, talking back to teachers, ignoring the rules. But by third grade he had been referred for mental health services. By fifth grade he was a regular in the juvenile justice system, brought up on charges of truancy, theft, and vandalism. This callous and criminal behavior qualified him for the diagnosis of "conduct disorder" by age ten.

When Maria had taken Frank out for walks, Leon had wailed in his crib at first. But he'd soon learned that crying would bring no aid, so he stopped. He lay there, alone and uncared for, with no one to talk to him and no one to praise him for learning to turn over or crawl (and not much room to explore anyway). For most of the day he heard no language, saw no new sights, and received no attention.

Like Laura and Virginia, Leon had been deprived of the critical stimuli necessary to develop the brain areas that modulate stress and link pleasure and comfort with human company. His cries had gone unanswered, his early need for warmth and touch unmet. At least Virginia had known consistent care in her foster homes, even though she was moved from one to another repeatedly, and at least Laura had known the constant presence of her mother, even if she hadn't received enough physical affection from her. But Leon's early life was maddeningly inconstant. Sometimes Maria would pay attention to him, others times she would leave him home alone for the whole day. Occasionally Alan was home and would play with him, but more often he was out working or too exhausted from his long days to cope with a baby. An environment of such intermittent care punctuated by total abandonment may be the worst of all worlds for a child. The brain needs patterned, repetitive stimuli to develop properly. Spastic, unpredictable relief from fear, loneliness, discomfort, and hunger keeps a baby's stress system on high alert. Receiving no consistent, loving response to his fears and needs, Leon never developed the normal association between human contact and relief from stress. What he learned instead was that the only person he could rely on was himself.

When he did interact with others, his neediness made him seem alternately demanding, aggressive, and cold. In vain attempts to get the love and attention he desperately required, Leon would lash out, hit people, take things, and destroy them. Receiving only punishment, his rage grew. And the "worse" he behaved, the more he confirmed to those around him that he was "bad" and didn't deserve their affection. It was a vicious cycle, and as Leon got older his misbehavior escalated from bullying into crime.

Leon could see that other people liked to be hugged and touched, but since his own needs for that had been neglected, he began to find it repellent. He could see that other people enjoyed interacting with each other, but because he'd been denied early attention, it now mostly left him cold. He just didn't understand relationships.

Leon could enjoy food, could enjoy material pleasures like toys and television, and could relish physical sensations, including those associated with his developing sexuality. But because he'd been neglected when key social circuitry of the brain was developing he couldn't really appreciate the pleasure of pleasing someone else or receiving their praise, nor did he suffer particularly from the rejection that followed if his behavior displeased teachers or peers. Having failed to develop an association between people and pleasure, he saw no need to do as they wished, felt no joy in making them happy, and didn't care whether or not they got hurt.

When he was two-and-a-half, Leon's behavioral problems qualified him for an early intervention preschool program, which could have been a great opportunity, but in fact only worsened his problems. Now his mother no longer left him alone during the day, and he was exposed to enough cognitive stimulation to learn to talk and to intellectually understand what was expected of him. But this didn't make up for what he'd missed. While well intentioned, the program had only one caregiver to handle five or six severely troubled toddlers, a child to adult ratio that may not be enough to give appropriate attention to normal children that age, let alone those with emotional disorders.

The cognitive development of his cortex did, however, allow Leon to take note of how other people behaved. Over time he became able to mimic appropriate behavior when he wanted to. This allowed him to manipulate others into getting what he wanted, though his underdeveloped limbic and relational neural systems limited him to shallow, superficial relationships. For him people were just objects that either stood in his way or acceded to his needs. He was a classic sociopath (the psychiatric diagnosis is antisocial personality disorder, or ASPD), and one I think who was almost entirely a product of his environment, not his genes. I believe that if he had been raised the way his brother Frank had been, he probably would have grown up to have a normal life, and would almost certainly have never become a murderer and rapist.

Even the steps taken to help him—for example the preschool

intervention program that placed him in a group of other disturbed children—only worsened his condition. Research has repeatedly found that surrounding a child with other troubled peers only tends to escalate bad behavior. This pattern of backfiring interventions would continue through his childhood and adolescence as he was shunted into "special ed" and other programs. There, he also found other antisocial peers who reinforced each other's impulsivity. They became partners in crime, egging each other on and modeling for each other the idea that violence is the best way to solve problems. Furthermore, through what he saw in his neighborhood, at the movies, and on the TV that was always on in most of the places where he spent his time, he also got the message that violence solves problems and that there was pleasure to be had in wielding physical power over others. Leon learned to copy the worst of human behavior, but remained unable to understand why he should imitate the best.

There are other brain disorders that affect the ability to empathize that provide insight on sociopathy like Leon's. Most notable are autism spectrum disorders (ASDs), including what was previously known as Asperger's syndrome, the less severe form of autism. ASDs appear to be strongly genetically influenced and range widely in their link to disability. About one-third of autistic children never learn to speak and all of them tend to isolate themselves from others, frequently focusing more on objects than on people. Autistic boys don't usually engage in imaginative play—and although many people on the spectrum desperately want to connect with others, they have great difficulty in forming and understanding relationships.

ASDs are almost always accompanied by sensory integration problems and differences in sensitivity, such as being unable to tolerate "itchy" fabrics and being overwhelmed by loud noises or bright lights. Autistic children also have repetitive behaviors like rocking and odd obsessions, typically with moving objects—for example, trains or the wheels on toy cars. Some autistic people are highly talented at understanding complex systems like math, music, and computer science, and most develop focused interests in particular objects or ideas.

People with Asperger's are better at connecting with others and functioning in society than those with more severe forms of autism, but their obsessions and inability to read social cues often keep them isolated. Their poor social skills can also make it hard for them to get or keep a job, although in some cases their mathematical and engineering abilities more than compensate for their awkwardness. Many children tagged as "geeks" or "nerds" because of their inability to relate to their peers may have an ASD or come close to meeting the criteria for one.

In order to function socially, people need to develop what is known as a "theory of mind." They need to know, in other words, that other people are distinct from them, have different knowledge about the world and have different desires and interests. In autism this distinction is blurred. One reason some autistic children may not talk is that they don't recognize the need to communicate; they aren't aware that other people don't know what they know. In one famous experiment, researchers put a pencil in a tube that ordinarily held candy and asked autistic children what someone outside the room would expect to find in it. Normal and even Down syndrome preschoolers said candy. But the autistic children insisted that others would expect the pencil, not realizing that people who hadn't seen the candy removed would think it was still there. The children knew the candy was gone, so their logical assumption was that everyone else must know, too. (The brain regions involved in coding "theory of mind" are believed to be in the left medial frontal cortex, just over the eyes.)

Unlike sociopaths like Leon, however, autistic people, although odd, do not tend toward violence or crime despite their problems with perspective taking and with recognizing, for example, that ignoring someone might be hurtful to him. Their problem with empathy is conceptual. Autistic people can be insensitive to the feelings and needs of others, but this usually occurs when they cannot fully perceive these feelings, not because they wish to cause harm or to be unkind. They have every capacity to love and feel emotional pain, but not the wiring that allows them to easily understand how to interact and have relationships. They may have difficulty imagining what it's like to be in someone else's shoes—sometimes called "mind-blindness"—but they do not lack sympathy for those people's experiences when they become aware of them.

Sociopaths like Leon are different. Their inability to empathize is a difficulty with mirroring the feelings of others coupled with a lack of compassion for them. In other words, they not only don't completely recognize what other people feel, but they don't care if they hurt them or they even actively desire to do so. They can imagine walking in someone else's shoes, and they can predict how other people will behave based upon this ability to put themselves in someone else's place, but they don't care what it's like there. Their only concern is how others will affect them.

In essence, they have a "theory of mind," but it is twisted. Not being able to fully experience love, they see it as something you promise in order to get sex, for example, not as a genuine feeling. Because they use other people's feelings as a way to manipulate them, sociopaths assume that's what everyone else does, too. Not feeling pleasure from relationships, they don't believe others genuinely feel it, either. Since they are selfish, they believe others act only in their own self-interest as well. As a result, they dismiss appeals for attention or mercy as manipulative attempts to take power, not as genuine emotional pleas. They are emotionally frozen, in an ice that distorts not only their own feelings, but also how they see the feelings of others and then respond to them.

UNSURPRISINGLY RESEARCH HAS now identified that some of the chemical correlates of sociopathy can be found in some of the same neurotransmitter systems that compose our stress response systems: alterations in serotonin, norepinephrine, and dopamine systems have been implicated in aggressive, violent, or antisocial behavior. Young people exhibiting antisocial traits and callous behavior tend to have abnormal levels of the stress hormone cortisol (which can be measured in a saliva test). Sociopaths are notorious for being able to fool lie detector tests, which actually measure physical responses related to anxiety and stress, not deception. It appears that their stress systems—either because they were placed on overdrive due to early trauma or because of genetic vulnerability or, most likely, some combination of both—are dysregulated, no longer responsive to anything except extreme stimulation. This makes them appear "cold" and unemotional and allows them to lie with impunity, as they do not show the signs of fear of detection that tend to give others away. It may also mean that far higher levels of painful or pleasurable stimulation are necessary in order for them to feel anything at all. Unlike people whose response to trauma is to get stuck in a highly sensitized state in which any stress at all triggers a massive response, sociopaths' systems appear to have gotten stuck at the other end of the spectrum, in deadening—and sometimes deadly—numbness.

While preparing my testimony, I thought hard about what I would say about Leon and what I believed about his own responsibility for his actions. Why did he kill? Why does anyone kill? Are these even the right questions? Maybe, I thought, I should try to understand what keeps the rest of us from killing, what didn't put the brakes on Leon's behavior. How exactly had things gone so wrong for this boy? How had he forged his misfortune, neglect, and trauma into hate—or did those things forge him entirely?

He was unquestionably guilty and did not meet the legal definition of insanity, which requires that a person be unable to tell right from wrong. Leon knew that murder was against the law and that it was reprehensible; he'd admitted it and he did not have any diagnosable mental illness that would impair his moral reasoning.

He met criteria for attention deficit disorder and conduct disorder during most of his childhood and youth. As an adult, Leon certainly fit the profile for both ADHD and ASPD, but those diagnoses, which simply describe symptoms like defiance, callous behavior, and an inability to focus attention, do not imply mental clouding that would overwhelm one's ability to know that killing and raping people is not acceptable. These disorders involve decreased impulse control, but impaired impulse control does not mean complete lack of free will.

But what about Leon's inability to give and receive love? Can we blame him for having a childhood that wilted the part of his brain that allows him to feel the greatest joys most of us have in life: the pain and pleasure of human connection? Of course not. He is responsible, I believe, for his reactions to his vulnerabilities. Virginia and Laura struggled with similar problems, but they did not become violent people, let alone murderers.

One might argue that this difference in outcome is due to gender and, indeed, male gender is the biggest predictor of violent behavior. Male murderers outnumber females by at least nine to one, though it appears that very recently, women have begun to close the gap. Nonetheless, throughout history, in every culture and even in most species, male violence predominates. Among our closest evolutionary cousins, the chimps, it is the males who make war on others, the males who are prone to use force. Yet I'd treated other adolescent boys with far worse histories of neglect, abuse and abandonment, and far fewer opportunities for love and affection than Leon had. Some had literally been raised in cages with no loving family at all, unlike Leon who had two parents and a brother, and who was neglected out of ignorance, not malice. Most of these boys who I'd treated grew up awkward and lonely, many were severely mentally ill, but the vast majority was not malign.

What about genetics? Could that explain Leon's behavior? Disadvantageous genetics combined with a less-than-ideal environment was likely a factor in how he was raised and who he became. If Leon had had an easier temperament, for example, Maria might not have been so overwhelmed by his needs; if Maria had been more intelligent, she might have discovered better ways to cope with her challenging baby.

But what I think happened in Leon's life was an escalation of small, in-themselves-inconsequential negative decisions made by him and for him that gradually led to a horrendous outcome for his victims, his family and himself. You may have heard of the "butterfly effect": the idea that complex systems—most famously, that which determines the earth's weather—are extraordinarily sensitive to minor fluctuations at certain critical points. Such systems are so responsive to tiny perturbations that, as the example goes, if a butterfly flutters its wings at the wrong instant in Brazil, it can trigger a series of events that may ultimately result in a tornado that devastates a small Texas town. The human brain, the ultimate complex system—in fact, the most complicated object in the known universe—is equally vulnerable to a version of the butterfly effect.

This might also be called a "snowball effect": when things go right early on, they will tend to continue to go right and even to self-correct if there are minor problems. But when they go wrong at first, they will tend to continue to go wrong.

This effect is literally built into the architecture of our brains and bodies. For example, it is a tiny chemical gradient that determines which of our early cells will become skin, which will become brain, and which will become bone, heart, and bowel. Other extremely tiny differences tell one neuron to become part of the cerebellum, another to become cerebrum, and similar slight differences in position and in concentration of certain chemicals determine which cells live and which will die.

We don't have nearly enough genes to begin to determine the location or even the type of every cell: there are just 30,000 for the whole body and yet the brain alone has 86 billion nerve cells (and supporting glial cells for each of those). Each one of those billions of neurons makes between 5,000 and 10,000 connections, producing extraordinarily complex networks. Our bodies and especially our brains are built to magnify practically imperceptible initial incongruities into massively differentiated results. And this, in turn, allows us to respond to the complicated social and physical environment that we face.

So, while for most babies, being born colicky does little more than frustrate their parents, for Leon it overwhelmed his mother's already limited emotional resources. Without the presence of her extended family, there was no one to hand him off to when she was at her wit's end, as there had been with Frank. Abandoning her infant during the day, she left him without the critical input he needed to soothe and, ultimately, organize his already slightly dysregulated stress response systems, making them even more chaotic and disorganized.

This, in turn, left Leon alternately clingy and aggressive, hampering his social skills, which could potentially have allowed him to elicit the warmth and care he needed from elsewhere. It also further alienated him from his parents and created a cycle of misbehavior, punishment and increasing rage and distress. Then he was placed with a negative peer group, from preschool onwards, which further magnified the harm.

Surrounded by normal peers, he might have found people who could reach out to him, who might have offered him healthy friendships that could have led him away from antisocial behavior. But in the company of other angry, distressed, and needy children, and additionally stigmatized by the labels applied to them, he instead became more distressed and out of control, leading him to react with escalating impulsivity and aggression.

At no one point did Leon make a conscious decision to become malevolent, but each small choice he or his family made pushed him further toward sociopathy, and each consequence of those choices made further negative choices increasingly likely. There were numerous forks in the road where different circumstances might have led Leon to become a better person, where better choices could have led to the start of a virtuous—not vicious—cycle. But unfortunately, he rejected every opportunity to turn away from his rage and impulsivity, and at none of those crossroads did he receive the appropriate help and support he needed from other people to pull him from the rut in which he'd become stuck.

The brain is built—our selves are built—from millions of tiny decisions—some conscious, most not. Seemingly irrelevant choices can result in tremendously different later outcomes. Timing is everything. We don't know when the smallest choice, or "stimuli," will push a developing brain onto the path of genius, or onto the highway to hell. I want to stress that this doesn't mean that parents have to be perfect. But it's important to know that young children are extraordinarily susceptible to the spiraling consequences of the choices we—and later they—make, for good and for ill.

Fortunately, the virtuous cycle is every bit as cascading and self-amplifying as the vicious cycle. A word of praise at just the right time, for example, can lead a child with a moderate interest in art to become more passionate about it. That intensity can escalate, leading him to develop greater skill, receive more praise, and, ultimately, build into his brain artistic genius, where once there may only have been modest potential.

Some recent research emphasizes the power of this effect in sports. Half of England's elite young soccer players on the teams that feed their professional leagues are born in the first three months of the year. The rest are equally distributed among the other months. Why should this be? Well, all youth teams have age cutoffs; if you are born earlier in the year, you are likely to be more physically mature, more skilled, and receive more rewards for your competence than those who are born later in that group. The pleasure of reward leads to more practice; we gravitate toward our competence. And, in the positive feedback cycle within the virtuous cycle, practice creates skill, skill attracts reward, and reward fuels practice. This small difference, enhanced over time by practice, leads to a huge difference, giving the earlier-born players a far better chance of making the cut by the time they reach the pros. These positive spirals are hard to predict, however. We just don't know when the butterfly will billow its tiny breeze into a hurricane.

So what could I tell the court about Leon, and what did I believe about his chances for rehabilitation? I would testify that the development of his brain had been skewed by what had happened to him as an infant. And I would confirm the diagnoses of attention deficit disorder and conduct disorder, which are mitigating factors, even if they do not absolve him of responsibility for his actions.

I would tell the court that his emotional, social, and cognitive problems and neuropsychiatric diagnoses were related to his mother's unintentional neglect. His stress response systems had certainly received aberrant input: being left alone as an infant amped them up, and there was no one around at that critical time to teach him how to calm them down. And at the same time that these lower systems of the brain became overdeveloped, the higher, cortical regions surrounding them, the areas that modulate our responses to the world, our focus, and our self-control, were left underdeveloped.

I would also have to take into consideration the fact that Leon had been drinking when he committed his crime. Alcohol is disinhibiting; it reduces self-control and increases impulsiveness. Leon was already prone to acting without thinking; alcohol only exacerbated this tendency, with deadly consequences for his victims. Would he have committed the crime had he not been drinking first? I suspect not. The alcohol released the already-overwhelmed and improperly developed brakes on his behavior, allowing his rage and lust to take over. Had he not been drunk, he might have stopped himself long before he killed or even assaulted the girls.

I ultimately testified about Leon's early childhood and its effects on his ability to maintain relationships, his impulse control, and his attentiveness. I discussed how early neglect can predispose children to reduced empathy and violence. I included all the mitigating factors that I had found. It was all I could do: there was no case to be made that he was not legally responsible for his actions, and I could not deny that he was an ongoing danger to those around him.

During a break I happened to be near the defendant as he watched the victims' families cry and try to soothe each other. They were despondent, tears running down their cheeks, clinging to each other like survivors on a life raft. Leon said to me, "Why are they crying? I'm the one who's going to jail." Again, his emptiness was chilling. He was emotionally blind.

Afterwards, when Leon had been removed as the jury retired to deliberate, Cherise's mother approached me. Her pain was visible in every step, in the slow movement of her hands, in her expression. "Doctor! Doctor!" she called to me, with great urgency, afraid I might leave before she could talk to me. I stopped, turned, and watched her slowly approach. Almost pleading, she asked, "Why did he do it? You talked to him. Why did he kill my baby? Please tell me. Why?"

I shook my head, acknowledging that, even with my expertise, I couldn't give her a satisfactory answer.

Crying and holding my arm, she asked again. "You know about these things. Why did he kill my baby?"

"Honestly, I just don't know for sure," I said, feeling embarrassed at the inadequacy of my words. I sought out something to help this grieving mother. "I think his heart is cold. Something in him is broken. He's not able to love like you can—like your daughter could. You hurt so much because you loved her so much. He doesn't feel things like you do—good things or bad."

She was quiet for a moment. I could see her bring her daughter's image to mind with a fleeting smile, then more tears. She sighed and nodded. "Yes. He must be broken inside to kill such a beautiful child. She never hurt anyone." I awkwardly hugged her for a moment and then she walked out toward the rest of her family. I thought of Maria and Alan and Frank. Our research is beginning to unlock the secrets of the brain and the causes of tragedies such as this one, but in that moment I was painfully aware of how much we still don't know.

CHAPTER 6

The Boy Who Was Raised as a Dog

WHAT ALLOWS SOMEONE TO MAKE the right choice, even if he hasn't been given the optimal developmental opportunities he needs? What made Virginia continue to seek help for her baby, rather than simply abandoning her? What could we take from Mama P.'s book and prescribe for other children like Laura? Could the right treatment help prevent children like Leon from becoming a threat? Is there anything new I could say today to Cherise's mom—and to Frank, Alan, and Maria—about why Leon had committed his terrible crimes?

Just as we only gradually came to understand how the sequential development of a child's brain is affected by trauma and neglect, it also only gradually dawned on us that this understanding could help us find possible treatments. These insights led us to develop what we came to call the neurosequential approach to therapeutic services for maltreated and traumatized children. One of the first children on whom we used this method had suffered neglect far, far worse than what had been done to Leon.

I met Justin in 1995 when he was six years old. He was in the Pediatric Intensive Care Unit (PICU). I had been invited by the PICU staff to come and, using *that-psychiatric-voodoo-that-you-do-so-well*, try to stop him from throwing feces and food at the staff. The PICU was almost always full and was typically busy 24/7. Nurses, physicians, aides and families crowded the unit. The noise from medical machines, phones, and conversations kept the large room filled with a nonstop buzz. There were always lights on, people were always moving around and, although each individual moved with purpose and each conversation was focused, the overall effect was chaos.

I walked unnoticed through the din to the nurses' station and studied the board to find the boy I'd been asked to see. Then, I heard him. A loud, odd shriek made me turn immediately to find a bony little child in a loose diaper sitting in a cage. Justin's crib had iron bars and a plywood panel wired to the top of it. It looked like a dog cage, which I was about to discover was terribly ironic.

The little boy rocked back and forth, whimpering a primitive self-soothing lullaby. He was filthy with his own feces, there was food all over his face and his diaper was heavy, soaked with urine. He was being treated for severe pneumonia, but he resisted all procedures and had to be held down to draw blood. He tore out his IVs, he yelled and screamed at staff and he threw his food. The closest this hospital had to a psychiatric unit was the PICU (where the ratio of staff to patients was very high), so Justin had been transferred. There, they had jury-rigged his crib/cage arrangement. And once placed in the cage, the boy began to throw feces and anything else he could get his hands on. That's when they called psychiatry.

Over the years I had learned that it is not a good idea to take a child by surprise. Unpredictability and the unknown make everyone feel anxious and therefore less able to process information accurately. Also, and importantly for clinical evaluation, the more anxious someone is the harder it is for him to accurately recall and describe his feelings, thoughts and history. But most critically, when a child is anxious it is much more difficult to form a positive relationship, the true vehicle for all therapeutic change.

I had learned the power of first impressions, as well. I could get a much better sense of a child's prognosis if he had a favorable or at least a neutral first impression of me. So rather than just start asking questions of an unsuspecting and usually frightened and disoriented child, I'd found it was best to give him a chance to meet me first. We'd have a brief humorous or engaging conversation, I'd let him size me up a little, provide a clear, simple explanation of what I wanted to learn from him, and then leave him alone for a while to process that information. I'd assure him that he was in control. The child didn't have to say anything if he didn't want to: if any topic came up that he didn't wish to share with me, I'd tell him to just let me know and I would change the subject. Any time he decided to stop, the conversation was over. Over the years I've only had one adolescent girl say that she did not want to talk. But later that week, she told the staff that the only person she would speak with was the "psychiatry guy with the curly hair."

When I saw Justin I knew this case was going to be different. I needed to know more about him before I could approach him. I took his chart, went back to the nurses' station and read his old records, occasionally glancing over to watch him rock with his knees up by his chin, his arms around his legs. He was humming or moaning to himself, and every few minutes he would let out a loud angry-sounding shriek. The PICU staff had become used to this; no one even glanced his way anymore.

As I read through his records it became clear that Justin's early life had not been normal. Justin's mother was a fifteen-year-old girl who left him with her own mother permanently when he was two months old. Justin's grandmother, by all accounts, was a kindhearted, nurturing woman who adored her grandchild. Unfortunately, she was also morbidly obese and had related health problems that made her very ill. When Justin was about eleven months old, she was hospitalized and died several weeks later.

During her illness, her live-in boyfriend, Arthur,* babysat for Justin. Baby Justin's behavior became difficult, surely a result of losing both his mother and his grandmother in such a short time. Arthur, still grieving himself, didn't know what to do with a crying, tantruming young child, and being in his late sixties, he wasn't physically or mentally prepared for such a challenge. He called Child Protective Services (CPS), seeking a permanent placement for the boy who, after all, was not even a relative. CPS apparently felt the boy was safe and asked if Arthur would keep Justin while they found alternate placement. He agreed. Arthur was a passive man, in general, and patient. He assumed that CPS would get around to finding a new home for Justin. But CPS is a reactive, crisis-focused agency and, with no one putting pressure on it to do so, it didn't act.

Arthur was not malicious, but he was ignorant about the needs of children. He made a living as a dog breeder and, sadly, applied that knowledge to the care of the baby. He began keeping Justin in a dog cage. He made sure the baby was fed and changed, but he rarely spoke to him, played with him, or did any of the other normal things parents do to nurture their children. Justin lived in that cage for five years, spending most of his days with only dogs as his companions.

If we could witness a child's moments of comfort, curiosity, exploration and reward—and his moments of terror, humiliation, and deprivation—we would know so much more about him, who he is and who he is likely to become. The brain is an historical organ, a reflection of our personal histories. Our genetic gifts will only manifest themselves if we get the proper types of developmental experience, appropriately timed. Early in life these experiences are controlled primarily by the adults around us.

As I read through Justin's chart I began to imagine his life as it unfolded. At the age of two, Justin had been given a diagnosis of "static encephalopathy," meaning that he had severe brain damage of unknown origin that was unlikely to improve. He had been taken to the doctor because he was severely developmentally delayed: he was unable to walk or say even a few words by the time most children are actively exploring toddlers who have begun to speak in sentences. Tragically, when Arthur had brought Justin in for medical check-ups, no one inquired about his living situation. And no one took a good developmental history. The boy had been tested for various physical ailments, and his brain had been scanned, revealing atrophy (shrinkage) of the cerebral cortex and enlargement of the fluid-filled ventricles in the center of the brain. In fact, his brain looked like that of someone with advanced Alzheimer's disease; his head circumference was so small that he was below the second percentile for children his age.

Back then, many doctors were still unaware of the damage that neglect alone can do to the brain. They assumed that something so clearly visible on scans had to be evidence of a genetic defect or intrauterine insult, such as exposure to toxins or disease; they couldn't imagine that early environment alone could have such profound physical effects. But studies done by our group and others later found that orphans who were left to languish in institutional settings without receiving enough affection and individual attention do indeed have visibly smaller head sizes and tinier brains. The brains show obvious abnormalities, virtually identical to those seen in Justin.

Unfortunately, as in Laura's case, Justin's problems were

exacerbated by a fragmented medical system. Over the years, even though he'd been given tests as complicated as high-tech brain scans and chromosomal analysis to look for genetic problems, he rarely saw the same doctor twice. No one followed his case over time or learned about his living situation. By age five a repeat screening showed he had made minimal progress in fine and large motor, behavioral, cognitive or speech and language capabilities. He still couldn't walk or talk. To the doctors, who didn't know about the deprivation the child was experiencing, it appeared as if most of his brain-mediated capabilities just did not work properly. They assumed that Justin's "static encephalopathy" was due to some, as of yet unknown and untreatable, birth defect. The unspoken conclusion with children exhibiting this kind of severe brain damage is that they do not respond to therapeutic interventions. In essence, the doctors had told Arthur that the boy was permanently brain damaged and might never be able to care for himself, so he wasn't given any incentive to seek further help.

Whether because of this medical pessimism or because of his irregular care, Justin was never provided any speech therapy, physical therapy, or occupational therapy, and no in-home social services were offered to his elderly caregiver. Left to his own devices Arthur made caregiving decisions that fit his understanding of child rearing. He'd never had children of his own and had been a loner for most of his life. He was very limited himself, probably with mild mental retardation. He raised Justin as he raised his other animals: giving him food, shelter, discipline and episodic direct compassion. Arthur wasn't intentionally cruel: he'd take both Justin and the dogs out of their cages daily for regular play and affection. But he didn't understand that Justin acted like an animal because he'd been treated as one, and so when the boy "didn't obey," back into the cage he went. Most of the time, Justin was simply neglected.

I was the first medical professional Arthur had told about his childrearing practices because, unfortunately for Justin, I was the first to ask. After interviewing Arthur, reading Justin's charts and observing his behavior, I realized that it was possible that some of the boy's problems were not due to a complete absence of potential. Maybe he didn't speak because he had rarely been spoken to. Maybe, unlike a normal child who hears some three million words by age three, he'd been exposed to far fewer. Maybe he didn't stand and walk because no one had coaxed him with her hand out to steady and encourage him. Maybe he didn't know how to eat with utensils because he had never held any in his hands. I decided to approach Justin with the hope that his deficits were indeed due to lack of appropriate stimulation, essentially a lack of opportunity and not lack of capacity.

The nursing staff watched as I walked carefully toward his crib. "He's gonna start throwing," one of them said cynically. I tried to move in slow motion. I wanted him to watch me. I figured that the novelty of my measured pace in contrast to the typical hurried motion in the PICU would catch his attention. I did not look at him. I knew eye contact might be threatening, just as it is for many animals. I pulled the curtains surrounding his crib partially closed so that all he could see was me or the nurses' station. That way he would be less distracted by the children in the adjacent beds.

I tried to imagine the world from his perspective. He was still ill, his pneumonia only partially resolved. He looked terrified and confused; he had no understanding of this new, chaotic realm in which he'd been placed. At least his home in the dog kennel had been familiar; he'd known the dogs around him and knew what to expect from them. Also, I was sure he was hungry, since he had thrown away most of his food over the last three days. As I got close, he sneered, scrambled around the small space of his crib, and gave out one of his screeches.

I stood still. Then I slowly started to take off my white coat, letting it slip to the floor. He stared at me. I slowly undid my tie and pulled it off. I rolled up the sleeves of my shirt. With each action I took one small step closer. I did not speak as I moved. I tried to be as nonthreatening as possible: no quick movements, no eye contact, trying to speak in a low, melodic, rhythmic tone, almost like a lullaby. I approached him as one would a terrified baby or a frightened animal.

"My name is Dr. Perry, Justin. You don't know what is happening here, do you? I will try to help you, Justin. See, I am just taking off my white coat. That's OK, right? Now let me come a bit closer. Far enough? OK. Let's see what might work here. Mmm. I will take off my tie. Ties are not familiar to you, I'll bet. Let me do that."

He stopped moving around the crib. I could hear his breathing: a rapid wheezy grunt. He had to be starving. I noticed a muffin on a lunch tray, far out of his reach but still within his view. I moved toward it. He grunted louder and faster. I took the muffin broke a small piece off, and slowly put it in my mouth and chewed deliberately, trying to indicate pleasure and satisfaction.

"Mmm, so good, Justin. Do you want some?" I kept talking and reached my arm out. I was getting closer. In fact, I was close enough now for him to reach my outstretched hand and the food. I stood still, keeping up my banter and holding the muffin out to him. It seemed like hours, but within thirty seconds he tentatively reached out of the crib. He stopped halfway to the muffin and pulled his arm back in. He seemed to be holding his breath. And then, suddenly, he grabbed at the muffin and pulled it into the crib. He scooted over to the furthest corner and watched me. I stood in the same place, smiled, and tried to bring some light into my voice, "Good, Justin. That is your muffin. It's OK. It's good."

He started to eat. I waved goodbye and walked slowly back to the nurses' station.

"Well. Just wait a minute and he'll be screaming and throwing things again," said one of the nurses, who seemed almost disappointed that he hadn't displayed his "bad" behavior for me.

"I expect so," I said on my way out.

From what I'd learned so far about the effects of neglect on the brain, I knew that the only way to find out whether Justin had unexpressed potential, or had no capacity for further development, was to see if his neural systems could be shaped by patterned, repetitive experience in a safe and predictable environment. But I hadn't yet learned the best way to structure this experience.

I did know that the first thing I needed to do was decrease the chaos and sensory overload surrounding Justin. We moved him to one of the PICU "private" rooms. Then we minimized the number of staff interacting with him. We began physical, occupational, and speech/language therapy. We had one of our psychiatric staffers spend time with him every day. And I made daily visits as well.

The improvement was remarkably rapid. Each succeeding day was better for Justin. Every day he appeared to feel safer. He stopped throwing food and smearing feces. He started to smile. He showed clear signs of recognition and comprehension of verbal commands. We realized he had received some social stimulation and affection from the dogs he'd lived with; dogs are incredibly social animals and have a sophisticated social hierarchy in their packs. At times he responded to unfamiliar people much like a scared dog will: tentatively approaching, backing off, and then moving forward again.

As the days went by he began to be affectionate with me and several other staff members. He even started to show signs of a sense of humor. For example, he knew that "throwing poop" made the staff crazy. So once, when someone gave him a candy bar, he let the chocolate melt into his hands and raised his arm as though he were about to throw it. The people around him moved back. And then he broke into a big, hearty laugh. It was this primitive sense of humor—which demonstrated that he understood the effects of his actions on others and connected with them—that rapidly gave me hope about his capacity for change.

At first, however, my colleagues thought I was wasting hospital resources by asking that physical therapists try to help him stand, to improve his large and fine motor strength and control. But within a week Justin was sitting in a chair and standing with assistance. By three weeks he had taken his first steps. Then an occupational therapist came to help him with fine motor control and fundamentals of self-care: dressing himself, using a spoon, brushing his teeth. Although many children who suffer this kind of deprivation develop a highly tuned sense of smell and often try to sniff and lick their food and people, Justin's sniffing was particularly pronounced and may have had to do with his life among the dogs. He had to be taught that this isn't always appropriate.

During this time speech and language therapists helped him begin to speak, providing the exposure to words he'd missed in his childhood. His once dormant, undeveloped neural networks began to respond to these new repetitive patterns of stimulation. His brain seemed to be like a sponge, thirsty for the experiences it required, and eagerly soaking them up.

After two weeks, Justin was well enough to be discharged from the hospital and placed in a foster family. For the next few months he made remarkable progress. This was the most rapid recovery from severe neglect that we had yet seen. It changed my perspective on the potential for change following early neglect. I became much more hopeful about the prognosis for neglected children.

SIX MONTHS LATER JUSTIN WAS transferred to a foster family who lived much further away from the hospital. While we offered our consultation services to his new clinical team, ultimately we lost track of him in the massive caseload that our group was beginning to attract. But we often talked about Justin when we consulted with other families who had adopted severely neglected children; he had made us reevaluate how we assessed and treated such children. We now knew that at least some of them could improve more dramatically than we'd previously dared to dream.

About two years after Justin's hospital stay a letter came to the clinic from a small town—a brief note from the foster family giving us an update on the little boy. He was continuing to do well, rapidly hitting developmental milestones that no one had ever expected him to reach. Now eight, he was ready to start kindergarten. Enclosed was a picture of Justin all dressed up, holding a lunch box, wearing a backpack, and standing next to a school bus. On the back of the note, in crayon, Justin himself had written, "Thank You, Dr. Perry. Justin." I cried.

TAKING WHAT I'D LEARNED FROM Justin's case—that patterned, repetitive experience in a safe environment can have an enormous impact on the brain—I began to integrate Mama P.'s lessons about the importance of physical affection and stimulation into our care. One of the next cases that would help us develop the neurosequential approach was that of a young teenager whose early life experience turned out to have been similar to that which had started Leon on his destructive and ultimately murderous path.

Like Leon, Connor had an intact nuclear family and an early childhood that, on the surface, did not seem traumatic. Connor's parents were both successful, college-educated businesspeople.

Like Leon, Connor had an above-average IQ but, unlike him, he did well in school. When we did a simple review of his previous psychiatric treatment, we noted that he had been given, at various points, more than a dozen different neuropsychiatric diagnoses starting with autism, then ranging from pervasive developmental disorder, childhood schizophrenia, bipolar disorder, ADHD, obsessive-compulsive disorder (OCD), major depression, anxiety disorder and more.

When the fourteen-year-old was first brought in to see me he was labeled with the diagnoses of intermittent explosive disorder, psychotic disorder and attention deficit disorder. He was taking five psychiatric medications and was being treated by a psychoanalytically trained therapist. He walked with an uneven, awkward gait. When he was anxious or distressed he would sway, rhythmically flex his hands and hum to himself in a tuneless drone that set most people's nerves on edge. He would frequently sit and rock back and forth, just like Justin had when I'd first seen him in that cage/crib. He had no friends: he hadn't become a bully like Leon, but he was a favored target for them. Connor had been placed in a social skills group in an attempt to address his isolation and poor relational skills but, so far, it had been an utter failure. It was, I would soon discover, as though the group had been trying to teach an infant calculus.

Connor was certainly relationally odd but he did not show the classic symptoms of either autism or schizophrenia. His behaviors were similar to children with those conditions, but he did not, for example, have the "mind-blindness" and apparent indifference to relationships linked with some types of autism or the disordered thought common to schizophrenia. When I examined him I could see that he sought to engage with other people, which is often missing in genuine autism. He was socially inept, to be sure, but he was far more social than autistic boys tend to be. He was also on so many medications that no one could tell which of his "symptoms" were related to his original problems and which were caused by medication side effects. I decided to stop the drugs. If medication turned out to be necessary, I would reintroduce it.

Connor's peculiar symptoms and their lack of concordance with typical cases of autism or schizophrenia reminded me of those I'd seen in other children who had suffered early trauma or neglect, like Justin. In particular, I suspected from the curious slanting gait that whatever had gone wrong had started early in infancy, because coordinated walking relies on a well-regulated midbrain and brainstem, regions crucial for coordinating the stress response. Since the brainstem and midbrain are among the earliest regions to organize during development, if something had gone wrong here, it had probably gone wrong in the first year of life.

I took a careful developmental history and questioned Connor's mother, Jane,* about her son's early childhood and about her own as well. She was a bright woman, but anxious and clearly near the end of her rope. Her own childhood hadn't been troubled. She had been an only child, brought up by loving parents. Unfortunately for Connor, however, she didn't live near extended family or spend much time babysitting as a teenager. As a result, until she had her own child, she had little experience with infants and toddlers. It's common in our mobile modern society to have fewer offspring, live further away from our families, and move in an increasingly age-segregated world, and therefore many of us aren't around children enough to learn about how they should behave at each stage of development. Furthermore, our public education includes no content or training on child development, caregiving, or the basics of brain development. The result is a kind of "child illiteracy," which would unfortunately play a large role in what went wrong for Connor, just as it did for Leon.

A few years before their son's birth, Jane and her husband, Mark,* moved from New Jersey to New Mexico to set up a new business, which thrived. Now that they were financially set, the couple decided to try for a child and soon Jane became pregnant. She received excellent prenatal care, had a normal delivery, and the child was born robust and healthy. But their family business was so demanding that Jane returned to the office just a few weeks after having her baby. Jane had heard horror stories about daycare, so she and her husband decided to hire a nanny. Coincidentally, a cousin of Jane's had recently moved to the community and was looking for work, so hiring her seemed to be the ideal solution to both of their problems.

Unfortunately, unbeknownst to Jane and Mark, the cousin took another job just after agreeing to work for them. Wanting to make extra money, she didn't tell Jane or Mark that she was leaving the child on his own and working another job. She fed and changed the baby in the morning, left for work, fed and changed him at lunch time, and then returned just before his parents came home from their jobs. She worried about diaper rash, or about the possibility of a fire or other danger while the child was on his own, but not about how damaging her actions could be. This cousin was even more ignorant of child development than Jane was: she didn't realize that infants need affection and attention just as much as they need nutrition, hydration, dry clothes, and shelter.

Jane told me she felt guilty about returning to work so soon. She described how, for the first two weeks after she returned to the office, Connor's cries as she left him were terribly distressing. But after that, he stopped crying, so Jane thought everything was fine. "My baby was content," she told me, describing how even when she accidentally stuck him with a safety pin, Connor didn't even whimper. "He never cried," she said, emphatically, not aware that if a baby never cries, this is as much a sign of potential problems as crying too much can be. Again, she was stymied by ignorance of basic child development. Like Maria, she thought that a quiet baby meant a happy baby.

Within a few months, however, Jane began to suspect that something was wrong. Connor didn't seem to be maturing as fast as her friends' babies did. He wasn't sitting up or turning over or crawling at the ages that others reached those milestones. Concerned about his lack of progress, she took him to the family's pediatrician, who was excellent at recognizing and treating physical diseases, but didn't know much about how to check for mental and emotional difficulties. She didn't have children of her own, so she was not personally familiar with their psychological development and, like most doctors, hadn't been given much education on it. The doctor also knew the parents well, so she had no reason to suspect abuse or neglect. Consequently, she didn't ask, for example, whether Connor cried or about how he responded to people. She simply told Jane that babies develop at different rates and tried to reassure her that he would catch up soon.

One day, however, when Connor was about eighteen months old, Jane came home from work sick. The house was dark, so she assumed the nanny had taken the child out. There was a terrible smell coming from Connor's room. The door was part way open, so she peeked in. She found her son sitting in the dark, alone, with no toys, no music, no nanny, and a full, dirty diaper. Jane was horrified. When she confronted her cousin, the woman confessed that she had been leaving Connor and going to the other job. Jane fired the cousin and quit her job to stay home with the baby. She thought she'd dodged the bullet: she thought that because he hadn't been kidnapped, harmed in a fire, or become physically ill, the experience would have no lasting effects. She didn't connect his increasingly odd behavior with over a year of near-daily neglect.

As he grew socially isolated and began to engage in peculiar, repetitive behaviors, no one in the mental health system, no one in the school system, not one of the special education teachers or occupational therapists or counselors to whom he was sent discovered Connor's history of early neglect. Hundreds of thousands of dollars and hundreds of hours were spent fruitlessly trying to treat his various "disorders." The result was this fourteen-year-old boy, rocking and humming to himself, friendless and desperately lonely and depressed; a boy who didn't make eye contact with other people, who still had the screaming, violent temper tantrums of a three- or four-year-old; a boy who desperately needed the stimulation that his brain had missed during the first months of life.

When Mama P. had rocked and held the traumatized and neglected children she cared for, she'd intuitively discovered what would become the foundation of our neurosequential approach: these children need patterned, repetitive experiences appropriate to their developmental needs, needs that reflect the age at which they'd missed important stimuli or had been traumatized, not their current chronological age. When she sat in a rocking chair cuddling a seven-year-old, she was providing the touch and rhythm that he'd missed as an infant, experience necessary for proper brain growth. A foundational principle of brain development is that neural systems organize and become functional in a sequential manner. Furthermore, the organization of a less mature region depends, in part, upon incoming signals from lower, more mature regions. If one system doesn't get what it needs when it needs it, those that rely upon it may not function well either, even if the stimuli that the later developing system needs are being provided appropriately. The key to healthy development is getting the right experiences in the right amounts at the right time.

Part of the reason for Justin's rapid response to our therapy, I soon recognized, was that he had had nurturing experiences during his first year of life, before his grandmother had died. This meant his lowest and most central brain regions had been given a good start. If he'd been raised in a cage from birth, his future might have been far less hopeful. It worried me that Connor, like Leon, had suffered neglect virtually from birth to eighteen months. The one hope was that during the evenings and weekend hours when his parents were caring for him there was at least some exposure to nurturing sensory experiences.

Drawing on these insights, we decided that we would systematize our approach to match the developmental period at which the damage had first started. By looking carefully at Connor's symptoms and his developmental history, we hoped we could figure out which regions had sustained the most damage and target our interventions appropriately. We would then use enrichment experiences and targeted therapies to help the affected brain areas in the order in which they were affected by neglect and trauma (hence, the name neurosequential). If we could document improved functioning following the first set of interventions, we would begin the second set appropriate for the next brain region and developmental stage until, hopefully, he would get to the point where his biological age and his developmental age would match.

In Connor's case it was clear that his problems had started in early infancy when the lower and most central regions of the brain are actively developing. These systems respond to rhythm and touch: the brainstem's regulatory centers control heartbeat, the rise and fall of neurochemicals and hormones in the cycle of day and night, the beat of one's walk and other patterns that must maintain a rhythmic order to function properly. Physical affection is needed to spur some of the region's chemical activity. Without it, as in Laura's case, physical growth (including the growth of the head and brain) can be retarded.

Like Leon and others who have suffered early neglect, Connor couldn't stand to be touched. At birth human touch is a novel and, initially, stressful stimulus. Loving touch has yet to be connected to pleasure. It is in the arms of a present, loving caregiver that the hours upon hours of touch become familiar and associated with safety and comfort. It seems that when a baby's need for this nurturing touch isn't satisfied, the connection between human contact and pleasure isn't made and being touched can become actively unpleasant. In order to overcome this and help provide the missing stimuli, we referred Connor to a massage therapist. We would focus first on meeting his needs for skin-to-skin contact; then, we hoped, we could further address his asynchronous bodily rhythms.

As we saw in Laura's case, touch is critical to human development. Sensory pathways involved in the experience of touch are the first to develop and are the most fully elaborated at birth compared to sight, smell, taste and hearing. Studies of premature babies find that gentle skin-to-skin contact helps them gain weight, sleep better, and mature more quickly. In fact, preemies who received such gentle massage went home from the hospital almost a week earlier on average. In older children and adults massage has also been found to lower blood pressure, fight depression, and cut stress by reducing the amount of stress hormones released by the brain.

Our reason for starting with massage was also strategic: research finds that parents who learn infant and child massage techniques develop better relationships with their children and feel closer to them. With children who have autism or other conditions that make them seem remote, creating this sense of closeness can often rapidly improve the parent-child relationship and thus escalate the parents' commitment to therapy.

This was particularly important in Connor's case because his mother was very anxious about our approach to his treatment. After all, previous psychologists, psychiatrists, counselors, and well-meaning neighbors and teachers kept telling her not to indulge his "babyish" behavior and to ignore his tantrums. He needed more structure and limits, they said, not more cuddles. Everyone else had told her that Connor was immature and must be forced to abandon his primitive self-soothing methods like rocking and humming. Now we were saying he should be treated gently, which seemed to her overindulgent. In fact, rather than ignore him when his behavior threatened to escalate out of control, as behavioral therapists often suggested, we were saying that he should actually be "rewarded" with massage. Our approach seemed radically counterintuitive, but because nothing else had helped, she agreed to give it a try.

Connor's mom was present during his massage sessions, and we made her an active participant in this part of his therapy. We wanted her there to comfort him and help him if he found the touch stressful. We also wanted her to learn this physically affectionate way of showing her love for her son, to help make up for the hugs and nurturing touches he'd missed during his infancy. This massage approach was gradual, systematic, and repetitive. The initial motions involved Connor's own hands, guided in massaging his arm, shoulders, and trunk.

We used a heart rate monitor to track the level of his distress. When his own touch to his own body did not cause changes in his heart rate we started to use his mother's hands in the same repetitive, gradual massage process. Finally, once his mother's massaging touch was no longer anxiety-provoking, the massage therapist started with more conventional therapeutic massage. The approach was very slow and gentle: the idea was to acclimate Connor to physical touch and, if possible, help him begin to enjoy it. After being taught to give her son neck and shoulder massages, Jane would continue the therapy at home, especially when Connor seemed upset or asked for a massage. We explained to both of them why we were trying this approach.

Nothing was forced. We knew that Connor found touch

aversive at first and instructed the therapist to carefully respond to any signals from him that it was "too much." She would progress to more intense stimulation only when the previous form and degree of touch had become familiar and safe. She would always start her work by having him use one of his own hands to "test" the massage, and then, when he was used to that, she began massaging his fingers and hands. She was gradually able to touch and then massage more deeply all of the appropriate bodily zones. Connor's mom was also instructed to follow her son's lead and not push contact if he found it overwhelming.

Over the course of six to eight months, Connor gradually began to tolerate and then enjoy physical contact with others. I could tell he was ready to move on to the next phase of treatment when he came up to me and reached his hand out, as if to shake my hand. He wound up patting my hand, like a granny would do with a young child, but for him, even a bizarre type of handshake was progress. He would never previously have sought—let alone initiate—physical contact. In fact, he would have actively avoided it.

Now it was time to work on his sense of rhythm. It may seem odd, but rhythm is extraordinarily important. If our bodies cannot keep the most fundamental rhythm of life—the heartbeat—we cannot survive. Regulating this rhythm isn't a static, consistent task, either: the heart and the brain are constantly signaling each other in order to adjust to life's changes. Our heart rate must increase to power fight or flight, for example, and it must maintain its rhythmic pulse despite the varying demands placed on it. Regulating heart rate during stress and controlling stress hormones are two critical tasks that require that the brain keep proper time.

Also, numerous other hormones are rhythmically regulated as well. The brain doesn't just keep one beat: it has many drums, which must all synchronize not only with the patterns of day and night (and in women, with menstrual cycles or phases of pregnancy and nursing), but also with each other. Disturbances of the brain's rhythm-keeping regions are often causes of depression and other psychiatric disorders. This is why sleep problems (in some sense, a misreading of day and night) almost always accompany such conditions.

Most people don't appreciate how important these rhythms are in setting the tone for parent/child interactions, either. If a baby's primary metronome—his brainstem—doesn't function well, not only will his hormonal and emotional reactions to stress be difficult to modulate, but his hunger and his sleep cycle will be unpredictable as well. This can make parenting him much more difficult. Babies' needs are much easier to read when they reliably occur at predictable times: if their infants become hungry and tired at consistent times, parents can adjust to their demands more easily, reducing stress all around. The implications of poorly regulated bodily rhythms, then, are far greater than one would initially suspect.

In the usual course of development a baby gets into a rhythmic groove that drives these various patterns. The infant's mother cuddles him while he eats, and he is soothed by her heartbeat. In fact, the infant's own heart rhythm may be partly regulated by such contact: some Sudden Infant Death Syndrome (SIDS) deaths, according to one theory, occur when babies are out of physical contact with adults and thus lacking crucial sensory input. Some research even suggests that while in utero the child's heart can beat in time with his mother's. We do know that maternal heart rate provides the patterned, repetitive signals—auditory, vibratory, and tactile—that are crucial to organizing the brainstem and its important stress-regulating neurotransmitter systems.

When a baby gets hungry and cries his levels of stress hormones will move upward. But if Mom or Dad regularly comes to feed him, they go back down, and over time, they become patterned and repetitive thanks to the daily routine. At times, nonetheless, the baby will feel distress and cry: not hungry, not wet, not in discernible physical pain, she will appear inconsolable. When this happens most parents hug and rock their children, almost instinctively using rhythmic motion and affectionate touch to calm the child. Interestingly, the rate at which people rock their babies is about eighty beats per minute, the same as a normal resting adult heart rate. Faster and the baby will find the motion stimulating; slower and the child will tend to keep crying. To soothe our children we reattune them physically to the beat of the master timekeeper of life.

In fact, some theories of language development suggest that humans learned to dance and sing before we could talk, that music was actually the first human language. It's true that babies learn to understand the musical aspects of speech—the meanings of tones of voice, for example—long before they understand its content. People universally speak to babies—and interestingly, to pets—in a high pitch that emphasizes a nurturing, emotional, musical tone. In all cultures even mothers who cannot carry a tune sing to their babies, suggesting music and song play an important role in infant development.

Connor, however, had missed out on music and rhythm when he most needed it. When he cried during the day in his early infancy no one came to rock him and calm him and bring his stress response systems and hormones back down into the normal range. Though he did get normal care at night and on weekends during his first eighteen months, those lonely eight-hour stretches left a lasting mark.

In order to make up for what he'd lost, we decided to have Connor participate in a music and movement class that would help him consciously learn to keep a beat and, we hoped, help his brain get a more general sense of rhythm. The class itself was nothing unusual: it looked a lot like what you would see in any kindergarten or preschool music class, where children learn to rhythmically clap their hands, to sing together, to repeat sounds in patterns and tap out beats with objects like blocks or simple drums. Here, of course, the children were older; unfortunately, we had many other patients who had suffered early neglect with whom to study this approach.

At first Connor was remarkably arrhythmic: he couldn't keep time with the most basic beat. His unconscious rocking had rhythm, but he couldn't deliberately mark out a steady beat or imitate one. I believe this was caused by the missing early sensory input to the brainstem, which created a weak connection between his higher and lower brain regions. We hoped that by improving his conscious control over rhythm we could improve these links.

Early on the class was frustrating for him, and Jane became discouraged. At this point we had been treating Connor for about nine months. The frequency of his outbursts had lessened, but one day he had a ferocious temper tantrum in school. School officials called Jane at work, demanding that she pick her son up immediately. I'd gotten used to regular, frantic calls from her several times a week, but this incident brought her despair to a new level. She thought that this meant Connor's treatment had failed, and I had to use all my persuasive powers to keep her committed to this admittedly unusual therapeutic approach. She had seen dozens of very good therapists, psychiatrists, and psychologists and what we were doing didn't look remotely like any of these previous treatments. She, like so many parents of struggling children, just wanted us to find the "right" medications and teach Connor to "act" his age.

That weekend, when I saw her number come up on my pager again, I cringed. I didn't want to call her back and learn about yet another setback or have to talk her out of trying some counterproductive alternate treatment from some new "expert" someone had told her about. I forced myself to return the call, taking a deep breath to calm myself first. I thought my worst fears were confirmed when it was immediately clear from her tone of voice that she'd been weeping.

"What's wrong?" I asked quickly.

"Oh, Dr. Perry," she said. She paused and seemed to have difficulty going on. My heart sank.

But then she continued, "I have to thank you. Today Connor came up to me, hugged me, and said he loved me." It was the first time he'd ever done that spontaneously. Now Jane, rather than worrying about our approach, became one of our biggest fans.

As CONNOR PROGRESSED IN THE MUSIC and movement class, we began to see other positive changes as well. For one, his gait became much more normal, even when he was nervous. Also, over time the rocking and humming gradually lessened. When we first got to know him, these behaviors were almost constant if he wasn't engaged in a task like schoolwork or playing a game. But now he only reverted to them if something seriously frightened or upset him. I wish all of my patients were as easy to read! Because of this trait I was able to know instantly if we had gone too far with any challenge and pull back until he could comfortably face it. After he'd been in treatment for about a year, his parents and his teachers began to see the real Connor, not just his weird behavior.

After he'd learned to successfully sustain a rhythm, I began parallel play therapy with him. The music and movement class and massage therapy had already improved his behavior: so far, he had had no further tantrums after the incident that had almost prompted Jane to end his therapy with us. But he still lagged in social development, was still being bullied, and still had no friends. A typical treatment for adolescents with such problems is a social skills group like the one Connor had been in when he first came to us. However, because of the developmental lag he'd experienced due to his early neglect, this was still too advanced for him.

The first human social interaction begins with normal parent/infant bonding. The child learns how to relate to others in a social situation in which the rules are predictable and easy to figure out. If a child doesn't understand what to do, the parent teaches him. If he persists in misunderstanding, the parent corrects him. Repeatedly. Mistakes are expected and rapidly and continually forgiven. The process requires enormous patience. As Mama P. reminded me, babies cry, they spit up, they "mess," but you expect it and love them anyway.

In the next social arena the child must learn to master—the world of peers—violating social rules is far less tolerated. Here, rules are implicit and are picked up mostly by observation rather than direct instruction. Mistakes can result in long-term negative consequences as peers rapidly reject those who are "different," those who don't understand how to connect and respond to others.

If someone hasn't developed the ability to understand the clearly defined rules of the parent/child relationship, trying to teach him peer relations is almost impossible. Just as higher motor functions, such as walking, rely upon rhythmic regulation from lower brain areas like the brainstem, more advanced social skills require mastery of elementary social lessons.

I had to approach Connor carefully because, at first, he was skeptical about me: talking to shrinks hadn't done him much good, and he found relating to others difficult in general. So I didn't attempt to engage him directly. I gave him control of our interaction; if he wanted to talk to me, I would talk to him, but if he didn't, I would let him be. He'd come in for therapy and would sit down in my office. I would continue to work at my desk. We simply spent time in the same space. I demanded nothing, he asked for nothing.

As he became more comfortable, he became more curious. He'd move a little bit closer to me, and then closer still, and pretty soon he'd come over and stand near me. Finally, after many weeks, he'd ask, "What are you doing?" And I'd say, "I'm working. What are you doing?"

"Uh, I'm in therapy?" he'd say questioningly. "Well, what's therapy to you?"

"We sit and talk?"

"OK," I'd say, "What do you want to talk about?"

"Nothing," he'd reply at first. I'd tell him that was fine, I was busy, he should do his homework and I'd do my work.

After a few more weeks, however, he said he did want to talk. We sat face to face and he asked, "Why are we doing this?" This had not been at all like the therapy he was familiar with. So I began to teach him about the brain and brain development. I told him what I thought happened to him when he was an infant. The science made sense to him, and he immediately wanted to know, "What's the next step? What do we do next?" That's when I talked about forming relationships with other people, saying that he didn't seem very good at it.

He said emphatically, but with a smile, "I know, I suck!" Only then did I start to do explicit social coaching, which he was instantly eager to start. It was harder than I'd thought it would be. Body language and social cues were unintelligible to Connor: they simply didn't register. Working with Connor, it hit me over and over again how sophisticated and subtle much of human communication is. I told him, for example, that people find eye contact engaging during a social interaction, so it is important to look at people while you listen to them and when you talk to them. He agreed to try it, but this resulted in him staring fixedly at me, just as he'd formerly fixed his gaze on the floor.

I said, "Well, you don't want to look at people all the time."

"Well, when do I look at them?"

I tried to explain that he should look for a little while, and then look away, because lasting eye contact is actually a human signal of either aggression or romantic interest, depending on the situation. He wanted to know exactly how long to look, but of course, I couldn't tell him because of how dependent such things are on nonverbal cues and context. I tried telling him to wait three seconds, but this resulted in him counting out loud and made matters worse. As we practiced I rapidly discovered that we use more social cues than I had ever realized, and I had no idea how to teach them.

For example, when Connor looked away after initiating eye contact, he would turn his whole face, rather than simply moving his eyes. Or, he'd look up afterwards, his eye rolling unintentionally signaling boredom or sarcasm. It was like trying to teach someone from outer space to make human conversation. Eventually, however, he got to the point where he could socially engage, even though he still often seemed a bit robotic.

Each step was complicated. Trying to teach him to shake hands properly, for example, resulted in alternately limp fish approaches and too firm grips. Because he didn't read other people's cues very well, he often wasn't aware that he'd said something that hurt someone's feelings, or perplexed them, or seemed frighteningly odd. He was a nice young man: when he came in, he would always say hi to the secretaries and attempt to engage them in conversation. But something about the interaction would be off, often his wording and tone of voice would be odd and he wouldn't notice the awkward silences. Once someone asked him where he lived, and he responded, "I just moved," and left it at that. From his tone and short reply the other person figured that he didn't want to talk. He would seem brusque or weird; Connor didn't understand that he needed to put the person at ease by providing more information. Conversations have a rhythm to them, but Connor didn't yet know how to play along.

At one point, too, I tried to address his fashion sense, which was another source of trouble with his peers. Style is partly a reflection of social skills; to be fashionable you have to observe others and read cues about "what's in" and "what's out," and then discover how to copy them in a way that suits you. The signals are subtle and a person's choices, in order to be successful, must reflect both individuality and appropriate conformity. Among adolescents, ignoring these signals can be socially disastrous—and Connor was clueless.

He'd wear his shirt buttoned all the way up to the neck, for example. One day, I suggested not buttoning the top button. He looked at me like I was crazy and asked, "What do you mean?"

I responded, "Well, you don't always have to button it."

"But there's a button there," he said, uncomprehending.

So I took a pair of scissors and cut it off. Jane was not pleased, calling me up to say, "Since when are scissors part of a normal therapeutic intervention?" But as he continued to improve, Jane calmed back down. Connor even made friends with another boy in our treatment program, a teenager who had also suffered neglect and who was at a similar level of emotional development. They'd been in the music and movement class together. When the other boy was frustrated about not being able to keep time, Connor had told him that he'd been just as bad at first, and then urged him to stick with it. They bonded even further over, of all things, Pokémon cards. At the time they were popular with elementary school-age children, but this was the emotional level of these boys' development, even though they were high school sophomores. They tried to share their obsession with their peers, but the other teens, of course, made fun of them.

Connor had one final out-of-control incident, incidentally, which was a result of the Pokémon obsession. He was defending his friend from some other adolescents who were teasing him about the cards, trying to tear them up. Jane, of course, panicked when she heard about it. She'd thought I shouldn't encourage the boys in their Pokémon games, fearing just such an incident. I did speak with both of them about when and where to flash their Pokémon cards, but I thought it was better to allow the connection between these two to flourish since it was giving both boys an opportunity to practice their social skills. I didn't think they'd be able to go from preschool to high-school socialization without elementary-school-like experiences (such as Pokémon) as intermediate steps, as awkward as I knew they'd be. We explained the situation to the school and Connor and his friend continued to enjoy Pokémon, but with a bit more discretion.

Connor went on to graduate high school and college without further outbursts. He continued his "sequential" development with just a bit of help from our clinical team; we saw him on breaks from school. He continued to socially mature. I knew the treatment had been a success when Connor—now a computer programmer—sent me an email with the header: "Next lesson: Girls!"

CONNOR IS STILL SOCIALLY AWKWARD and may always be "geeky." However, even though he suffered almost exactly the same kind of neglect during a similar developmental period as Leon did, he never showed anything like the other teen's malicious, sociopathic behavior. He became a victim of bullies, not a bully himself; while he was an outsider, he was not someone filled with hate. His behavior was bizarre and his tantrums appeared threatening, but he didn't attack other children or steal from them or enjoy hurting people. His rages were prompted by his own frustration and anxiety, not by a desire for vengeance or a sadistic wish to make others feel as bad as he did.

Was it treatment—from us and all of the other clinicians before us—that made the difference? Was it important that his family pushed for intervention when he was young? Did it matter that we were able to intervene early in Connor's adolescence? Probably. But did any of that truly count in keeping him from becoming a raging sociopath like Leon? It is, of course, impossible to know. However, in our work with children like these two very different boys who experienced severe early neglect, we have found a number of factors that clearly do play a role in which path they follow, and we try to address as many of them as possible in our treatment.

A number of genetically influenced factors matter. Temperament, which is affected by genetics and intrauterine environment (influenced by maternal heart rate, nutrition, hormone levels, and drugs) is one. As noted previously, children whose stress response systems are naturally better regulated from birth are easier babies, so their parents are less likely to get frustrated with them and abuse or neglect them.

Intelligence is another critical factor, one that is often poorly understood. Intelligence is basically faster information processing: a person requires fewer repetitions of an experience to make an association. This property of intelligence appears to be largely genetically determined. Being able to learn with fewer repetitions means that brighter children can, in essence, do more with less. Hypothetically, for example, if it takes a normal child 800 repetitions of having his mother feed him when he is hungry in order for him to learn that she will come and help modulate his distress, it might take only 400 repetitions for a "smarter" child to make the connection.

While this doesn't mean that smart children need less affection, it does suggest that if they are deprived, brighter kids may be better equipped to cope. Needing fewer repetitions to build an association may allow smarter kids to more quickly connect people with love and pleasure, even when they don't receive what is usually the bare minimum of stimulation required to cement those links. This quality might also allow them to benefit more from brief experiences of loving attention outside the family, which can often help severely abused and neglected children recognize that the way it is at home is not necessarily the way it is everywhere, a realization that can offer them much-needed hope.

Intelligence may also help protect young people in other ways from developing the kind of rage and sociopathy we saw in Leon. For one, it allows them to be more creative when making decisions, giving them more options and decreasing the likelihood they'll make bad choices. This also helps them avoid a defeatist attitude, thinking "there's nothing else I can do." Being able to envision alternate scenarios may also help increase impulse control. If you can think of a better future, you may be more likely to plan for it. And being better able to project yourself into the future may also improve your ability to empathize with others. If you're planning for consequences, in some sense, you are empathizing with your "future self." Imagining yourself in another setting is not a far leap from imagining the perspective of others—in other words, empathizing. However, intelligence alone is probably not enough to keep a child on the right track. Leon, for example, tested above average in some areas. But it does seem to help.

Another factor is the timing of the trauma: the earlier it starts, the more difficult it is to treat and the greater the damage is likely to be. Justin had nearly a year of loving and nurturing care before he was placed in that dog cage. That affection built the basics of so many important functions—including empathy—into his brain and, I believe, greatly aided his later recovery.

But perhaps the most important factor in determining how these children fare is the social environment in which the child is raised. When Maria and Alan lived among their extended families, other relatives were able to make up for Maria's limitations, and Frank had a normal, happy childhood. Leon's neglect occurred only when Maria no longer had a supportive social network to help her cope with parenting. In Connor's case, while his parents had more financial resources, they were stymied by a lack of information about child development. Better knowledge would have allowed them to recognize his problems much sooner.

In the last fifteen years numerous nonprofit organizations and government agencies have focused on the importance of education about appropriate parenting and early childhood development, and on just how much critical brain development goes on in the first few years of life. From Hillary Clinton's "It Takes a Village" to Rob Reiner's "I Am Your Child" Foundation to the Zero to Three organization and the United Way's "Success by Six," millions of dollars have been spent to educate the public about the needs of young children.

The hope of these efforts—some of which I have been involved with—is to make this kind of neglect far less likely to occur due to ignorance. I believe they have had a significant impact. However, the age segregation in our society, the lack of integration of these key concepts into public education and the limited experience many people have with young children before they have their own still puts far too many parents and their children at risk. Currently, there's little we can do to change a child's genes, temperament or brain processing speed, but we can make a difference in their caregiving and social environment. Many of the traumatized children I've worked with who have made progress report having had contact with at least one supportive adult: a teacher who took a special interest in them, a neighbor, an aunt, even a school bus driver. In Justin's case, his grandmother's early kindness and love allowed his brain to develop a latent capacity for affection that unfurled when he was removed from his later deprived situation. Even the smallest gesture can sometimes make the difference to a child whose brain is hungry for affection.

Our work using the neurosequential approach with adolescents like Connor also suggests that therapy can mitigate the damage done by early neglect. Affectionate touch, appropriate to the developmental age at which the harm was done, can be given through massage therapy, and then repeated at home in order to strengthen the desired associations. Rhythm-keeping can be taught through music and movement classes, which can not only help a dysregulated brainstem to improve its control over important motor activities like walking, but also, we think, strengthen its role in stress response system regulation. Socialization can be improved by starting with teaching simpler, rule-based, one-on-one relationships and then moving to more complex peer group challenges.

I believe if Leon's maternal neglect had been discovered earlier, there is a good chance that he would not have turned out the way he did. It took a long chain of deprivation of developmentally necessary stimuli and poor responses to Leon's needs and bad choices by Leon himself for him to become a vicious killer. At any one of these crossroads, particularly those at the beginning of his life, a change in direction could potentially have led to a completely different outcome. If we had been able to treat him as a young adolescent, like Connor, or, better still, during the elementary school years, like Justin, I think his future could have been altered. Had someone intervened when he was still a toddler he would have become a completely different person, far more like his brother than the predatory young man I met in the prison cell.

Because trauma—including that caused by neglect, whether deliberate or inadvertent—causes an overload of the stress response systems, which is marked by a loss of control, treatment for traumatized children must start by creating an atmosphere of safety. This is done most easily and effectively in the context of a predictable, respectful relationship. From this nurturing "home base," maltreated children can begin to create a sense of competence and mastery. To recover they must feel safe and in control. Consequently, the last thing you want to do is force treatment on these children or use any kind of coercive tactics.

The next chapter illustrates some of the harm coercive methods can cause.

CHAPTER 7

Satanic Panic

"I DON'T DO SATAN," I TOLD THE EAGER young man from the Texas governor's office. He was trying to enlist my help with a complex case involving a group of children who reportedly had been ritually abused by members of a Satanic cult. The boys and girls were in foster care at this point, safe from their supposedly devil-worshipping parents and their coven of friends, but the state attorney general's office had become worried that local Child Protective Services (CPS) workers had taken these children out of Beelzebub's frying pan and into hell on earth.

IT WAS LATE 1993, AND I HAD BEEN trying to stay out of the contentious "memory wars" then raging over whether previously unrecalled incidents of severe abuse "remembered" by adults during therapy were true. There was also debate about whether children's accounts of recent abuse or molestation were

171

accurate. I knew for sure that there was an awful lot of genuine child abuse going on: every day I saw wrenching, concrete evidence of it.

But I also knew from my training in neuroscience and my clinical work with traumatized children that narrative memory is not simply a videotape of experiences that can be replayed with photographic accuracy. We make memories, but memories make us, too, and it is a dynamic, constantly changing process subject to bias and influence from many sources other than the actual event we are "storing." What we experience first filters what comes afterwards—just as Tina's early sexual abuse shaped her perception of men and Leon and Connor's neglect altered their respective worldviews. However, this process works both ways: what we feel now can also influence how we look back and what we recall from the past. As a result, what we remember can shift with our emotional state or mood. For example, if we are depressed we tend to filter all our recollections through the haze of our sadness.

We know today that, just like when you open a Microsoft Word file on your computer, when you retrieve a memory from where it is stored in the brain, you automatically open it to "edit." You may not be aware that your current mood and environment can influence the emotional tone of your recall, your interpretation of events and even your beliefs about which events actually took place. But when you "save" the memory again and place it back into storage, you can inadvertently modify it. When you discuss your memory of an experience, the interpretation you hear from a friend, family member, or a therapist can bias how and what you recall the next time you pull up that "file." Over time, incremental changes can even lead to the creation of memories that did not take place. In the lab, researchers have been able to encourage test subjects to create memories of childhood events that didn't happen: some as common as being lost in a mall, others as extreme as seeing someone possessed by a demon.

Back in 1993, however, the nature of memory and its incredible malleability weren't as well researched and what was known about traumatic memory had not been widely taught to clinicians or other professionals working with children. Survivors of incest were bravely speaking out about their experience for the first time and no one wanted to question their stories or the reality of their pain. Children's claims of being abused were also being taken much more seriously than they had been in the past. People didn't want to go back to the bad old days when abusive adults could count on a child's accounts of mistreatment being met with disbelief. Unfortunately, this desire to give the benefit of the doubt to victims, the naïveté of some therapists and their ignorance of how coercion can affect memory combined to cause serious harm.

Perhaps nowhere was that more evident than in the Satanic panic that swept Gilmer, Texas, in the early 1990s. The governor's aide explained to me what he knew of the situation.

A seven-year-old boy, Bobby Vernon, Jr., was lying in a hospital in an irreversible coma, having been pushed down a flight of stairs by his recently adoptive father. Both this adoptive father and his wife had then committed suicide after their other adopted and foster children were taken away following Bobby's hospitalization; the father by shooting himself in the head the next day and the mother by an overdose a day after that.

The seven-year-old's skull had been fractured and he had severe brain damage. Little Bobby had refused to continue running up and down the stairs, which he had been being forced to do by his "parents." According to siblings who witnessed the assault, either one or both of the adults had smashed his head on a wooden floor until the back of his head "was mushy." To make matters worse, when the adults finally stopped the beating long enough to realize that the boy was unconscious, instead of immediately calling 911 they waited for an hour to get help, trying bizarre things like spraying Windex in the child's face in an unsuccessful attempt to revive him.

EMS (Emergency Medical Services) workers were appalled by how these foster/adoptive parents appeared to be disciplining the ten children in their care. The children described being starved, isolated and repeatedly beaten. The paramedics told the parents, James and Marie Lappe, that they were required to call CPS, whereupon they were informed that the couple was actually employed by CPS. Theirs was a "therapeutic" foster home. The children, according to the Lappes, had been victims of Satanic Ritual Abuse (SRA) by their parents; what looked like harsh discipline was actually "therapy" for these children. Surprisingly, the family's CPS caseworkers in east Texas backed them up, insisting that the children had been in good hands at the Lappe home. The Lappes, however, were no longer in east Texas. They had moved to a west Texas community "in secret" to get away from what they believed was an active and dangerous Satanic cult, which wanted its children back and was prepared to do anything to get them. The local CPS workers in west Texas knew nothing about this "therapeutic" home in their community or about this alleged cult. It was at this point that higher-level state CPS officials were notified about the situation.

The east Texas caseworkers said, based upon testimony that they and the Lappes had elicited from these children, that a murderous Satanic cult had finally been exposed. There were reports of ritual killings, dead babies, blood drinking and cannibalism. Eight cult members were now in prison awaiting trial, not only for child abuse, but also for the gang rape and ritual murder of a seventeen-year-old high school cheerleader. One of those arrested and incarcerated was the police officer who had originally been in charge of investigating the cheerleader's disappearance. Two experts on Satanism and a special prosecutor were on the case, seeking further indictments.

But now CPS officials in the state office began to wonder about the integrity of these investigations. They asked the state attorney general to get involved. The caseworkers' immediate supervisor feared that she was about to be arrested in retaliation for voicing doubts about the investigation. Her fears seemed well founded: the police officer who'd been accused of being a murderous cult member and subsequently arrested had incurred scrutiny and ultimately an indictment himself after he'd expressed similar doubts. Prior to that he'd had an impeccable record and had won numerous law enforcement awards and plaudits. Indictments were being planned for other police officers, sheriff's deputies, an animal control officer and even an FBI agent, as well as the Gilmer police chief. Sixteen children had already been taken from their parents during the investigation and no one knew where it would go next.

Could it all have been a terrible mistake? Had innocent parents lost their children to a bout of Satanic hysteria propelled by poor investigative techniques? What had really happened in Gilmer, Texas? As soon as I had learned what had been done to those sixteen children—then aged from two to ten—in foster care, I felt obliged to get involved.

The main thing the state wanted me to do was to help CPS determine which of the children currently in foster care had genuinely been the victims of parental abuse and which had been taken from their parents as the result of false accusations made by other children who'd been led to "remember" incidents of abuse during the course of the investigation. To do this I would need to reconstruct each child's history. Fortunately there were boxes upon boxes of old records and hours of audio and videotape of interviews with some of the children and their "cult member" parents. Our clinical team started to put together a detailed chronology of the case. The chronology document would soon run to dozens of pages.

It had all started in 1989, in a tar-paper house surrounded by a collection of dilapidated trailers on Cherokee Trace Road, on the periphery of Gilmer. Gilmer is a small, east Texas town of 5,000 located near where the Lone Star state meets Louisiana and Arkansas. It is the county seat of Upshur County, an unremarkable Bible Belt community but for one fact: it has one of the nation's highest illiteracy rates. One in four adult residents cannot read. At that time, Bette Vernon* reported to the police that her then-husband, Ward Vernon,* had been sexually abusing their two daughters, aged five and six. Both parents were soon implicated in the child abuse, and all four of their offspring were taken into foster care. As a result of the abuse investigation, Ward Vernon was convicted of child sex abuse. Incredibly, he was sentenced to probation.

While on probation, Ward Vernon set up house with a woman named Helen Karr Hill,* who had five children of her own. When CPS discovered this liaison, they removed those children as well and Helen, who ultimately married Ward, gave up her parental rights. During the course of the child abuse investigation initiated by Bette Vernon's call, the children also accused their grandparents and their uncle (Ward's brother, Bobby Vernon*) of molestation, and his five children were taken into care. Later, two children of family friends would join them in foster homes, based on the accusations of the children who had preceded them.

In the course of my work with maltreated children, I have come across a number of extended families in which abuse is this pervasive; families that have harmful multigenerational "traditions" of pansexuality and insularity, in which sexual and physical abuse and ignorance are handed down almost the way other families pass on heirlooms and Christmas recipes. At this point I didn't see any "red flags" to suggest that child welfare caseworkers were acting incorrectly or overzealously. Physical evidence of sexual abuse—anal and genital scarring, in some cases—had been found. Corporal punishment had also left marks on the bodies of some of the sixteen children.

But the choice of foster placements was where things started to go terribly wrong. The children were placed in two fundamentalist Christian "therapeutic" foster homes, where two seemingly incongruous cultural trends of the late 1980s and early 1990s would merge, with appalling results.

America had discovered an epidemic of child abuse, much of which was real and deserved genuine exposure and attention. One of the reasons abuse was being discussed in the news and on talk shows was the popularity of the "recovery movement," which had encouraged Americans to find their "inner child," and help it recover from wounds inflicted on it by negligent or abusive parents. At this time it was hard to read a newspaper or turn on the TV without coming across some celebrity discussing her (or, occasionally, his) history of being sexually abused as a child. Some self-help gurus claimed that more than 90 percent of families were dysfunctional. Some therapists eagerly propagated the idea that most of their clients' problems could be traced back to childhood abuse, and then set about helping them dig through their memories to discover it, even if they originally claimed no recollection of maltreatment. As some people searched their memories with the aid of certain poorly trained and overly confident therapists, they began to recall ugly perversions that had been perpetrated upon them, even as these "memories" became increasingly divorced from any plausible reality.

The second trend was a rise in evangelical Christianity. Converts and adherents warned that the devil must be behind these widespread sexual atrocities. How else to explain the soul sickness that could lead so many people to perform such violent and pro-fane acts on innocent children? Soon moral entrepreneurs made a business of the problem, selling workshops on how to identify children who were survivors of what came to be known as Satanic Ritual Abuse. As unlikely an ally of the Christian right as the feminist flagship *Ms.* magazine would feature on its front page a first person account by a "survivor" of such abuse in January 1993. The cover declared "Believe It—Child Ritual Abuse Exists," and inside, the magazine told the story of a woman who claimed she'd been raped with crucifixes by her parents and forced to eat the flesh of her decapitated infant sister.

The CPS caseworkers and foster parents involved with the Vernon case were immersed in this cultural confluence at its peak. Around the time these children were taken into care in 1990, the foster parents and the caseworkers who supervised them had attended a seminar on "Satanic Ritual Abuse." When the local DA recused himself from these cases because he had previously represented one of the defendants, the CPS case-workers convinced a local judge to appoint a special prosecu-tor. This special prosecutor ultimately brought on board two special "Satanic investigators" to help make their case for the existence of a devil-worshipping cult, led by the Vernon family, operating in Gilmer, and practicing child sex abuse and human sacrifice. These "investigators" were reputed to be experts in uncovering cult crimes. One was a former Baptist minister from Louisiana; the other was a gym instructor for the Texas Department of Public Safety. Neither had experience with police investigations.

None of the material related to Satanic Ritual Abuse or "recovered memory" therapies had been scientifically tested before it became widely popularized. The "recovered memory" therapists and workshop trainers taught that children never lie about sexual abuse, even though there was no empirical evidence on which to base such a claim. They also told adult patients who weren't sure whether they'd been abused that "if you think it happened, it probably did," and that the presence of conditions like eating disorders and addictions, even without any memories of abuse, could prove that it had happened. The checklists for determining the presence of "Satanic Ritual Abuse" were based upon even flimsier evidence, yet they were propounded as diagnostic tools during hundreds of workshops conducted for therapists, social workers and child welfare officials.

If these methods had been tested, as they were later, the studies would have found that memories recalled under hypnosis, and even during ordinary therapy, can easily be influenced by the therapist, and that while many people have strong feelings about their childhoods, this does not necessarily mean that they were abused or that all of the events they recall are literally true. While children rarely lie spontaneously about sexual abuse (although this, too, can happen), they can readily be led to concoct tales by adults who may not be aware that the child is simply telling them what they want to hear. Overt coercion is not needed, though, as we shall see, it can certainly make matters worse. The "Satanic" checklists, like similar checklists that circulated around the same time for incest survivors and for "codependents" who had addicted loved ones, were so vague and over-inclusive that any adolescent with even the most minor interest in sex, drugs and rock-n-roll—in other words, any normal teenager—could qualify as a victim. And any younger child with nightmares, fears of monsters and bedwetting could as well.

Another dangerous form of quackery was also being widely touted at this time and was unfortunately inflicted on these foster children. It came in various forms and had a number of different names, but was most commonly known as "holding therapy," or "attachment therapy." During this "treatment," adults would tightly restrain children in their arms and force them to look into the eyes of their caregivers and "open up" about their memories and fears. If the child did not produce a convincing story of early abuse, he would be verbally and physically assaulted until he did. Frequently practiced on adopted or foster children, this was supposed to create a parental bond between the child and his new family. One form, invented in the early 1970s by a California psychologist named Robert Zaslow, involved several "holders," one assigned to immobilize the child's head, while the others held down their limbs and dug their knuckles into the child's ribcage, moving the knuckles roughly back and forth. This was supposed to be done with enough force to cause bruising. Zaslow's "technique" was picked up and elaborated on by a group of therapists originally based in Evergreen, Colorado. Zaslow, however, lost his professional license after being charged with abuse. Evergreen-associated therapists, too, would ultimately be charged in several child abuse deaths associated with their "therapy."

"Holding" therapy was intended to go on for hours, with no breaks to eat or use the bathroom. Meanwhile, the adults were supposed to verbally taunt the child to enrage him, as if the torture being performed on the small body wasn't enough. "Releasing" his anger in this way was supposed to prevent future explosions of rage, as if the brain stored rage like a boiler and could be emptied of it by "expressing" it. The session would end only when the child was calm, no longer reacting to the taunts and seemingly in thrall to his caregivers. To end the assault he would have to declare his love for his tormentors, address his foster or adoptive parents as his "real" parents and display complete submission. The Lappes and a woman named Barbara Bass who housed the Vernon children used this version, improvising their own additions, such as making the kids run up and down stairs until they were exhausted and crying before beginning a "holding" session.

This is one of the many cases where a little knowledge can

be a dangerous thing. Supporters of "holding" believe (unfortunately, some are still around) that traumatized children's problems result from poor attachment to their caregivers due to early childhood abuse and/or neglect. In many cases, this is probably true. As we've discovered, early deprivation of love and affection can make some children manipulative and lacking in empathy, as in Leon's case. "Holding therapy" advocates also believe, in my view appropriately, that this missing or damaging early experience can interfere with the development of the brain's capacity to form healthy relationships.

The danger lies in their solution to the problem. Using force or any type of coercion on traumatized, abused or neglected children is counterproductive: it simply retraumatizes them. Trauma involves an overwhelming and terrifying loss of control, putting people back into situations over which they have no control recapitulates this and impedes recovery. This should go without saying, but holding a child down and hurting him until he says what you want to hear does not create bonds of affection but, rather, induces obedience through fear. Unfortunately, the resulting "good behavior" that follows may look like positive change and these youth may even appear to be more spontaneously loving toward their caregivers afterwards. This "trauma bond" is also known as Stockholm Syndrome: children who have been tortured into submission "love" their foster parents the way kidnapped newspaper heiress Patty Hearst "believed in" the cause of her Symbionese Liberation Army captors. Incidentally, children's "love" and obedience also tend to fade over time if the abuse is not continually repeated, as did Hearst's commitment to the radical politics of the group once she was freed.

The east Texas foster parents apparently knew nothing about the potential for harm inherent in "holding therapy," nor did the CPS caseworkers who monitored their care and sometimes participated in the holding sessions of the Vernon children. The ideology of "holding" fit easily into the families' religious beliefs that children who were spared the rod would be spoiled and that children's wills must be broken in order for them to learn to avoid sin and temptation. The foster families and caseworkers were convinced that the widespread abuse and incest in the children's biological families could only have resulted from involvement in a Satanic cult. Besides, the children had all the symptoms they'd been told to look for at the Satanic Ritual Abuse workshop. One of them even reportedly told a caseworker that "Daddy said that if we go into the woods, the devil would get us." Of course, the same warning could have come from a parent who practiced almost any religion, but no one considered this alternate explanation.

So, in order to "help" the children "process" their trauma and to bond with them, both the Lappes and Barbara Bass began "holding." It was here that another pernicious belief came into play, one that unfortunately is still widely held in the mental health field. I call it the "psychic pus" theory. This is the idea that, like a boil that needs to be lanced, certain memories are toxic and must be excavated and discussed in order for people to recover from trauma. Many people still spend hours in therapy searching for the "Rosetta stones" of their personal histories, trying to find the one memory that will help their lives make sense and instantly resolve their current problems.

In fact, memory doesn't work this way. The problem with traumatic memories tends to be their intrusion into the present, not an inability to recall them. When they intrude, discussing them and understanding how they may unconsciously influence our behavior can be extraordinarily helpful. For example, if a child avoids water because of a near drowning experience, talking it through when he is about to go to the beach may help him safely begin to swim again. At the same time, some people heal by fighting their fears and never discussing or explicitly recalling their painful memories at all. For people whose memories don't negatively affect them in the present, pressuring them to focus on them may actually do harm.

It's especially important to be sensitive to a child's own coping mechanisms if they have a strong support system. In one study we conducted in the mid-1990s, we found that children with supportive families who were assigned to therapy to discuss trauma were more likely to develop post-traumatic stress disorder than those whose parents were told to bring them in only if they observed specific symptoms. The hour per week that the children assigned to therapy spent focusing on their symptoms exacerbated them, rather than exorcised them. Each week, in the days prior to their therapy session, these children would begin thinking about their trauma; each week the children would have to leave school or extracurricular activities to travel to the clinic for therapy. In some cases children became hyperaware of their normal stress reactions, keeping tabs of every blip so they'd have something to say to the therapist. This disrupted their lives and increased rather than decreased their distress. Interestingly, however, if the child did not have a strong social network, therapy was beneficial. It probably gave them somewhere to turn that they did not have ordinarily. The bottom line is that people's individual needs vary, and no one should be pushed to discuss trauma if they do not wish to do so. If a child is surrounded by sensitive, caring adults, the timing, duration, and intensity of small therapeutic moments can be titrated by the child. We observed this in practice with the Branch Davidian children and we feel the same principles hold for all children dealing with loss and trauma living in a healthy social support system.

Believing that you cannot recover unless you remember the precise details of a past trauma can also become a self-fulfilling prophecy. It can keep you focused on the past rather than dealing with the present. For example, some studies have found that depression can be exacerbated by ruminating on past negative events. Because of how memory works, such rumination can also lead you to recall old, ambiguous memories in a new light, one that, over time, becomes darker and darker until it eventually becomes a trauma that never actually occurred. Add the coercive, physically assaultive practice of "holding" to the malleability of the memories of young children, and you have a recipe for disaster.

During "holding" sessions the foster parents and sometimes their caseworkers and the "Satan investigators" would interrogate the youth about their devil-worshipping parents. They would ask lengthy, leading questions and dig their knuckles into the child's side until he agreed with their version of events. The children soon learned that the "holding" would stop a lot sooner if they "disclosed" their parents' cult involvement and described its rituals. Rapidly, they confirmed the tales of sacrificed babies, cannibalism, devil masks, hooded figures circling fires in the woods and Satanic altars, all originating from the questions and prompts of the interviewers, confirming the foster parents' ritual abuse "diagnosis." Soon, the children were saying that they had been videotaped for child pornography in a warehouse and had witnessed numerous murders. When the foster parents began to ask about whether other children were being abused by the cult, in desperation to escape the "holding," they began to give up the names of their friends. As a result, two other children were taken from their parents, and many more were named as possible abuse victims.

Fortunately, many of these "holding sessions" and related "interviews" were audio or videotaped. As awful as they were to watch and hear, they allowed some incredible facts to emerge as we tried to figure out which children had actually been victimized by their parents, and whose parents had been accused because the Vernon children needed to name new names to please their interrogators. One thing became clear right away: if the caseworkers knew and liked the families who were accused (remember, this was a very small town, so most people knew each other), they would dismiss the Vernon siblings' accusations and ask for other names. If they didn't like the family, however, the parents would be investigated and their children taken.

That was how Brian came to be among the sixteen children in "therapeutic" foster care. Brian was a bright second-grader with a crew cut and a conscientious nature. He enjoyed watching the news, so before the sheriffs came to arrest his parents for sexually abusing him and his younger brother, he'd heard about the Vernon case on TV. The Vernons lived across the street from him and he was also friends with their children, so he had heard plenty of local gossip as well. From the media and from what neighbors were saying, Brian's parents figured out that they were likely to be the next family targeted as Satanic sexual abusers. On the day CPS came to take him away, Brian was playing outside and saw the sheriff's cars approaching, so he ran in and warned his parents. Unfortunately, he could do nothing but watch as caseworkers jolted his one-year-old brother awake from his nap and his parents were taken away in handcuffs. Brian was permitted to take one beloved item from home with him; that he chose a Bible and not a toy should have been an early clue that he was not a being raised in a Satanic cult.

Unfortunately, from the news, Brian had also learned about another horrifying local crime. Seventeen-year-old Kelly Wilson, a wide-eyed, blonde cheerleader out of central casting, had abruptly disappeared on January 5, 1992. She was last seen leaving work at a Gilmer video store. Today, neither her remains nor any signs of her continued existence have been found. The officer on duty when her parents called about her disappearance, Sergeant James York Brown, was assigned the case.

By all accounts, Sergeant Brown worked it diligently, placing posters about the missing girl all over town, even working through the following Thanksgiving when a report (later found to be false) came in that her body might be in a local field. He convinced a local business to fund and erect a billboard requesting any information the public might have about Wilson's whereabouts. Brown rapidly identified the most likely suspect: a young man whom the cheerleader had dated and who had a prior conviction for an assault with a knife. That man's car had mysteriously been sold days after the girl's disappearance. Even more suspiciously, when the vehicle was finally located, a giant piece of its interior carpeting was missing. But the car had been washed thoroughly, inside and out, and no definitive physical evidence could be found.

That suspect, however, wasn't of interest to the social workers and the special prosecutor in the Vernon case. The ex-boyfriend had no connection to the Vernons. If he had killed Kelly, it would be just another case of a teenage love affair gone wrong, not a body that could be linked to the tales of human sacrifice the Vernon children were telling. The Vernons and their Satanic followers, the investigators were sure, must be guilty of more than beating and raping a few children and sacrificing some animals. But no one could find any bodies, nor had any local people been reported missing. Until Kelly Wilson.

The caseworkers and "cult crimes" investigators became convinced that there must be a connection between the Vernons and the young girl's disappearance. They subjected seven-year-old Brian to an entire day of "holding" to find it. Brian's intelligence meant the stories he was forced to produce were far more coherent than those of the others. When nine adults surrounded him, held him down and shouted at him until he was so terrified that he soiled himself, he came up with the story that would lead to Sergeant Brown's indictment. He reported seeing Wilson victimized at the Vernon's Satanic rites. He said that "a man in a blue uniform" was there, and he made remarks about police officers being "bad."

One of these "bad" cops became James Brown when the investigators and the prosecutor conducted a ten-hour taped interrogation of a woman with a reported IQ of seventy. Patty Clark* was the common-law wife of one of the Vernon brothers. She had a long history of abusive relationships and had herself been raised in foster care. She was facing child abuse charges related to the Vernon children, which she was told she could mitigate if she told the "truth" about Kelly Wilson's murder and James Brown's involvement in it. She later said that her testimony had literally been scripted on a white board because her interrogators had become so frustrated by her inability to reliably repeat what they told her to say. The transcripts of her interrogation vividly show the coercion used to get her statements, with interrogators repeatedly telling her that they knew that Brown was at the scene of the crime and threatening her with the consequences of "not telling the truth." If you read them, it is hard to tell who is displaying less intelligence: the interrogators who try to make the mentally subnormal woman use the same terms for anal sex that were used by the children during their "holding" sessions, or poor Patty Clark who tries at least seven different phrases before finally being prompted by investigators with the right term.

Clark's "testimony" ultimately described a ten-day period of torture endured by the kidnapped cheerleader, capped off by a gang rape, the removal of one of Wilson's breasts, the hanging of her body to drain its blood for drinking, and cannibalism. It was Clark's child, Bobby Vernon Jr., whom the Lappes would later beat into a coma.

COERCED CONFESSIONS ARE problematic in many ways. Not least is the potential they have for leading to the convictions of innocent people. Another is that facts unknown to the interrogators may later surface to destroy their witnesses' credibility and, by extension, their own. Such facts ultimately halted Gilmer's Satan investigators and its special prosecutor. Sergeant Brown himself uncovered the most damning evidence, which is why, many believe, the special prosecutor and his minions eventually decided that the police officer had to be named as part of the cult. The problems with the evidence were multiple: there was no physical evidence linking the Vernons and the missing cheerleader; the children's claims that they were taken to warehouses to film child pornography could not be corroborated since no such warehouses (every one in the county was checked), films, photos or videos could be found; the bones found buried in the Vernons' back yard turned out to be animal, not human; a "devil mask" found in their home turned out to be a cheap Halloween costume that could serve as evidence to make the case that millions of Americans were Satanists.

But the worst piece of evidence for the prosecutor's case was that on the night of Kelly Wilson's disappearance cult "leaders" Ward Vernon and his wife Helen, who were reported to have been key perpetrators in the girl's kidnapping and death, were in New York. There were multiple documents attesting to this: Ward was a truck driver and his employer kept records of his travels, including the bills of lading required to prove delivery of the shipments. Ward even had gas station credit card receipts from New York to prove that he'd been there. When Sergeant Brown insisted that this meant that the Satan investigators had the wrong suspects in Wilson's death and that their witnesses' testimony was unreliable, the special prosecutor told him, "If you get into my investigation in any way, I will ruin you personally, professionally, financially and in every other way."

That prosecutor made good on his threat. The Patty Clark interrogation that turned young Brian's "man in the blue uniform" into James Brown followed. Brown's arrest—complete with a brutal takedown by a SWAT team—occurred shortly thereafter.

HOW WAS I GOING TO DETERMINE which abuse allegations were coerced by interrogators and which had really occurred? How were we going to figure out the safest place for these traumatized children? Should they be returned to parents who were possible abusers or should they be placed in new, much more closely scrutinized foster or adoptive homes? I was pretty sure from the chronology that Brian and his little brother had been removed from their home in error, but what if their parents were genuinely abusive and the Vernon children had known about it? Then again, what if the second group, Bobby and Patty's children, had been removed only because their cousins had been coerced into naming more victims? Our chronology suggested that there was physical evidence to support the allegations of abuse against both Vernon brothers, their wives/partners and the Vernon grandparents, but the investigation was so tainted that it was hard to know what to believe.

Fortunately, I'd discovered a tool that could, in conjunction with other evidence, help us sort through the wreckage. I'd stumbled onto it by accident. Back in Chicago and just after I had moved to Houston in the early 1990s, I'd run a few marathons. While training, I wore a continuous heart rate monitor. One day, right after a practice run, I'd gone to do a home visit with a boy who was in foster care, so I was still wearing the monitor when I arrived at the house. The little boy asked me what it was, and I let him try it out, explaining what it did. When I put it on him, his heart rate was one hundred, quite normal for a boy his age at rest. Then, I realized I'd left some paperwork that I needed in my car, so I asked him if he wanted to come with me to get it. He seemed not to have heard my question, but I could see that his heart rate had shot up to 148. I thought that perhaps my monitor had broken, so I moved closer to take a look. In case I'd mumbled, as I sometimes do, I repeated what I'd said. The boy remained motionless and his heart rate moved even higher. I was perplexed, but I saw no reason to press him to come with me. I went out to get the paperwork, returned and finished the visit.

Before my visit, I hadn't known this particular child's history; I was just there to see how he was doing in his current placement. When I got back to my office I looked up his chart. It turned out that he'd been sexually abused by his mother's boyfriend—in a garage. When this man had said to him, "Let's go out and work on the car," what he really meant was, "I'm going to abuse you now." Inadvertently, I'd given him a traumatic cue by suggesting that he come to the car with me. I decided to see if heart-rate monitoring might help me figure out what cues triggered trauma symptoms in other children.

Frequently, I saw the same reaction: if a child was exposed to a scent, sight, sound, or, as in this case, a verbal suggestion that lead him to recall the trauma, his heart rate would rise dramatically. For some, if cues made them experience dissociative symptoms rather than hyperarousal responses, their heart rates would go down, rather than up. Hyperarousal prepares people for fight and/or flight, which requires an increased heart-rate; dissociation prepares them for inescapable stress, slowing their heart rate, breathing and other functions. Although it doesn't work in every case and needs further study, heart-rate monitoring has been very useful in my work. Knowing that something or someone provoked traumatic memories in a child could often help us narrow down who or what had harmed them, especially with toddlers who were too young to tell us what had happened.

I tried this method with Brian, who by now was living in a group home. He'd been away from his parents for almost two years by this point, and it was obvious that he missed them terribly. I stressed repeatedly that if there was anything he didn't want to discuss, he should say so, and that no harm would come to him if he admitted to having lied about something in the past. I told him that this would be the chance for him to tell his side of the story. And then I colored with him for a while. Brian had stayed with Barbara Bass. Much of the "holding" therapy and "investigation" involving the Satanic abuse took place at her home.

When I first asked him about her "therapeutic" foster home, he said that it was "kind of fun." I encouraged him to tell me more, without prompting him about whether I wanted to know good or bad things.

"One thing I didn't like, we had holding there," he said immediately.

"Tell me what holding is," I said.

"She makes you run the stairs till you cry so you're, like, tired and then we go in the room and get on the bed and she lays down with ya, and she rubs your sides, like your ribs and it hurts and you scream and you get all your anger out and you talk to her about what you're mad about."

"When she says, 'Get your anger out,' what does she mean by that?"

"Stuff that you're just mad about. And then she makes you say stuff that you don't want to say."

"Like what?"

"Like stuff that your parents did that they didn't do."

"She'd want you to say that?"

Brian, who was on the brink of tears, his heart racing, nodded his head.

"Give me an example."

"Like say that they hurt you or something. And we'd usually always have holding right before we'd come down to see a therapist or something."

"How many times a week would you have it?"

"Probably once a month, but it depended where we were going. If we were going to testify or see a therapist or something like that, we'd have it like that day or the day before."

I asked him how Barbara got him to say things that weren't true. "She'd rub your sides till it hurts and after a while, you know, you're going to give in. It hurts."

"What kinds of things did she make you say?"

Brian began to cry openly, tears running down his face and dripping from his nose. "That my parents did stuff that they didn't do," he said, weeping. I reassured him, again, that he didn't have to tell me anything and that I wouldn't try to make him say anything that he didn't want to say, or that he didn't think was true. But he was brave and, after I gave him some tissues, he insisted on telling me the whole story. He described the day when he was taken from his parents, how he knew when his mother began to cry that "I was going," and how he was allowed to bring "one thing he really liked" with him and chose his Bible. He talked about how he tried to calm his one-year-old brother, saying that "he didn't know what was going on," and "was grumpy because they woke him up from his nap." (The younger child didn't even recognize his mother by the time he was finally returned home.)

When I questioned Brian about the "Satanic" ritual killing of Kelly Wilson and other atrocities he'd claimed to have witnessed or taken part in, he didn't cry and his heart rate remained steady. He was very matter-of-fact and said that he'd made up those stories in order to stop from being hurt. He did not express any fear, either verbally or physically, when discussing things like "killing babies," which was in complete contrast to when he discussed being taken from his home or the "holding" procedure. His compassion for his brother and his distress over being made to lie about his parents made clear that this was a highly sensitive, moral and caring boy. Such a child would have responded to being made to watch or participate in murder and cannibalism with agony and terror; only a sociopath could have reacted unemotionally when recalling such memories if they had been true. Brian simply would not have been able to respond so differently to these two sets of experiences, which was something I had to testify to in great length in order to get the judge who was presiding over the custody cases to allow Brian and his brother to return home.

Figuring out what had really happened to the Vernon children was more complicated. No one wanted to return children with anal and genital scarring to people who had repeatedly raped them. But the false allegations of murder and Satanic rites had so warped their credibility that their parents could now claim, quite believably, that everything the kids had said about who abused them and what had gone on was suspect. I hoped to use heart rate monitoring and other physiological and emotional cues to try to find out who had hurt these children, and find the best permanent placement for them.

I spoke with one little girl who had been a toddler when she was removed from her parents' home. Annie had had so many conversations with professionals by this time that she could mimic us. At one point in our interview she sat on a swivel chair, swinging herself back and forth, and said, "Tell me about yourself. My name is Annie and I have brown hair and brown eyes and I've been in 10,000 foster homes." She was drinking soda from a can, and very much enjoying burping after each sip. I asked her about where her reports about Satan and killing people had come from.

"It came from my birth dad, he killed all these babies and

he made me kill them or I was going to die and the babies were going to die, too," she said, and smiled, burping up some soda. There was no movement on the heart rate monitor.

"How can you remember that?" I asked.

"I remember because my sister told me," she said, swinging her legs. When I asked if she could remember any of this herself, she said that she couldn't, explaining that she couldn't remember anything much before she was three.

When I asked her if she remembered "holding," her mood immediately darkened. She said in a serious tone, "Yes I do and I don't want to talk about it." But then she described how her foster parents and caseworkers, "kept on making me talk about my past and saying that I killed babies."

Later, when I asked her about whether she'd been sexually abused by her father, she was even more reluctant to talk. "He made me touch his privates and I said I didn't want to and he stuck my hand down there," she said, and got up out of her chair to look out the window. When I asked if this had happened more than once, she nodded, keeping her eyes down. "He made me rub it and when I said no he said 'You don't tell me what to do or I'll kill you.'"

Now you could see signs of fear, in the dissociative response as she physically tried to escape the question by walking away, and in her heart rate. She later returned to her chair, saying, "I can't stand the name Ward Vernon." She bore down on the pencil with which she'd been drawing earlier, scribbling back and forth, as if to blot out his name forever. The little girl responded similarly to discussions about her stepmother, but insisted that her real mother had never harmed her.

When I spoke with one of her older sisters, Linda, she told me that the initial idea that there had been Satanic abuse, "came from Barbara's mouth. She would say, 'OK, you're in the dungeon with Helen, right,' and she'd press on you until the tears start running, until you say yes. She would put words actually in your mouth." Linda, too, described sexual abuse by her father and stepmother, detailing how her grandparents were often involved. "They do it almost every day," she said, and when I pressed her about whether she remembered this or whether she'd been told to say it, she got stern with me and said, "You would remember too if it happened in your life when you were seven years old." Again, her physiological responses were consistent with having been sexually abused by family members, but not with her having taken part in Satanic rituals and murder. None of the Vernon children were ultimately returned to their biological parents because it was clear that they were at great risk for further abuse in that extended family.

One of the most troubling aspects of the case—and something that is important for parents to keep in mind when dealing with emotionally charged situations—was how the fear sparked by this pathetic investigation spread and caused otherwise rational people to behave in bizarre ways. Once the allegations of Satanic Ritual Abuse were made public, they took on a life of their own. Even highly trained professionals in mental health and law enforcement, even some of my own staff, were not immune.

Once the children had been removed from their homes and the accusations of Satanic abuse surfaced, nearly everyone involved in their care became convinced that Satanists were going to kidnap the children and slaughter those who were now trying to help them. Despite the fact that the "cult leaders" and almost everyone else believed to have been involved in the child abuse and murder had already been incarcerated, the Satan investigators, the caseworkers and the foster parents were sure there was a larger conspiracy and that they were all in mortal danger. They began behaving in an extremely paranoid fashion, even moving the children to west Texas (where Bobby Vernon was beaten into a coma) in order to evade what they believed were the still-thriving tentacles of the cult. The Lappes' suicides were seen as evidence that the cult had somehow "gotten to them." Once belief in the power of the cult and its evil activities had been established, it was almost impossible for people to acknowledge contrary evidence.

Explaining the Lappes' suicides would seem straightforward to most people: the couple had just beaten a child they'd presumably cared for so ferociously that they'd smashed his skull, leaving him in a permanent vegetative state. Guilt, shame, sorrow—any one of these motivations would do, no Satanic cult necessary. But rather than reexamine their initial assumptions, those involved with the investigation simply became further and further detached from reality.

The town of Gilmer itself was split. Some believed that a Satanic cult resided there and had killed people and was continuing to wreak havoc, while others thought innocent people had lost their children and had been accused of unspeakable and frankly impossible crimes. Kelly Wilson's own parents exemplified the divide. Kelly's mother believed that Sergeant Brown was involved with a Satanic cult that had kidnapped and killed her daughter, while Kelly's father argued just as strenuously that Brown and the others had been railroaded and his daughter's true killer has not been found.

The judge who presided over the custody hearings for the children was convinced that Satanic rituals had taken place. The grand jury that had indicted Brown refused to reverse its indictment when the Texas attorney general's office tried to explain to them why the evidence that had previously been presented to them was unreliable. Ultimately another judge dropped the indictments, but many in Gilmer remained convinced that Satan worshippers had gathered there to abuse and kill children. During the course of my work on this case, I was accused of involvement in the cult, my staff members reported things like dead cats on the road as evidence of "spookiness" in Gilmer, and a general atmosphere of fear predominated. Without any evidence other than the coerced testimony of sixteen children, twentieth-century adults were ready to convict half a dozen people, including a police officer who'd randomly been assigned to investigate the crime and a man whose employer's records and gas station receipts put him halfway across the country on the day of the crime.

Humans are social animals, highly susceptible to emotional contagion. Training, logic, and intelligence are often no match for the power of groupthink. Early humans who couldn't quickly pick up on and follow the emotional cues of others would not have been able to survive. Following such cues is a key to social success, and being unable to perceive them is a serious handicap, as we saw in Connor's case. But the "side effect" of this legacy can lead us to witch hunts like the one in Gilmer, Texas.

CHAPTER 8

The Raven

SEVENTEEN-YEAR-OLD AMBER had been found unconscious in a high school bathroom. Her breathing was shallow, her heart rate sluggish, her blood pressure far too low. Unsurprisingly, her mother, Jill,* who had arrived at the emergency room after being called by the school, was distraught. I had just walked into the ER as well. I was the attending physician there that month and was reviewing the evaluation of a suicidal adolescent by one of the child psychiatry fellows.

As a group of doctors was trying to evaluate Amber, the girl's heart had suddenly stopped. The medical team had quickly revived and stabilized the girl, but it had been terrifying for Jill to see. Despite the physicians' best efforts, Amber was still unconscious and unarousable. Now Jill was hysterical. I was asked to help calm the mother so the other doctors could focus on her daughter's problems. Toxicology screens, which would have found any drugs in Amber's system, were negative, ruling out the most likely cause of teen unconsciousness in such a situation: an overdose. Jill could recall no previous health problems that might explain her state. Consequently, the doctors were thinking rare heart disease, or perhaps brain tumor or stroke.

I found Jill sitting by her daughter's bedside, holding her hand and crying. A nurse was adjusting Amber's IV. Jill looked at me, pleading with her eyes. I tried to reassure her that the hospital was excellent and that her daughter was receiving the best possible care. But when she asked me what kind of doctor I was and found out that I was a child psychiatrist, she became more, not less, upset.

"Are you here because she's going to die?" she demanded.

"No," I responded quickly, explaining that the rest of the team was busy trying to figure out exactly what was wrong with Amber. They knew that it would help Jill if she could talk with someone and I'd been assigned that role. She looked me in the eye and saw that I was telling the truth. She relaxed perceptibly and I thought, not for the first time, that simple honesty was vastly underrated and underused in medicine.

"Why won't they tell me what is going on?" she asked. I explained that the other doctors probably weren't withholding information, but that they most likely didn't know themselves what was wrong with Amber. I told her I'd look at her chart myself to find out what I could.

I left the room, read the chart, and spoke with the resident and one of the other doctors. They described how Amber's school had called EMS after a student had found the teen in the bathroom. Her vital signs had been stable; however, her heart rate was remarkably low: running between forty-eight and fifty-two beats per minute. A normal heart rate for a girl her age at rest is between seventy and ninety. The paramedics brought her to the hospital and the clinical team had been in the middle of their evaluation when her heart stopped. Then she had to be revived, in a scene now familiar from hundreds of episodes of medical dramas like "ER."

By this time Amber had been in the emergency room for about four hours. During that period she'd been seen by neurology and a CAT scan had shown no brain abnormalities. Other neurological tests were equally normal. The cardiology service had also seen her and they could find no heart problem that would explain her symptoms. All of her blood work appeared normal and her toxicology screens were repeatedly negative. My suspicion had been correct: no one had told Jill what was going on because no one knew.

I went back into the room and told Jill what I had learned. And then, using a simple technique I had learned as a way of helping people relax before beginning hypnosis, I began to ask about Amber's life, hoping to calm the mother while simultaneously finding some clue about whether something had gone wrong in the daughter's past.

"Tell me about your daughter," I said. Jill looked confused by this seemingly irrelevant question. "Where was she born?" I prompted. Jill started to think back, and then offered me the same stories she had probably happily told a hundred times since her daughter's birth. Most people's mood changes noticeably when they reminisce like this. As she talked about her daughter's birth, Jill smiled for the first time in our conversation. Whenever Jill began to falter, I would re-prompt her, always sticking to topics that were likely to be neutral or positive, like Amber's first day of school or the books she enjoyed as a small child.

I noticed, however, that she seemed to skip over long periods of time, and just by looking at her, I could also see that she'd had a difficult life herself. She looked ten years older than her actual age in her mid-thirties; her bleach-blonde hair was thin and her face haggard. Of course, no one looks especially good in a hospital room hovering over a seriously ill child, but Jill struck me as someone who had been through a great deal and had struggled hard to get where she was in her life. I could tell that she was leaving a lot out but, eventually, she filled in some of the blanks, admitting to a string of failed relationships and lousy jobs that had kept her and Amber moving around the country, rootless, for years. But now, at last, she had a good job as an administrative assistant and seemed committed to making Texas her home.

As Jill spoke, I also studied her daughter. Amber had dyed black hair. Triple piercings in one ear, double in the other. Then I noticed something that I immediately recognized might be important: her forearm had dozens of short shallow cuts on it. The cuts were perfectly parallel with an occasional crosscut. The location, the depth, and pattern were all characteristic of self-mutilation.

Trying to figure out if the cuts might be relevant to Amber's medical problems, I asked Jill if anything had happened recently that might have upset Amber. The mom thought for a moment and then covered her mouth with her hands, as if to suppress a scream. It turned out that the night before, one of Jill's former partners, Duane,* had phoned. Jill had broken up with Duane eight years back after discovering that he'd repeatedly raped her daughter, then age nine. The abuse had gone on for several years. Amber had answered the phone the night before she was hospitalized. Duane had suggested a visit before Jill got on the line and told him that neither she nor her daughter would have anything to do with him.

Many "cutters"—as I would soon find out Amber was— have a history of trauma. When they mutilate themselves, they can induce a dissociative state, similar to the adaptive response they'd had during the original trauma. Cutting can be soothing to them because it provides an escape from anxiety caused by revisiting traumatic memories or just the challenges of everyday life. In dissociative states, as we've discussed, people can become so disconnected from reality that they move into a dreamlike consciousness where nothing seems real and they feel little emotional or physical pain. These experiences are linked with the release of high levels of opioids, the brain's natural heroin-like substances that kill pain and produce a calming sense of distance from one's troubles. Research on rodents has shown that when these animals are totally restrained—a highly stressful experience for them—their brains flood with natural opioids, known as endorphins and enkephalins. People who suffer life-threatening experiences often describe a sense of "disconnection" and "unreality" and a numbness that is similar to what people feel when they take opioid drugs. Endorphins and enkephalins are an integral part of the brain's stress response system, preparing the body to handle both physical and emotional pain.

It occurred to me that Amber's physiological state as she lay in the ER was very much like that of someone who has overdosed on heroin, although, unlike most overdose victims, she was breathing on her own. Considering her self-mutilation and the unexpected contact with her abuser that she'd had the night before, I thought: Could this be an extreme dissociative response, which had essentially caused her brain to OD on its own opioids?

When I first broached this possibility, the ER docs thought it was absurd. Even I had to admit that it seemed far-fetched and that I had never heard of any similar cases. Still, I knew that the antidote to opioid overdoses, a drug called naloxone, is safe. In fact, it is so unlikely to prove harmful that some needle exchange programs provide it to people with addiction to reverse overdoses that they may witness. In our clinic we also use a similar, but longer acting, drug called naltrexone to help children who are prone to dissociative states modulate their reactions when they encounter trauma-related cues. After Amber continued to be unresponsive for a few more hours and more tests came back without offering any additional insight into her condition, her doctors decided to give naloxone a try.

And as with ordinary opioid overdoses, the results were rapid. Ninety seconds after receiving the injection, Amber blinked, came around and, within minutes, sat up and asked where she was. As I was soon to find out by learning more about her life, my theory that a dissociative reaction to traumatic memories had caused her symptoms was the most plausible explanation for both the loss of consciousness that brought her to the hospital as well as her response to the naloxone.

She was kept overnight in the hospital for observation. The next morning I went to see her. I found her awake and sitting in her bed. She was drawing and writing in a journal. I introduced myself, saying, "I met you yesterday but I'm sure you don't remember. You were a little bit disoriented."

"You don't look like a doctor," she said, looking me up and down, focusing on my T-shirt, jeans and sandals, not on my white coat. She seemed suspicious. But she also seemed confident and self-assured, and immediately went back to her drawing.

"Are you that shrink?" she asked, not looking up again. I tried to take a surreptitious glance at her work. The journal contained elaborate designs reminiscent of ancient calligraphy. There were serpent-like creatures around the edges of the corner of each page. She caught me watching her and slowly closed her journal. It was an interesting way to simultaneously conceal and reveal: as she shut the book, she turned it toward me so I could more easily see the pages as they were being obscured by the book's cover. So she does want to talk, I thought.

"I had a chance to talk with your mom a little bit about you," I said, "She loves you very much but she is worried. She thinks it would be helpful for you to talk with someone about what happened earlier in your life." I paused, giving her a moment to digest what I had just said, and listened. "My mom likes you," she replied, looking me straight in the eyes as she spoke. Then, she looked away for a moment as if she was thinking. Would I become another man her mother brought into her life who hurt her? I wondered if she distrusted all men, the way my first patient, Tina, had? Did some part of her brain loathe any man her mother liked? Should I have had one of our female clinicians work with her? Yet my instinct told me she would be OK with me. Ultimately, she would need, over time, to replace some of her bad associations with men, to experience an honest, predictable, safe and healthy relationship.

"Well, I think your mom likes that we were able to help you," I said, trying to reframe the issue. "She told me what happened with Duane; that's how I figured out what we should do to help you. And I think it would be really helpful for you to talk with somebody about all of that. It might help prevent something like yesterday from happening again."

"What happened with *him* is *over*," said Amber, emphatically.

I reached over to her hand, opened up her palm and exposed her forearm. I looked at the cuts and then looked at her and asked, "Are you sure?"

She pulled back, crossed her arms, and looked away from me.

I continued, "Listen, you don't know me, you don't know anything about me and you shouldn't trust me until you get to know me. So I'm going to say a few things. After I leave, you will have a chance to think about whether or not you want to spend any time talking with me. Whatever you decide is final. You don't have to agree to see me, it is your choice. You are in control." I described our clinic's work with traumatized children in simple terms, explaining how it might be of help to her and how we might be able to learn more from her to aid our work with other maltreated children as well.

I stopped for a moment and watched her. She looked at me, still unsure what to make of me. I wanted her to know that I did understand something of what she had experienced, so I continued.

"I know that when you feel anxious, you feel pulled to cut yourself. And that when you first put the razor to your skin and feel that first cut, you feel relief." She looked at me as though I was revealing a deep secret. "I know that sometimes in school, you feel the tension build inside you and you can't wait to get to the bathroom and cut yourself, even just a tiny bit. And I know that even on warm days, you will wear long-sleeved shirts to hide the scars."

I stopped speaking. We looked at each other. I put my hand out to shake hands with her. She looked me over for a moment and then slowly put her hand out as well. We shook hands. I told her I'd be back to answer any questions and see if she wanted to make an appointment.

When I returned, Amber and her mom were waiting for me. "I think you're ready to go home," I said to the girl, adding, "So what about you coming in to see me next week?"

"Sure," she responded and gave me an uncomfortable smile. "How did you know all that stuff?" She couldn't resist asking.

"We can talk about that next week. Right now you get out of that stupid gown and go home and have a nice night with your mom." I tried to keep the moment light. Trauma is best digested bit by bit. Both mother and daughter had had enough in the past two days.

WHEN AMBER STARTED THERAPY, I was surprised by how quickly she opened up to me. It is not unusual for several months to pass before a patient shares her intimate thoughts during a weekly psychotherapy session. It took only three or four weeks before Amber started to talk about having been abused by Duane.

"Don't you want me to talk about being abused?" she asked one day.

"I figured that when you're ready to talk about it you'll bring it up," I said.

"I don't think about it very much. I don't like to remember it."

I asked her when she did think about it.

"Sometimes when I'm going to sleep," she said, "But then I just go away."

"Go away?"

I knew she was talking about dissociation but I wanted her to describe what happened. There was a change in her posture: she cocked her head and stared into space, her eyes fixed down and to the left. I knew she was running some painful images through her mind.

"When it first started to happen I was so scared," she said in a quiet, almost child-like voice. "And it hurt. Sometimes I couldn't breathe. I felt so helpless and so small and so weak. I didn't want to tell my mom. I was so embarrassed and confused. So when it would happen, I would close my eyes and try to think about other things. Pretty soon, I was able to go to a safe place in my head."

As she described it, she seemed to change. "Little by little, I made that place my special retreat. Whenever I thought about going there and being there, I felt safe. Nobody knew where it was. Nobody could come in there with me. Nobody could hurt me there." She paused. She was now speaking in a low tone of voice, in a monotone, almost robotically. She was staring off into space as she spoke. She hardly blinked. We sat in silence for a moment and then she continued.

"I felt like I could fly when I was in that place. And I began to imagine that I was a bird, a raven. I tried being a beautiful bird, a bluebird or a robin but I couldn't be beautiful there. I tried being a majestic bird, like an eagle or a hawk, but that didn't work either. My mind kept making me something dark. Like a raven. But I was powerful. I could control other animals. I was wise and I was kind, but I was absolutely ruthless in hunting down and using my power to kill evil. To those creatures, the bad ones, I was the Black Death."

She paused again. This time, she looked at me. Her words had been moving. I knew she'd never shared this with anyone and that she felt that some of the power of her fantasy to comfort her lay in its secret nature. It is critical to protect someone when they are vulnerable in moments like this.

"Are you still the Black Death?" I asked. She looked away for a moment and then back at me and started to cry. That was the real start of our work.

AS THE WEEKS WENT BY I LEARNED more and more about her. Amber's story would ultimately teach me a great deal about the dissociative response to trauma and how to help those who suffer from it.

The sexual abuse that Amber had experienced was violent and terrifying, beginning when she was about seven years old. Her parents had split when she was two, and her mother found a new partner several years later and relied upon him to support the family. Duane would only molest her when he'd been drinking, which was about once every ten days or so. Then, for days afterwards, he would seem remorseful, showering her with gifts and praise, trying to make up for what he'd done. Since his drinking was unpredictable, Amber lived in a constant state of fear, always worrying about when it would happen next and about the pain and terror of the event itself. Her grades began to decline and she went from being a happy, outgoing child to being a withdrawn and anxious little girl.

She was too frightened to tell her mother what Duane was doing; he threatened her with even worse if she told. Feeling that the situation was inescapable, Amber did what she could to get control over it. She began to serve Duane drinks and behave provocatively, with the aim of getting the abuse over with. Knowing when it would happen allowed her to study and sleep through the night rather than worrying about when he'd come into her bedroom. In essence, she could schedule and isolate her terror so that it didn't interfere with the rest of her life. Her grades improved again and, to those around her, she seemed to be back to herself. Although her behavior probably doubled the frequency of the molestation, the control she gained over the situation allowed her to manage her anxiety such that it minimized the effects that the abuse had on her daily life. Unfortunately, of course, this would later produce a whole new set of problems related to her guilt over her feelings of complicity in his actions but, at the time, it helped her cope with the trauma.

When she was actually being raped or sodomized, Amber dissociated, withdrawing into her Black Death/Raven fantasy world. She would be chased by evil creatures and demons, but she would always triumph over them, as in a role-playing video game. The fantasy was elaborate and detailed. In fact, it was so encompassing that she literally no longer felt what was actually happening to her body. She encapsulated the trauma in a way that allowed her to function and cope, although, of course, she still suffered its effects when she was exposed to cues that reminded her of what had gone on, such as Duane's scent or the smell of certain drinks that he favored. Such cues would prompt a dissociative response that she could not control, in which she retreated to her "safe" world and did not respond to outside stimuli. The most extreme reaction was the one that had put her in the hospital the day after he called.

The abuse had continued for several years. Then, when Amber was around nine, her mother caught Duane in bed with the little girl, and immediately kicked him out. She didn't blame Amber, as many mothers unfortunately do in such situations, but, other than calling the police, she didn't seek help for her, either. Sadly, the district attorney didn't pursue the case after the perpetrator moved out of state. And Jill had problems of her own to deal with: as a single mother with few skills, she now had to struggle to support herself and her daughter. She and Amber made many moves from state to state, seeking better employment opportunities. Jill eventually managed to go back to school and get a higher paying job, but the instability and the abuse had done its damage to Amber.

Amber continued to cope on her own, getting decent, but not spectacular, grades. Intelligent as she was, she almost certainly could have done better but, probably at least in part because of what had happened to her, she stayed a B-student and an under-achiever. Though she was not the most popular girl in her class, she was not the least popular either. She hung out with a group of teens in the middle of the social spectrum who were "Goths," dressed in black but not especially extreme in their behavior. They didn't drink or take drugs, for example, but their interest in mysticism and alternative culture made them tolerant of those who did. A recent study of Goth youth culture, in fact, found that it tends to attract adolescents like Amber who have histo-ries of self-harm. Interestingly, becoming a Goth didn't increase self-harm: before these teens found a community that accepted their "dark" interests, in fact, they were more prone to cut or otherwise harm themselves.

In school, Amber discovered that pinching or deeply scratching her arms relieved some of her anxiety. And later, in private, she found that cutting her skin could produce a disso-ciative state, allowing her to escape what she experienced as an intolerable buildup of stress. "It's like I have magical skin," she told me, describing how cutting into it with a knife or razor prompted an incredible sense of relief and access to her "safe" place. Many teens, of course, find similar escape with drugs.

Though teen drug use is often seen as simple hedonism or rebellion, in fact, the teenagers who are most at risk for lasting drug problems are those like Amber, whose stress response systems have suffered an early and lasting blow. Research on addicts and alcoholics finds dramatically increased numbers of early traumatic events, as compared to those who have not suffered addictions. The most severe addicts' histories—especially amongst women—are filled with childhood sexual abuse, loss of parents through divorce or death, witnessing severe violence, physical abuse and neglect and other trauma. Brain scans of those who've experienced trauma often reveal abnormalities in areas that also show changes during addiction. It may be that these changes make them more vulnerable to getting hooked.

While self-mutilation, too, is often seen as an act of rebellion or attention-seeking, in most cases it is probably better understood as an attempt at self-medication as well. Cutting releases brain opioids, which makes it especially attractive to those who have been previously traumatized and found relief in dissociation. Although anyone who cuts will experience some degree of opioid effect, the experience is far more likely to be perceived as pleasurable and attractive to those who have a sensitized dissociative response from previous trauma and are in emotional pain. The same is true of people who use drugs like heroin or OxyContin. Contrary to popular belief, most people who try these drugs do not find them overwhelmingly blissful. In fact, most people don't like the numbing sensation they produce. But those who suffer the after-effects of severe stress and trauma are likely to find the substances soothing and comforting, not deadening.

Curiously, stimulant drugs like cocaine and amphetamine replicate the other common natural reaction to trauma: the hyperarousal response. Both drugs increase the release of the neurotransmitters dopamine and noradrenaline (also called norepinephrine). Both of those brain chemicals skyrocket during hyperarousal. Just as the dissociative experience bears a physiological and psychological resemblance to the opioid "high," the stimulant high is physiologically and psychologically comparable to the hyperaroused state. In both stimulant "highs" and hyperarousal, the person experiences an elevated heart rate, heightened senses and a feeling of power and possibility. That feeling is needed to fuel fight or flight, but it also explains why stimulants increase paranoia and aggression. Brain changes related to hyperarousal may make some trauma victims more prone to stimulant addiction, while those related to dissociation may prefer opioids like heroin.

AS MY COLLEAGUES AND I BEGAN to recognize how trauma affects the brain and body, we began to look for pharmacological methods to treat some of its symptoms. We hoped that this might prevent the children we were able to reach at an early age from developing problems like drug addiction and self-mutilation later on. We knew, for example, that opioid-blocking drugs like naloxone and naltrexone might reasonably be tried to blunt sensitized dissociation. We had already studied clonidine as a way to reduce hyperarousal. Though Mama P. had, with some justification, been afraid that we might "drug up" the children she cared for if we used medications—or that we might decide that medications were all that was needed, and leave out love and affection—we found that the right medication can be helpful if used in the right context.

One of the first patients we tried naltrexone with was a sixteen-year-old boy named Ted. Like Amber, he had come to our attention because of his physical symptoms, not his psychological problems. Ted had what seemed to be unpredictable fainting episodes; sometimes at school, he would pass out. As in Amber's case, medical tests revealed no discernable heart disorder, nor did he have a diagnosable neurological problem like epilepsy or a brain tumor that might cause such symptoms. Throwing up their hands and deciding that Ted was inducing unconsciousness in some kind of bizarre teenage attention-seeking gesture, the doctors who had ruled out these other problems called in psychiatry.

Ted was tall, rail-thin, and good-looking, but he carried himself as though he were depressed: slouching, moving with little confidence, seeming as though he wanted to disappear. He didn't meet the criteria for depression, however. He didn't report unhappiness, lack of energy, suicidal thoughts, social distress, sleeping problems, or any of the other classic symptoms of the disorder. His only apparent problem was that about twice a week, he would suddenly faint.

When I began to talk to him, though, I discovered that there was more. "I feel like a robot sometimes," he told me, describing how he felt removed from the emotional aspects of his life, almost like he was watching a movie or going through the motions without fully experiencing what was happening around him. He felt detached, disconnected, numb: classic descriptions of dissociation. As I got to know him I began to find out what had prompted his brain to protect him from the world. Starting before elementary school, Ted had been a continual witness to domestic violence. His stepfather frequently beat his mother, and this was not just the occasional slap or push, but rather full-on assaults that left her bruised, scarred, and terrorized into complete submission. More than once, his mother had to be hospitalized. As Ted got older he began to try to protect his mother and found that he could redirect the man's rage from her to him. As he put it, "I'd rather get a beating then watch my mother get beat up." Although it didn't happen immediately, it was seeing her child hurt that finally prompted Ted's mom to end the relationship.

But by this point, Ted was ten years old. He'd lived most of his life with the daily threat or actual occurrence of serious violence. He'd become socially withdrawn and isolated. His teachers called him a "daydreamer," noting that he often seemed to be "miles away" rather than paying attention to the class around him. However, he participated enough to get average, though not outstanding, grades. Even more so than Amber, he seemed to have discovered a way of fading into the background, recognizing that earning grades that were either too low or too high would bring him attention. He didn't care if the attention for high grades was positive, since he found any attention stressful, even threatening. Ted seemed to have made up his mind that the best way to avoid any potential for further abuse was to be invisible, to disappear into the vast undifferentiated gray middle. And, until he began fainting in junior high school, that's what he did.

I proposed a trial of naltrexone to see if it would stop the fainting episodes. As noted earlier, when people suffer extreme traumatic stress, their brains can become "sensitized" to future stressors, and it takes smaller and smaller amounts of stress to set the system off and prompt a full-blown stress response. As part of this stress response, especially when the stress is severe and appears inescapable, the brain releases opioids. By using a long-acting opioid blocker like naltrexone, I hoped to prevent these opioids from having an effect when they were released by his sensitized system, and thereby stop the fainting.

Ted agreed to try it and to continue seeing me for therapy.

He took the medication for four weeks, during which he had no further fainting episodes. But because the drug blocked the opioid response that allowed Ted to dissociate, he now became very anxious when he faced new or stressful experiences. This is a common problem with many drugs in psychiatry, and in general medicine. A drug may be excellent at eliminating a particular symptom, but does not treat the whole person and deal with the full complexity of his problem, and therefore it may exacerbate other symptoms. In fact, we found that parents and teachers often thought that naltrexone "made the child worse" because rather than "spacing out" in response to perceived stress, many children began to have hyperarousal symptoms instead. These "fight-or-flight" reactions appeared far more disruptive to adults because the children now appeared more active, more defiant and sometimes even aggressive. We could give clonidine to minimize the hyperarousal, but without helping the child learn alternative coping skills, the medications had no enduring effects. We ultimately decided that while there were certain cases in which naltrexone could be helpful, it had to be used with great care.

Ted had problems that ran much deeper than occasional fainting. He had a dissociative disorder that had deeply affected his ability to deal with emotional and physical challenges. In order to help this young man, and not just "resolve" the medical issue that had brought him to us, we needed to help him learn how to cope with his stress. Thanks to the naltrexone, his brain was no longer automatically responding to minor stresses by shutting down the whole system, but now we needed to help his mind learn how to handle life stress in a healthier, more comfortable and more productive way.

As with Amber, it was not only Ted's sensitized stress system that had led to his problems, it was also the associations he'd made related to his abuse that were getting in his way. When Ted and I began to talk, I started to understand that his fainting was most often triggered by interactions with men and with the trappings of masculinity—cues that reminded him of his abuser, who had been an extremely macho military man. The fainting itself had been precipitated by his entry into late adolescence, a situation that exposed him to mature men far more often than before. Now, not only did he have contact with male teachers and coaches, but also he, along with his peers, was beginning to show signs of adult manhood. As a young boy he could avoid many of these triggers, but now they were everywhere.

In order to teach him to respond to these cues without overreacting and engaging a dissociative response once he was no longer taking the naltrexone, I needed to have him experience them in a safe setting. I decided to give him the shorter-acting opioid blocker, naloxone, at the beginning of his therapy session with me, expose him to male-related cues and help him face them so that they would no longer be so powerfully stressful to him. By the end of our session, the naloxone would wear off, so that if he did experience cues later on, he could dissociate if he felt extremely threatened.

To maximize the effect, I had to act a lot more stereotypically masculine and macho than I usually do, which was a lot easier back then when I was a bit younger and in pretty good condition! On days I had therapy with Ted, I would tuck my shirt into my pants to emphasize the male characteristics of my waistline and roll up my sleeves to expose my forearm muscles. It seems silly (and sometimes it felt silly), but it allowed him to develop a healthy relationship with a male and get used to such cues. When he began to experience feelings and memories related to the abuse, I could calm him and reassure him that he was safe, and he could see for himself that he could handle things without having to shut down.

Ted was highly intelligent, and I explained the rationale for our treatment to him. He soon came up with his own ways of furthering the process. He got assigned to record statistics for the school basketball team, which would let him be around young men in situations where he would be safe and comfortable and could develop new associations to replace those that had previously prompted his symptoms. His fainting never returned and, while he continued to try to "fade into the background," he became better at fully experiencing his own life.

I made progress with Amber, too. We met each week for the first ten months following her ER visit. Since she did not have regular fainting episodes and had some degree of control over her dissociative symptoms, I decided not to use naloxone or naltrexone. I looked forward to our sessions. Her intelligence, creativity and sense of humor allowed her to articulate her story in ways that gave me greater insight into other children who weren't able to be as clear about what they were going through. But she was also fragile, overly sensitive, dark and tired inside. It takes a great deal of energy to remain vigilant and "on guard" the way Amber was; it is exhausting to view the entire world as a potential threat. She didn't just fear physical threats, either. She tended to twist positive comments from others into neutral remarks, neutral interactions into negative exchanges and any negative cues into catastrophic personal attacks.

"They hate me," she would say. She was constantly perceiving slights where none were intended, which made the relationships she did have difficult and eliminated many others before they could start. As a result, much of our time was spent trying to get her to see these interactions as clearly as she could see so much else about her life. This part of our work was basically cognitive therapy, which is one of the most effective treatments for depression. Amber's abuse had produced a number of depressive symptoms, one of which was self-hatred. Often, people like Amber believe that others can "sense" that they are unworthy and "bad," that they deserve to be hurt and rejected. They project their self-hate onto the world and become sensitized—indeed, hypersensitive—to any sign of rejection.

The key to recovery, then, is to get the patient to understand that her perceptions aren't necessarily reality, that the world might not be as dark as it seems. With Amber, it was slow work. I wanted to help her understand that not everyone was out to hurt her. There were people—teachers, peers, neighbors—who could be kind, supportive and positive. But she often shut out people to protect herself from the pain and terror Duane had brought to her in the past.

One day as she walked through my office door, she asked, "Did you know that the raven is the smartest bird?" She looked me in the eyes, almost challenging me. She plopped into a chair, putting her feet up on a little coffee table.

"No, I didn't know that. Why do you say that?" I shut the door to my office and sat down in my desk chair, swiveling it to face her.

"Corvus Corax." She spoke the Latin species name for the common raven.

"You know Latin?"

"No. That is the official name of the raven."

"You like ravens."

"I am a raven."

"You look like a girl."

"Funny. You know what I mean."

"Kind of." She was quiet. I kept going. "You want to talk animals. Let's talk about the animal world."

"OK."

"Many animals have ways to send signals to other animals—their own species and their predators." As I spoke she settled deeper in the chair. She grew quiet. I could see that I was getting close to pushing her to shut down. "Sometimes those signals say don't mess with me, I'll hurt you," I continued. "A bear rises on both feet and huffs; dogs growl and bare their teeth, the rattlesnake rattles." I paused and let the silence fill the room. I was trying to get her to understand how she gave off such powerful "leave me alone" signals. I knew she was often creating the self-fulfilling prophecy that "people don't like me." She emitted negative signals—and elicited negative responses. Then, of course, those reactions further reinforced her perception that the world is full of people who didn't like her.

She blinked and looked at me. She wasn't tuned out yet. "What does the raven do?" I asked. She smiled a little.

"The raven does this." She sat forward, leaned toward me and pulled her long sleeved shirt up. I expected to see fresh cuts. But all I saw was a new tattoo, entirely in black ink. It was a raven sitting with spread wings. She held her arm out for me to study it a bit.

"Nice ink. Who did the work?" At least she knew by now that her dark clothes, piercings, and new tattoo were sending signals.

"Bubba, down on Montrose." She rolled her sleeve back down.

"So tattooing now. Does that have the same effect as cutting?"

"Not really. It didn't hurt that much though."

"Are you cutting?"

"No. I'm trying to use those relaxation exercises. Sometimes they work OK." I had taught her a form of self-hypnosis to use in situations when she felt the urge to cut. Hypnosis helps people access their own dissociative capacity in a controlled way. I wanted Amber to gain a healthier control over when and to what degree she would use this powerful adaptive response.

I had taught her an induction technique that involved focusing on her breathing. After simply observing each breath she took for a moment or two, she would then take a number of deep, controlled breaths and count them down, from ten to one. With each inhalation she would imagine taking one step down a staircase. At the bottom of the staircase was a door, and when she opened that door she would be in her "safe" place, where no one could hurt her and where she was in total control. Once she had that technique down, we worked on helping her use it whenever she was distressed or overwhelmed, rather than cutting herself.

LITTLE BY LITTLE SHE WOULD OPEN up and then close back down. She'd discuss a bit of the hurt and shame that she carried around and then, when it got too painful, she'd withdraw again. I didn't push. I knew that her defenses were there for a reason and that, when she was ready, she'd tell me more. She kept getting more tattoos, most of them small, all of them black. There was a black rose. A black Gaelic knot. Another small raven. And still, she always dressed entirely in black.

In a later visit we talked more about how people are designed to read and respond to others. We talked about the signals we send.

"Did you know that the human brain has special neural systems that are designed to read and respond to the social cues from other people?" I held up a neuroscience journal I had been reading. I was trying, again, to get her to recognize the negative signals she was sending out to people, and that she might be misreading the social cues of others.

"Are you saying my social cue neurons are fucked up?" She had immediately jumped way past the point I was trying to make; her response itself precisely illustrated the problem I was trying to get her to address. I needed to back off a bit.

"Yikes. Where did that come from?"

"I know it's what you're thinking."

"So now your powers extend to mind reading? Can you read everyone's thoughts or just mine?" She didn't see the humor in my comment. I decided that the safest way to move forward was to approach her at a cognitive, rather than emotional, level.

"When these special neurons in the brain fire, they are almost a reflection of similar neurons firing in the brain of someone you are interacting with. They're called mirror neurons, in fact. And they're a part of the systems that our brain has to help us connect with and communicate to others. Pretty cool, right?"

She was listening. I hoped that she was processing some of this, maybe thinking about what it might mean for her. I continued, "When a mother holds her newborn baby and smiles and coos, all of the primary sensory signals—the visual input from the mother's smile, the auditory input from the cooing, the olfactory signals from the scent of the mother and the tactile information from the warmth and pressure of the mother's touch—all get turned into patterns of neural activity that go up into the brain of the baby and actually stimulate the parts of the brain that match the parts of the brain that the mother uses to smile, coo, rock, and so forth. The baby's brain is being shaped by the patterned, repetitive stimulation of the interactions from the mother!"

She was listening now. I could see that she was fully engaged, nodding her head. I said, "Pretty amazing. I love the brain." I dropped the journal back on my desk and looked at her for a response.

"You are a strange dude." She smiled. But I was pretty sure that she recognized that she had misinterpreted my comment, that I'd never said nor implied that her brain was "fucked up." She was beginning to see how her perception could differ from reality and how her reactions to people might be based on a skewed vision of the world.

AND OVER TIME, AMBER GOT BETTER. Her resting heart rate was now above sixty beats per minute and was no longer frequently dipping dangerously low. She had not had any further spells of unconsciousness. All reports from home and school suggested that she was doing well. She became more animated in our sessions. Now she talked about a small group of friends, all of them a bit marginalized, but overall healthy.

Then one day she came in, slouched down onto the chair and announced, "Well, we are moving again." She tried to act nonchalant.

"When did you find this out?"

"Yesterday. Mom got a better job in Austin. So we're moving." She stared into space, her eyes filling with tears.

"Do you know when you are going to move?"

"In a few weeks. Mom starts on the first of the month."

"Well. Let's talk about this some."

"Why?"

"Because I would guess that this feels pretty bad to you."

"So who is reading minds now? You don't know how I feel."

"Mmmm. I believe I said that I would *guess* that this feels pretty bad. Is my guess wrong?" She pulled her legs up underneath her and dipped her head to prevent me from seeing her tears. A tear dripped onto her black pants. I reached over and handed her a tissue. She took it from my hand.

"I hate this," she said quietly. I let silence fill the room. I pulled my chair closer to hers and put a hand on her shoulder, leaving it there for a few moments. We sat.

"What part do you hate the most?"

"All of it. New school, new kids, new freak in town. I hate starting over all the time."

"That must be hard." I didn't want to invalidate her feelings by trying to put a positive spin on it. I knew that we would have time later to talk through some of the potential positive aspects of a new start. I just let her spill out her frustration and sadness. I listened.

The next week, she came in, announcing, "I can't wait to get out of this town." She had already flipped to the "who cares?" mode. It is easier to leave people places if you "don't care" about them.

"So I guess all those tears last week were . . . ?" She looked at me, angry. I held her gaze and allowed her to read my face, my expression, which told her that I was sad and concerned about her, and her anger melted. We started the hard work of helping her with this transition.

During those last few weeks she struggled with how to

present herself to her new school. Was she ready to "start over?" Did she need to always project anger, darkness? Did she always have to wear black? She was beginning to think that she might be able to be softer, more open and more inviting to new relationships. Our discussions about the animal world and how the brain works had seeped into her understanding of herself.

"I can't decide what to do. I don't know if I should try to start over and be myself, or to protect myself. I don't know what to do. I don't know how to be."

"When the time comes, you will make the right choice."

"What do you mean?"

"If *you* make the choice it will be right. Just don't let anyone else choose for you; don't let your mom, or your friends, or me, or . . ." I paused and caught her eye, "the ghost of Duane make the choice for you."

"How does Duane have anything to do with this?"

"I think that the darkness is not your own. I think those things that worked when you were being abused—the disengaging, the fantasizing, the darkness you projected to the world—were forced on you by Duane."

"No. I made that world."

"Remember when you told me that when you first retreated to that world you wanted to be a songbird? A bluebird or a robin. And it didn't work?"

"Yeah."

"Those beautiful, colorful songbirds were your first choice, Amber. Maybe they didn't work then because they were too vulnerable; and you needed something more powerful, dark, menacing to protect you."

"Yeah."

"Maybe you don't need that now, Amber. Maybe it would be ok to let the birds sing."

"I don't know."

"Me neither. But when the time is right, you will know. And when the time is right you will make good choices."

Before the move, I tried to encourage her and her mother to see a new therapist in Austin. I gave Jill a list of names and reassured her that I often worked with colleagues from a distance. I told her that I would remain available by phone or for occasional consultation visits to track Amber's progress. But ideally, I hoped that she would find a primary therapist in Austin where she could continue the work we had started. Amber didn't like that idea.

"I don't need to see a shrink. I'm not crazy."

"Have I been treating you like you are crazy?"

"No." She was quiet. She knew her argument was ridiculous.

"Listen, it's up to you. My opinion is that it would help you if you take the time to find the right person. Meet with these folks and you can see who you might feel comfortable talking with."

"OK." She looked at me knowing that I knew she wouldn't really try.

"Well. Just make sure that whatever choice you make, it's truly yours."

And I reached my hand out to seal the deal. She shook my hand. "Sure thing, Doc."

WE DID HEAR FROM AMBER'S MOTHER a few times in the first six months after they moved. She had taken her daughter to the first therapist on the list of referrals we'd provided, but Amber didn't like the woman. They hadn't gotten around to trying again. All too often when things seem OK, parents aren't motivated to follow through with the expense and inconvenience of therapy. Since Amber was "doing great" her mom didn't push it when Amber resisted finding a new therapist.

More than a year after Amber moved to Austin, I signed onto my email and saw a note from BlueRaven232. At first, I thought it was spam and almost deleted it. Then I saw the subject: "New Tattoo." I read it:

Dear Doc:
Wanted you to be the first to know. I got a new tattoo;
a bouquet of flowers—orange, red, purple and blue.
Real girly girl. No black ink. Blue Raven

I wrote back.

Thanks for the note, sounds like a nice choice. Good
work. One question: Sky Blue Raven?
Dr. P.

Later that day, she wrote back:

No. Navy Blue Raven. Hey, it's a start, right?

I smiled as I typed back:

It's a good start, Amber.

Every now and again, I get email from Blue Raven. She is now a young adult. She went to college and graduated in four years. Like all of us, she has had her ups and downs. But from what I can tell she is a healthy, productive and caring young woman. She works with young children now and can't decide whether to go back to school to become a social worker, police officer or a teacher. I suspect, however, that she will make the right choice for her. And I know that because of what she's been through and what she learned about how trauma can shape a child's view of the world, in whatever capacity she works with children they will be very lucky to know her.

CHAPTER 9

"Mom Is Lying. Mom Is Hurting Me.
Please Call the Police."

ONE OF THE HAZARDS OF RUNNING a clinic for maltreated and traumatized children is success: if you develop a reputation for being able to help these young people, you will inevitably be unable to keep up with the demand. It can be hard to increase staff and services and still maintain the high-quality, individualized, and time-intensive care the children need. This was why our working group ultimately decided to maximize our ability to get the best care to the most children by focusing on research and training. Our educational efforts target all of the adults who live and work with maltreated children—from psychiatrists to policy makers to police officers and parents. We continue to do clinical work with multiple service partners across the country, but back in 1998 most of this work was based at our large clinic in Houston. James, a six-year-old boy became one of our patients. Our work in his case was not therapy; I had been asked to provide expert input on his complex situation. James taught me a great deal about courage and determination, and reminded me how important it is to listen, paying close attention to the children themselves.

James was referred to us by a judge who had received so many different opinions about the boy's situation that he hoped we could clarify what was going on. A children's legal advocacy organization was worried that he was being abused by his adoptive parents. Numerous therapists and Child Protective Services, however, believed that he was such a troublemaker that his adoptive family had needed a break from him. Teachers reported unexplained bruises and scratches. The boy had been adopted before his first birthday by a couple who had also taken in three other children and had one biological child. James was the second oldest. When we met him, his oldest sibling was eight and the youngest, a girl, was an infant.

According to his mother, Merle,* James was incorrigible and uncontrollable. He frequently ran away from home, he tried to jump out of moving cars, he attempted suicide and wet his bed. By age six he had been hospitalized numerous times, once after jumping from a second story balcony. He lied constantly, especially about his parents, and seemed to enjoy defying them. He was being prescribed antidepressants and other medications for impulsivity and attention problems. He'd seen numerous therapists, psychiatrists, counselors and social workers. His mother said he was so unmanageable that she called Child Protective Services on herself, pretending to be a neighbor concerned that his mother could not handle him and that he was a danger to himself and his siblings. The last straw was an overdose of medication he'd taken that had landed him in an intensive care unit. He was so close to death that he had to be flown to the hospital in a helicopter for rapid treatment. Now he'd been taken to a residential treatment center to give his mother a "respite." The judge had been asked to determine what should happen next.

CPS caseworkers and several therapists believed he had Reactive Attachment Disorder (RAD), a diagnosis frequently given to children who have suffered severe early neglect and/or trauma. Leon, who ultimately killed two girls, may have had this disorder: it is marked by a lack of empathy and an inability to connect with others, often accompanied by manipulative and antisocial behavior. RAD can occur when infants don't receive enough rocking, cuddling and other nurturing physical and emotional attention. The regions of their brains that help them form relationships and decode social cues do not develop properly, and they grow up with faulty relational neurobiology, including an inability to derive pleasure from healthy human interactions.

RAD symptoms can include the "failure to thrive" and stunted growth we saw in Laura's case. The disorder is often seen in people like Laura's mother Virginia, who was moved to a new foster home every six months and not allowed to develop a lasting early attachment with one or two primary caregivers. Children raised in institutions like orphanages are also at risk, as are children like Justin and Connor. In addition to being unresponsive to people they know, many children with RAD are inappropriately affectionate with strangers: they seem to see people as interchangeable because they were not given the chance to make a primary, lasting connection with a parent or parent-substitute from birth. These indiscriminately affectionate behaviors are not really an attempt to connect with others, however, but rather they are more accurately understood as "submission" behaviors, which send signals to the dominant and powerful adults that you will be obedient, submissive and no threat. RAD children have learned that affectionate behaviors can neutralize potentially threatening adults, but they don't seem to engage in them as a way to form lasting, emotional ties.

Fortunately, RAD is rare. Unfortunately, many parents and mental health workers have latched onto it as an explanation for a wide range of misbehavior, especially in adopted and foster children. Treatments like "holding," which were so harmful to the Gilmer, Texas, children, are pitched as "cures" for RAD, as are other coercive and potentially abusive treatments that involve emotional attacks and heavy-handed discipline. James's therapist, for example, had recommended that his mother lock him in a closet when his behavior got too wild.

The therapist and the mother's description of James's behavior did seem to fit the diagnosis. But there was something decidedly odd about James's records. When he was in the hospital or in a residential treatment center, he was well behaved. He didn't try to run away, didn't threaten suicide. His behavior in school was unremarkable aside from some minor aggression toward other boys, nothing like the out-of-control demon his mother consistently complained about. And there was something else, too: his adoptive parents' behavior was unusual. They would show up for his appointments with us (he was living in a treatment center at the time) when they had explicitly been told not to do so; one time his father came with a gift for him and waited around for hours. When one of our staff interviewed James's mother, she seemed entirely focused on herself and her own problems, repeatedly expressing her distress about being separated from him, but not any concern about what he might be going through.

When I met James, I instantly liked him. He was a bit small for his age, with curly blond hair. He was engaging, behaved appropriately and reciprocated eye contact and smiles. In fact, he laughed and joked with me and seemed to like my company. Stephanie, his primary clinician on our interdisciplinary team, felt the same way about him. After four sessions we had planned to stop seeing him because we felt we had enough information for our evaluation.

At our clinic we coordinate and discuss a patient's care in

staff meetings, where everyone involved in a particular child's case comes together to "staff" the child. We thoroughly discuss each person's interactions with the patient and their impressions of him or her. In the staffing for James, Stephanie became emotional; she'd liked the boy and was sad that she wouldn't be working with him anymore. When I saw her near tears, my perspective on the case shifted.

If a child has RAD, the lack of connection and attachment goes both ways. There is a reciprocal neurobiology to human relationships—our "mirror neurons" create this. As a result, these children are difficult to work with because their lack of interest in other people and their inability to empathize makes them hard to like. Interacting with them feels empty, not engaging. Stephanie shouldn't have been so upset at disconnecting from a child with RAD; there should have been no loss of relational contact to miss. Therapists are as human as anyone else, and the lack of rewarding interactions with RAD children tends to make working with them feel like a burden, not a joy. The anger and despair that their coldness and unpleasant behavior can provoke may be the reason why so many parents are attracted to therapies for it that are harsh and punitive and why therapists so often converge on these harmful techniques. Most therapists feel relieved if the therapy ends. But James had endeared himself to Stephanie and me and, as we discussed him, I realized that he could not have genuine RAD.

We began to look more closely at his records and at the different versions of the events contained there. That overdose, for example. With a little additional research we discovered that James had run away from home earlier the same day and had been returned to his mother by sheriff's deputies. Within an hour, according to Merle, he'd "taken an overdose" of an antidepressant. She called the poison control hotline and operators told her to get the child to the hospital immediately. Inexplicably, Merle hadn't driven to the hospital. Instead, she went to a nearby super-market, and what should have been a ten-minute drive from her home to that shop somehow took her half an hour. After parking, she ran screaming into the store, seemingly hysterical about her unconscious child. EMS was called. Recognizing the urgency of the situation, paramedics rapidly called in a Life Flight helicopter to take him to the hospital.

Now we learned that medical staff had been suspicious of Merle almost every time she'd had contact with them. As EMS workers fought frantically to stabilize the boy at the market, she'd sat calmly, sipping a soda, her hysterics and worry about the child mysteriously ended, even though his survival was still far from assured. At the hospital, upon being given the good news that he would pull through, Merle shocked the doctor by asking that the boy be removed from life support. One ER nurse suspected her of tampering with the medical equipment. As soon as he was conscious and his mother was not present, James told hospital staff, "Mom is lying. Mom is hurting me. Please call the police."

Suddenly, James's behavior made sense to us. There had been numerous aspects of his story that didn't "fit," that made no sense in the context of what I knew about child behavior. Over time one's sense of how certain kinds of youth are likely to behave in certain circumstances becomes intuitive and, when something doesn't "seem right," it's a signal one should give close attention. That's how I knew, for example, that Stephanie and I weren't reacting the way we would if James had really had RAD. Such "trained intuition" is a large part of what distin-guishes experts from amateurs in most fields. We don't always consciously know what it is that doesn't fit, but somewhere our brain recognizes that part of the puzzle is missing, and it sends up a signal that something's askew. (This "gut feeling" is actu-ally a low-level activation of the stress response system, which is acutely attuned to combinations of incoming signals that are out of context or novel.)

It was clear to me that James had run away because his mother was harming him, not because he was defiantly misbehaving. Running away is uncommon among children his age, even those who are abused: even the most severely battered and neglected elementary school children tend to fear change and strangeness more than they fear losing the only parents they have ever known. They prefer the certainty of misery to the misery of uncertainty. The younger the child, the more important familiar people and situations usually are. Many such children have begged me to return them to violent and dangerous parents. But James was different. His behavior was that of someone seeking help, not of someone who had difficulty forming attachments and relationships.

From this new perspective I could see that the boy hadn't jumped off the second-floor balcony or tried to leap out of moving cars. He'd been pushed. James hadn't voluntarily swallowed a whole bottle of antidepressants: the "overdose" had been forced on him. He was not manipulative nor was he "acting out," he was simply trying to get help for himself and his siblings in the only ways he knew how. And he refused to give up, despite being disregarded, ignored, disbelieved and even punished for telling the truth.

Merle had almost succeeded in killing James at least twice: his helicopter ride following the "overdose" had not been his first experience with Life Flight transportation. He'd been helicoptered to the hospital following the "fall" from the second-story balcony as well. James was scheduled to return to her home after the "respite care" and, worse, his adoptive siblings were, as we sat around discussing the case, still in that dangerous household. I am ordinarily extremely cautious, but I knew once we figured out what had happened that those children were in imminent danger. I contacted the authorities and asked the judge to have CPS remove the other children immediately and seek permanent termination of parental rights.

James's case plunged me into the heart of one of the key conflicts in child psychiatry: although the patient is the child, he is not the one that gets to make most decisions about his care and treatment, and he is often not the person who provides the initial information about the case. We'd been told by Merle that James was sick, but James was sick only because Merle had been making him that way. James's case had been framed as that of a "difficult" child with "behavior problems." But he was really a courageous, persistent and ethical child who'd been placed in an impossible situation—one in which his every attempt to help himself and his siblings was framed as evidence of his "bad behavior."

Those of us who work with troubled children have to guard constantly against our preconceptions about a situation; one person's "troubled teen" may be another person's "victim of sexual abuse," and the label given to the child often determines how he is treated. A child seen as "bad" will be treated differently from one viewed as "mad," and both will have their behavior seen in a very different light depending on whether the clinician sees a "victim" or a "perpetrator." Further, depending upon one's point of view, the exact same behavior can be framed as "running away" or "seeking help" and the perspective will profoundly affect decisions about what to do for and to the child.

While most parents have their children's best interests at heart, it is also true that disturbed children often have disturbed parents who may be the direct cause of the children's problems. It is a serious challenge to engage the parents and to keep the child in therapy, but to avoid supporting them in ongoing actions that will do him harm. Many children are lost to treatment because the parents are either unwilling or unable to change harmful behavior patterns, and such parents often rapidly become suspicious of any treatment that doesn't place the blame for any difficulties squarely on the child.

In James's case, Merle continuously "doctor shopped," seeking professionals who viewed him as a case of RAD and dropping those who questioned her actions or judgment too closely. She was able to present the opinions of therapists and social workers in support of her case to child welfare authorities, leaving out the views of those who disagreed with the diagnosis.

However, to be fair, I should also point out that many parents also do have good reason to avoid stigmatizing, parent-blaming theories of mental illness: not long ago, schizophrenia was believed to be caused by "schizophrenogenic mothers" and autism was blamed on "refrigerator moms," (mothers who are "cold" and uncaring). We now know that genetics and biology play the major role in the etiology of those conditions. But abuse and trauma can also produce similar symptoms. As we have seen, children like Connor and Justin, whose problems were solely due to abuse and neglect, are often labeled autistic, schizophrenic, and/or brain damaged. Their problems, however, were the result of a damaging environment. It is an ongoing challenge for child psychiatry to distinguish between diseases like schizophrenia and autism and disorders caused by early abuse and neglect, and it is even more difficult to understand and take into account how early childhood trauma can express underlying genetic vulnerabilities. For example, people with genuine schizophrenia are far more likely than others to have a history of childhood abuse or trauma; all complex human conditions, even those that involve a strong genetic component, can also be affected by the environment. The challenge of treating these children and dealing with their parents becomes even more daunting in cases like that of James, in which the parents are deliberately deceptive.

Merle would turn out to have a condition called Munchausen syndrome by proxy. Munchausen syndrome is named after an eighteenth-century German Baron, Karl Friedrich von Munchausen, who was known for the exuberantly exaggerated tall tales he told. Patients with Munchausen syndrome, usually women, deliberately make themselves ill in order to get medical attention and sympathy from others. They go from doctor to doctor, undergoing unnecessary painful and invasive tests and procedures. In order to produce convincing symptoms they go to great extremes—contaminating IV lines with feces to cause infection, for example. In Munchausen by proxy syndrome (MBPS), the patient tries to make another person, usually a child, sick, in a similar ploy for attention and support.

The cause is not known, but it clearly involves problems with dependency. People like Merle have a pathological need to be needed and their identities revolve around being seen as nurturers and helpers. Having a sick or injured child allows them to display this aspect of themselves; they live for the concerned glances, hugs of support, and medical attention they get when the child is hospitalized. Often they attract partners who are extremely passive and whose own needs for care and direction are met by being with someone who has such a strong desire for control and utility. Merle's husband fit that description perfectly. What people with MBPS cannot cope with is a child's maturation and the decreased neediness and increased independence that goes along with it. Often, they "solve" this problem by having or adopting additional younger or sicker children, but in Merle's case, she seemed to have a specific need for James in particular to be ill. And his resistance and running away, which was not getting her the attention and support from professionals she thought she'd get, became increasingly threatening to her. Since a mother whose young child has died is the ultimate object of sympathy, and since James's behavior could expose her and lead to her losing custody of her other children, his life was increasingly in jeopardy. Mothers with Munchausen by proxy are extremely dangerous. They may succeed in killing several children before they are caught because the very idea of a mother killing a child is so monstrous. The sympathy for parents who have lost children is also so natural and automatic that the deaths are often not thoroughly investigated. In many cases the children are killed in infancy and their demise ascribed to Sudden Infant Death Syndrome (SIDS). In fact, the research paper originally used to claim that SIDS has a genetic origin was based primarily on the case of a mother who had supposedly lost five successive children to SIDS. It turned out that the mother had MBPS and had smothered the children to death. She was ultimately convicted of the murders.

One of the earliest studies of Munchausen by proxy involved covertly videotaping mothers suspected of having the condition. Thirty-nine mothers with MBPS were caught on tape; some tampered with life support machines, some smothered their babies with pillows, and one even forced her fingers down her infant's throat. Twelve siblings of these children were found to have died suddenly and, when confronted with the videotapes, four of the mothers confessed to having killed eight of the babies.

Unfortunately, increased attention to the disorder has also led to wrongful prosecutions of women whose children genuinely did die of SIDS. Because, thankfully, both multiple SIDS deaths in one family and Munchausen by proxy are exceptionally rare, the limited data available has made distinguishing between the two causes of death tricky. The British pediatrician who originally named the syndrome, Roy Meadow, devised the basis of what became known as Meadow's law regarding infant deaths: "One sudden infant death is a tragedy, two is suspicious and three is murder until proved otherwise." Recently, however, he lost his medical license after his expert testimony on the foundations of his "law" turned out not to be supported by the data. The convictions of numerous women based on this "law" are being revisited, although Meadow's license has now been returned. At least three convictions have already been overturned.

The Meadow debacle has led some to doubt even the existence of Munchausen's as a specific form of child abuse, but there are clear cases like Merle's and like those of the parents in the videotapes who deliberately harm their children in order to get support and medical attention. Around 9 percent of children born to women with this disorder die at their hands, and many more suffer serious injuries and are subjected to hundreds of unneeded and painful medical procedures. Unfortunately, because so little is known about its cause, there are very few clues to diagnosing it. Few males have MBPS; and MBPS may be overrepresented in women who work in the health care field. Many seem to have suffered childhood trauma or abuse themselves—often severe neglect—but the overwhelming majority of women who work in health care or who were victims of childhood trauma never develop this condition. It may be on the pathological end of a spectrum of healthy behaviors stemming from a desire to nurture others and be valued for it—a case of too much of a good thing. The same dependency may drive other people to extreme acts of caring and altruism. How some slip from desperately wanting to help others into feeling compelled to hurt them so that help will always be needed, I cannot say.

Thankfully, the judge took our advice and, on an emergency basis, removed James and his siblings from the custody of Merle and her husband. A civil jury later agreed that James had been abused by his adoptive mother and that the father had not intervened to prevent it. Evidence was presented that proved how James's mother had twisted his words and actions to portray him as a troubled child and hide her own depravity. The couple's parental rights in relation to all five children—including their one biological child—were terminated and criminal child abuse charges were also filed against them.

I hear occasionally from the prosecutor in the case, who has stayed in touch with James and his new adoptive parents. His name has been changed and, last I heard, he was thriving in his new life. His "disruptive" behavior and running away was entirely a product of his attempt to get help. I believe he saved not only his own life, but those of his siblings as well. His story reminds me to trust my gut and always keep listening to the child, no matter what other therapists, official reports and even parents may say.

CHAPTER 10

The Kindness of Children

I watched them a few moments before I walked into the waiting room. The boy's behavior had an innocent sweetness to it: I could see him smiling, crawling into his mother's lap, squirming so that he could sit face-to-face with her. Then, he tenderly reached his hand up to her mouth and touched her, playful, exploring. The quiet interaction between the two was classic bonding behavior between a mother and an infant, even a toddler. But Peter was seven. As I watched them, I could tell that mother and child had frequently engaged in this gentle, soothing game. When I walked in I also noticed that Amy*, the mom, was embarrassed by it. Her husband, Jason,* Peter's father, seemed even more ashamed when I appeared to have "caught" them.

"Sit up, Peter," Jason said as he stood up and shook my hand.

I walked over to the boy, stood over him, looked down, and smiled, "Hi, Peter." I put my hand out. Peter reached up to touch my hand.

"Peter, stand up and shake Dr. Perry's hand," Jason said. Amy tried to push Peter off her lap to his feet. Peter went limp and laughed. It seemed like part of their game.

"Peter, stand up," Jason said again, his voice patient but firm. I could feel his frustration and exhaustion. I knew they had their hands full.

"That's OK. You guys just get comfortable. I just wanted to see how you think things went today." I sat down across from them. "This first visit is really just to give Peter a chance to come and meet some of us and start to get familiar with us. Hopefully, you had some fun today."

Peter nodded.

"Use words, honey," Amy said.

Peter sat up and said, "Yes."

The family had just spent three hours in our clinic for an intake appointment. They had come to see us because Peter had a long history of speech and language problems, as well as difficulties with attention and impulsivity. Not surprisingly, he also had social and academic problems in school. Occasionally he had bizarre and ferocious outbursts in which he seemed to completely lose control. They were terrifying and, unlike ordinary temper tantrums, could last for hours.

Peter's parents had adopted him from a Russian orphanage when he was three years old. They had immediately fallen in love with the blonde, blue-eyed boy with rosy cheeks who looked like a little angel. The operators of the orphanage had proudly shown off how well fed he was and how clean their facility was but, in truth, Peter and the other children who lived there had been profoundly neglected. Amy and Jason had heard about our work with maltreated children from other adoptive parents. We were at the end of the first day of a two-day consultation visit at our clinic. The family had traveled over five hundred miles for the evaluation.

"So, Peter, will you come back and visit us tomorrow?" I asked.

"Yes," he said with a big smile.

Our clinicians had a lot of work to do before then. During a typical evaluation, our interdisciplinary group of psychologists, social workers, child psychiatry fellows, and child psychiatrists usually spread multiple visits out over a few weeks to get to know a child and his family. In Peter's case the process was condensed because he lived so far away. Records from the schools, the child's pediatrician, previous mental health providers and other professionals were available to review, process and integrate into our impressions of the child and family. We also did a brain scan, an MRI, as part of a study we were working on to see how early neglect affected the brain. The data from our research has shown that significant early life neglect such as that seen in formerly institutionalized children like Peter leads to smaller brain size over all, brain shrinkage in certain regions, and a host of brain-related functional problems. By finding which areas were most affected in Peter's case, we hoped to target our treatments to maximal effect.

During the evaluation period, sometimes as many as a dozen staff members would meet to talk about what we were seeing and experiencing with this child. It was a process designed to identify the child's strengths and vulnerabilities, and carefully determine his current developmental stage in a host of domains—from perceptual abilities to motor skills, from emotional, cognitive and behavioral abilities to moral sentiments. This enabled us to come to a preliminary diagnosis and make our initial recommendations for intervention. Although it would be too time consuming and expensive to replicate in many settings, we hoped to develop models of care based on this process that would be less staff intensive.

At the time we began working with Peter and his family, we'd made good progress on our neurosequential approach to mal-treated children. We'd recognized that victims of early trauma and neglect need experiences—such as rocking and being held—appropriate for the age at which they'd suffered damage or deprivation, not for their chronological age. We'd found that these developmentally appropriate enrichment and therapeutic experiences had to be provided repeatedly and consistently in a respectful and caring manner. Coercive, punitive and forceful delivery only made things worse. We'd also started to incorporate music, dance and massage in order to stimulate and organize the lower brain regions, which contain the key regulatory neurotransmitter systems involved in the stress response. As we've seen, these areas are more likely to be affected by early trauma because they undergo important, fast-paced development early in life. Finally, we'd begun to use medications to help children with troublesome dissociative or hyperarousal symptoms.

But while we had realized that ongoing relationships are critical to healing, we hadn't yet fully understood how important peer relationships are, especially as children get older.

The details of Peter's past brought the critical role of relationships into vivid focus for me. Peter had been raised without adult attention for the first three years of his life. He'd been kept in what was basically a baby warehouse: a big, bright room with sixty infants in seemingly endless, straight rows of perfectly sanitized cribs. The two caretakers on duty for each shift would work methodically from one bed to the next, feeding each child, changing his or her diaper, then moving on. That was all the individual adult attention the babies received: roughly fifteen minutes each per eight-hour shift. The infants were rarely spoken to or held other than during these brief intervals; they were not rocked or cradled or cooed at because there simply wasn't time for staff to do more than feed and change, feed and change. Even the toddlers spent their days and nights caged in their cribs.

With no one but each other to turn to, the children would reach their tiny hands through the bars into the next crib, holding hands, babbling and playing patty-cake. In the absence of adults, they became parents to each other. Their interaction, as impoverished as it was, probably helped to mitigate some of the damage such severe deprivation can cause.

When Peter's adoptive parents first brought him home, they discovered that he was trying to communicate with them. Delighted, they sought a Russian translator. But the Russian translator said his speech wasn't Russian—perhaps the orphanage workers had been immigrants from elsewhere in Eastern Europe who had taught the children to speak their native tongue? A Czech speaker said it wasn't Czech, however, and soon Amy and Jason learned that Peter wasn't speaking Hungarian or Polish, either.

To their surprise, they found that the words Peter spoke didn't belong to any known language. Apparently, the orphans had developed their own rudimentary language, like the private speech of twins or the improvised signing of deaf children raised together. Like King Psamtik of Egypt, who, according to Herodotus, isolated two children to learn what language they would "naturally" speak without the opportunity to learn from people around them, the operators of the orphanage had created a harsh and accidental experiment in linguistics. On their own, the children had apparently created and agreed upon several dozen words. One word the translators were able to figure out was that "Mum" meant "adult or caregiver," just as similar sounds mean mother in almost every known human language, since the "mm" sound is the first one babies learn to make while suckling.

In our clinical meeting, my team and I went over everything we knew about the boy's early history, including his limited exposure to adults and his linguistic deprivation. We also discussed his adoptive parents. My initial impression of Amy and Jason was confirmed by the rest of the staff: everyone agreed that they were remarkable. Even before they'd adopted Peter, they had read parenting books, watched parenting videos and talked extensively with their pediatrician about what to expect when adopting a child like him. After they brought Peter home they worked with speech and language therapists, occupational therapists, physical therapists and mental health providers to help Peter catch up.

They followed the advice they were given diligently. They spent money, time and energy trying to give Peter what he needed to grow up healthy, happy, productive and compassionate. Yet, despite all of their best efforts, and the efforts of the dozens of specialists, Peter continued to struggle. He had improved dramatically in many regards, but his progress was spotty, slow and incremental.

He would learn new skills only after hundreds of repetitions, not dozens like other children. He learned English but his enunciation was strange and his grammar was mangled. His movements were also uncoordinated, and even when he tried to sit still, he would sway. Also, he would rarely establish or maintain eye contact appropriately. At seven, he still had several primitive self-soothing behaviors, primarily rocking and sucking his thumb. He would sniff extensively at everything that he ate before putting it into his mouth and also tried noticeably to catch the scent of people whenever he met them. He was easily distracted and often laughed and smiled to himself, giving the impression that he was in "his own little world." And in the last year he seemed to have hit a developmental plateau, and perhaps even regressed a bit.

We first discussed Peter's strengths, starting with his friendly, almost goofy manner. He was also well above average in some aspects of language and seemed to have some mathematical talents. He was extremely nurturing, but in a blatantly immature fashion, responding to peers and adults the way a toddler might.

It became clear through our discussions that while Peter was in some ways cognitively seven, in other domains, he acted much younger. Confirming our observations regarding the use-dependent nature of brain development, the areas where he was doing better were related to brain regions that had received stimulation, and those where he had deficits represented brain regions that had either been more severely deprived or had not yet received enough stimulation to make up for the earlier neglect. The scans of his brain reinforced our observations of this fractured neurodevelopment: he had cortical atrophy, large ventricles (which meant that spinal fluid was taking up space that would normally have been occupied by brain tissue) and lower-brain structures that were small for his age and likely underdeveloped.

Such splintered development is common in children who grow up in chaotic or neglectful environments. It causes tremendous confusion for parents, teachers and peers. From the outside, Peter looked like a seven-year-old boy, but in some ways he was only a three-year-old. In terms of other skills and capabilities, he was eighteen months old, and he was eight or nine years old in still other respects.

This inconsistency was a major source of the family's problems. There were also important differences in the way each parent interacted with Peter. When he was home and alone with Amy, she was extremely attuned to his needs. If he acted like a baby, she would engage him at that age level, and if he acted like an older child, she would interact with him that way. I believe that her intuitive capacity to meet his developmental needs was the primary reason he had made as much progress as he had. But as Peter got older Jason began to question some of Amy's "babying" of the boy. This caused tension in the marriage, with Jason arguing that Amy was responsible for Peter's lack of progress because she was "smothering" him, while Amy insisted that he needed the extra affection because of his past. Such differences are an almost universal feature of parenting. However, when disagreements are profound as they were becoming in Amy and Jason's case, they can lead to serious marital problems.

I had seen the conflict in my brief interaction with the family in the waiting room. Part of my job would be to help the couple understand Peter's needs and explain to them how it was necessary to meet him where he was developmentally. That way, they would be able to learn to avoid overwhelming Peter and frustrating themselves by requiring age-appropriate behavior in a domain for which he did not yet have the capacity.

When the family came in for the second day of the evaluation we gave Peter some formal psychological tests. Later we observed more parent/child interactions and sent the boy off for another play break. Finally, it was time to tell the parents what we thought about Peter's case and what we proposed to do to help him. I could see that Amy and Jason were anxious as soon as I walked into the room.

"What do you think?" Jason said, clearly wanting to get bad news out of the way.

"I think Peter is really a very lucky boy," I began. "You are wonderful parents. And he has shown remarkable progress over the last four years." I paused for a moment to let that sink in. Then, I added, "Your efforts are heroic. You must be exhausted." Amy started to cry. Her husband tenderly put his arm around her. I got some tissue and handed it to her. She wiped her eyes.

I began to tell them what I thought, asking them to interrupt if I said anything that they thought wasn't accurate or didn't make sense. I related Peter's history as I understood it, recounting the details of the orphanage and the list of developmental delays he had experienced.

Then I asked if I was right in suspecting that when Peter became upset, all of his developmental progress would seem to disappear and he would act in primitive, almost frightening ways. Perhaps he'd lie on the floor in the fetal position, moaning and rocking, or perhaps he'd let out unearthly screams. I added that I thought that once he started to get stirred up or overwhelmed he probably reached a "point of no return," and that he seemed to regress before slowly coming back to himself. They nodded. That's when I explained how changes in our emotional state can affect how we learn. Skills that we've mastered like comprehension of certain concepts or even use of language itself may dissipate when we get "worked up." I talked about how new or frightening situations would be stressful to a child like Peter and would likely prompt this kind of regression.

Wrapping up what we'd learned from the evaluation, I said, "So, I think we have a pretty good idea about Peter's problems and how he ended up with them. We also know some of his strengths—not all, but some. The key now is whether we can use what we know to help him." I paused, struggling to strike a balance between hope and caution.

"Let me take a moment and talk with you about how the brain develops," I began, "I think if you understand this a little bit more you will feel better about the progress that Peter has made, and I think you will better understand why progress now seems so slow." As I spoke, my thoughts about the theory and practice I'd been working on for so many years seemed to crystallize for the first time as a coherent whole.

I drew several charts on a blank piece of paper. The first (see Appendix, Figure 1) showed a simple comparison of the growth of the brain relative to the growth of the rest of the body, making the point that while the body doesn't reach its adult height and weight until adolescence, the brain's growth follows a much different path. By age three it has reached 85 percent of its full adult size.

"The human brain grows most rapidly early in life," I

explained, "In fact, the majority of brain growth takes place in the first three years of life." I wanted to help them understand the full significance of the fact that Peter had been in a sterile, neglectful institution during that critical period when the brain is rapidly organizing itself.

Then I drew a pyramid and turned the page upside down (See Appendix, Figure 2). "The brain is organized from the bottom to the top," I said. "The top part here," I noted as I pointed to the wide base of the upside-down pyramid, "is the cortex, the most complex part of the brain, responsible for our ability to think and for integrating many of our functions." I also described how some of the lower regions work, how the central emotional areas allow us to make social connections and control our stress and how the core brainstem areas drive the stress response itself. I explained how these regions "awaken" sequentially during development, starting from the innermost brainstem and moving out toward the cortex as the child grows. I discussed how the development of higher, more complex brain regions relies on proper organization of the lower, simpler areas. I explained how deprivation could affect these regions and cause the wide variations in their son's behavior.

"The key is to parent Peter where he is developmentally, not where he is chronologically," I said. Jason nodded, beginning to understand what I was saying. "Which is a very difficult thing to do, right?"

Now, both parents nodded.

"The challenge is that, in one moment, you will need to have expectations and provide experiences that are appropriate for a five-year-old, for example, when you are teaching him a specific cognitive concept. Ten minutes later, however, the expectation and challenges will have to match those for a younger child, for example, when you are trying to teach him to interact socially. He is, developmentally, a moving target. This is why parenting these children is such a frustrating experience. One moment you are doing the correct thing and the next, you are out of sync."

Amy and Jason had experienced this dichotomy many times, but until this conversation they hadn't been able to articulate it. My explanations helped them enormously, immediately reducing their conflict over "babying" Peter and helping Jason not worry when his wife engaged in it. Now, in fact, he could allow himself to do it as well. Amy, however, could also see from what we'd taught her that there were times when Jason's more demanding parenting style would be useful.

But explanations alone would not be enough. The core challenges of parenting Peter would remain the same—and it would be close to impossible for either parent to be attuned to him always or even most of the time without more support. Both parents were spent, emotionally and physically. We would need to help them get some respite care. We suggested bolstering their social network, taking time for themselves as a couple and doing things they enjoyed so that they could "recharge their batteries" for their time with Peter.

Amy and Jason were open to all of our suggestions. Since they did not live near our clinic, we had to work with and through their local providers. Fortunately, most of the pieces of a good clinical team were in place. Peter had an excellent speech therapist, occupational therapist, master's level therapist and an understanding pediatrician. We had talked with all of them. We wanted to add therapeutic massage and a music and movement class to his routine, which had been useful for other children who suffered early neglect, such as Connor.

But what I thought, at first, would be just another piece of the puzzle turned out to be the most important element: Peter's school and, especially, his classmates. As I looked over his history, I suddenly recognized that most of Peter's progress had come in the first three years after he came to the United States: when he spent his time alone with his parents, or with adults, or one or two peers selected by them.

When he began attending kindergarten, however, his progress had ceased and his behavior problems had intensified. His mother had intuitively understood that he was chronologically six but behaviorally two, but his classmates couldn't comprehend why he behaved so strangely. Even his teacher didn't know how to handle him, despite having been told of his background. Peter would grab toys from other children without asking, missing the social cues the other kindergartners understood about when it was OK to take something and when it wasn't. He didn't understand when he should share his things and when to keep them to himself, when he should speak and when he should be quiet. At circle time he'd suddenly get up and slip into the teacher's lap or begin to wander around without realizing he wasn't supposed to. And he'd sometimes shriek and have his terrifying tantrums.

As a result the other children began to fear and marginalize him. His oddly accented English didn't help. His classmates viewed him as a strange and frightening boy. He'd done well in the sheltered world of his adoptive home, with one-on-one relationships with adults who knew and loved him. But the complex social world of kindergarten, with its varying peer and teacher relationships to negotiate, was beyond him.

Instead of the patient, nurturing, loving responses he got at home, at kindergarten his behavior was met with suspicion and, often, outright rejection. The classroom filled with noisy children and loud toys and frequent movement was overwhelming to him. Where once he understood what was expected of him and was treated gently if he wasn't able to do it, now he couldn't figure out what was going on. No matter how many hours of healthy positive experiences Peter had each week, the hours when he was marginalized or teased could easily overshadow them.

Peter had no real friends and preferred to play with much younger children; he felt most comfortable with three- or four-year-olds. His own classmates didn't know what to make of the boy who talked funny and often acted like a baby. In many situations children can be kind and nurturing to someone who appears to be younger and more vulnerable. But Peter frightened them.

The behavior of his classmates was predictable. What was happening was a small version of what happens all across the planet in various forms every day. Human beings fear what they don't understand. The unknown scares us. When we meet people who look or act in unfamiliar or strange ways, our initial response is to keep them at arm's length. At times we make ourselves feel superior, smarter, or more competent by dehumanizing or degrading those who are different. The roots of so many of our species's ugliest behaviors—racism, ageism, misogyny, anti-Semitism, to name just a few—are in this basic brain-mediated response to perceived threat. We tend to fear what we do not understand, and fear can so easily twist into hate or even violence because it can suppress the rational parts of our brain.

Faced with Peter's growing ostracism and social rejection, Amy and Jason wanted to know what to do: should they hold him back in kindergarten, hoping he'd learn more socially the second time around? Yet his cognitive abilities were clearly on grade level for first grade, perhaps higher.

Peter was intellectually advanced, but socially clueless. I realized that if he was going to catch up, he was going to need the help of his peers. It seemed to me that we might as well try letting him start first grade. When I had worked with adolescents, some of them had allowed me to talk with their classmates about their traumatic experiences and the effect it had on their brain. A bit of understanding had gone a long way in helping improve their social lives. But could this work with first graders? And would Peter find it acceptable?

I knew that I would be in his hometown several weeks after his evaluation and could talk to his classmates at that time. I went back to explore this possibility with Peter. As we were coloring, I asked, "Peter, do you remember living in Russia?"

He stopped and looked at me for a moment. I kept slowly coloring, not looking back at him. The pace of his coloring slowed. I was just about to ask again when he took a new sheet of paper and drew a big blue circle around the entire page.

"This is Russia." He held the page up to me. He placed the paper back on the floor, took a color and made one tiny, delicate, almost invisible dot. "And this is Peter." I looked at him; he was clearly sad. He was eloquently expressing how he felt at the orphanage, where he'd been special to no one, just one of dozens of anonymous babies.

I smiled sympathetically at him, then raised my eyebrows and said, "But that isn't Peter anymore, is it?" He shook his head no, and smiled back.

"Peter, I was thinking that I would come to your first grade class to visit." I wasn't sure he would understand, but I wanted him to know what I wanted to do and why.

"OK."

"You know how we have talked about how your brain is growing and changing? I was wondering if you would mind if I talked to your class about the brain. And maybe a little about the way you lived before you came to live with your parents?"

"OK," he said, thoughtfully, adding, "Will you bring the pictures?"

"Which pictures?"

"The pictures of my brain."

"Sure. You won't mind if I show pictures of your brain to your class?"

"No. My brain is cool."

"You know, Peter, you are so right. Your brain is cool." And so, with his permission and with that of his parents and his school, I decided to see if I could make first graders into a new community of "therapists" for Peter.

I addressed his first grade class at the beginning of the school year. "I'm Peter's friend," I said. "I study the brain and Peter asked me to come from Houston to tell you some of the things about the brain that I taught him." I had Peter come up to the front of the class and serve as my assistant.

I told the first graders about the brain, and about how in some ways, it acts like a muscle. I talked about how they were exercising their "ABC" muscles in school and about the importance of repetition. I described how they had many other similar kinds of "muscles" in their brains that also needed certain kinds of attention in order to grow big and strong. I talked about how the brain develops and what makes everyone's brain work, emphasizing how the brain changes.

"Remember, Peter, when we were talking about how it takes a lot of practice to learn anything new? That is because the brain changes when you use it, use it, use it."

I looked at the children and then back at Peter, "Right, Peter?" He smiled and nodded. "And that is why your teacher keeps having you practice writing again and again; and practice your letters again and again and again."

I showed some slides; I brought a model of the brain and Peter passed it around. I answered questions. What part of the brain makes you talk? What color is the brain? Does the brain keep videos of your life?

I told the children how important it was for a developing baby's brain to get stimulation from talk and touch and human interactions. I told them the same things that I told parents, judges, pediatricians and my own staff, just with fewer big words.

Then I talked a little bit about how different children grow up in different homes. How Japanese children learn Japanese; how in some cultures mothers carry their babies around all day long during their first year of life. How some children don't get as much touch or talk or love early in life, and how that can change the brain. They were having fun. We laughed.

Peter was smiling. Then, it was time. I didn't know how much I would say, or even what I would say. I would let the response of the children—and Peter—guide me. I jumped in, "Well. Thank you for letting me come to your classroom. Peter told me about you guys when he came to visit me in Houston. I know he went to kindergarten with many of you." A few of the children raised their hands. "We asked Peter to come to our clinic in Houston because we wanted to learn from him about his amazing brain."

The children looked at Peter. "See, when he was a little boy he spent every minute of every day for the first three years of his life in one crib." The children looked interested, but kind of confused. "Peter was born in another country where they did not know very much about the brain. His parents could not take care of him so Peter went to an orphanage when he was just a baby. In this orphanage each baby was put in a crib and that was their home. They didn't get to wander around, crawl anywhere, or even practice standing so they could learn to walk. Until his parents came to get him when he was three, Peter never had a chance to walk around, to play with friends, to get a hug from any loving grown-ups. His brain didn't get very much stimulation." The room was completely silent: twenty-six six-year-old children didn't move, speak, or fidget.

"And then when he was three, his new parents came and brought him to live in Tulsa." I paused to let some of the tension dissipate. "And that is when Peter's amazing brain started to learn so many things. Even though he had never heard English, he learned English in just a couple years. He had never had a chance to walk or run or skip and he learned to do all of those things." Peter looked embarrassed. I didn't want to push too much. "And so even today, Peter's amazing brain is learning. He has really done great. And that is why we wanted to meet Peter and learn more about how any person with such a hard start in life could do so well."

Then I ended with, "Part of what we learned is that every day in school, Peter learns things from all of you. He watches how you do things, he learns from playing with each of you and he learns from just being your friend. So thank you for helping Peter. And thanks for letting me come and talk about the brain."

It was a short and simple talk. I tried to take an unknown— Peter—and make him less frightening to these children. And over time, their natural goodness emerged. No longer an odd and scary boy, Peter became popular—so popular, in fact, that his peers would argue over who got to sit next to him, who got to be his partner, who got to be in his group. The brightest and strongest children in his class took a special interest in him and their leadership made all the difference. They included him, protected him and, ultimately, provided therapeutic experiences that helped Peter catch up.

They were tolerant of his developmental problems, patient in correcting his social mistakes and nurturing in their interactions. These children provided many more positive therapeutic experiences than we ever could have given Peter.

Children, just like us adults, react badly to the unknown, to the strange and unfamiliar, especially when they themselves are trying to adjust to a new situation like the start of a school year. Although their social hierarchies aren't always so easy to influence, most bullying and social rejection begins with fear of the unfamiliar, and adults have much more influence over the process than they may believe. When children understand why someone behaves oddly, they give him or her more slack, generally. And the younger the children are, the more easily they are influenced by both obvious and subtle cues of rejection and acceptance from adults. These cues often set the tone for the children's status systems, and teachers and parents can either minimize bullying or unfortunately, maximize it, by either strongly discouraging or tolerating the scapegoating of those who are "different."

Knowing that Peter's immature behavior came from his history of deprivation helped his classmates reinterpret it. When he grabbed something or talked out of turn, they no longer saw it as a personal affront or jarring oddity, but simply as a remnant from his past that they'd been taught to expect. The results were rapid: almost immediately he stopped having tantrums and outbursts, probably because what had prompted them was frustration, a sense of rejection and feeling misunderstood. Because the other children were more forgiving and more explicit about the social cues they were giving him, he was able to read them better and thus able to fit in better. What had been a downward spiral of rejection, confusion and frustration became instead a cascade of positive reinforcement, which fed on itself. The huge gaps in developmental age across emotional, social, motor and cognitive domains slowly filled in. By the time Peter reached high school he no longer stood out and he has continued to do well, both academically and socially.

His peers and his family healed him by creating a rich social world, a nurturing community. While the neurosequential approach helped us provide the specific stimuli his brain had lacked—massage offering the physical affection that he'd missed, and music and movement to help restore his brain and bodily rhythms—none of that would have been enough without Amy and Jason's love and sensitivity nor without the patience and support of his classmates. The more healthy relationships a child has, the more likely he will be to recover from trauma and thrive. Relationships are the agents of change and the most powerful therapy is human love.

CHAPTER 11

Healing Communities

IT HAS BEEN AN EXTRAORDINARY privilege to work
with the children whose stories I have shared here—and I have
learned a tremendous amount from them. I have been consistently amazed by their courage, their strength, and their ability
to cope with situations that most adults would find unbearable.
But while emerging therapeutic models like the neurosequential approach hold great promise, my experience as well as the
research suggests that the most important healing experiences in
the lives of traumatized children do not occur in therapy itself.

Trauma and our responses to it cannot be understood outside the context of human relationships. Whether people have
survived an earthquake or have been repeatedly sexually abused,
what matters most is how those experiences affect their relationships—to their loved ones, to themselves, and to the world. The
most traumatic aspects of all disasters involve the shattering of
human connections. And this is especially true for children. Being
harmed by the people who are supposed to love you, being abandoned by them, being robbed of the one-on-one relationships that

allow you to feel safe and valued and to become humane—these are profoundly destructive experiences. Because humans are inescapably social beings, the worst catastrophes that can befall us inevitably involve relational loss.

As a result, recovery from trauma and neglect is also all about relationships—rebuilding trust, regaining confidence, returning to a sense of security and reconnecting to love. Of course, medications can help relieve symptoms and talking to a therapist can be incredibly useful. But healing and recovery are impossible—even with the best medications and therapy in the world—without lasting, caring connections to others. Indeed, at heart it is the relationship with the therapist, not primarily his or her methods or words of wisdom, that allows therapy to work. All the children who ultimately thrived following our treatment did so because of a strong social network that surrounded and supported them.

What healed children like Peter, Justin, Amber and Laura were the people around them, their families, their friends, the folks who respected them, who were tolerant of their weaknesses and vulnerabilities and who were patient in helping them slowly build new skills. Whether it was the coach who allowed Ted to keep team statistics, Mama P. who helped teach Virginia how to nurture Laura, the first graders who took Peter under their wing and protected him, or the incredible adoptive parents of so many of my patients—all of them provided the most important therapy that these children ever received. Because what they needed most was a rich social environment, one where they could belong and be loved.

What maltreated and traumatized children most need is a healthy community to buffer the pain, distress and loss caused by their earlier trauma. What works to heal them is anything that increases the number and quality of a child's relationships. What helps is consistent, patient, repetitive loving care. And, I should add, what doesn't work is well-intended but poorly trained mental health "professionals" rushing in after a traumatic event, or coercing children to "open up" or "get out their anger."

However, because it is exactly those children who are most vulnerable to trauma who are least likely to have a healthy, supportive family and community, it is exceedingly difficult to provide effective help through the current systems we have in place. Because healthy communities themselves are often what prevents interpersonal traumatic events (like domestic violence and other violent crime) from occurring in the first place, the breakdown of social connection that is common in our highly mobile society increases everyone's vulnerability.

If we are to successfully raise healthy children, children who will be resilient in the face of any traumatic experience they may encounter—and some 40 percent of children will experience at least one potentially traumatic event before they become adults—we need to build a healthier society. The wonderful thing about our species is that we can learn; our memories and our technologies allow us to benefit from the experience of those who came before us. But at the same time those technologies, even the ones that are presumably meant to bring us together, are increasingly keeping us apart. The modern world has disrupted and in many cases abandoned the fundamental biological unit of human social life: the extended family. There has been so much emphasis on the breakdown of the nuclear family, but I believe that in many cases the extended family, whose dissolution has been much less discussed, is at least as important. It certainly, as you may recall from Leon's story, can make the difference between a young couple who are able to cope and raise a healthy child and one where one or both parents becomes overwhelmed and neglectful.

For countless generations humans lived in small groups, made up of 40 to 150 people, most of whom were closely related to each other and lived communally. As late as the year 1500, the average family group in Europe consisted of roughly twenty people whose lives were intimately connected on a daily basis. But by 1850 that number was down to ten living in close proximity, and in 1960 the number was just five. In the year 2000 the average size of a household was less than four, and a shocking 26 percent of Americans live alone.

As technology has advanced, we have gotten farther and farther away from the environment for which evolution shaped us. The world we live in now is biologically disrespectful; it does not take into account many of our most basic human needs and often pulls us away from healthy activities and toward those that are harmful. My field, unfortunately, has been part of this trend.

For years mental health professionals taught people that they could be psychologically healthy without social support, that "unless you love yourself, no one else will love you." Women were told that they didn't need men, and vice versa. People without any relationships were believed to be as healthy as those who had many. These ideas contradict the fundamental biology of human species: we are social mammals and could never have survived without deeply interconnected and interdependent human contact. The truth is you cannot love yourself unless you have been loved and are loved. The capacity to love cannot be built in isolation.

I believe we're at a transitional point in history where people are recognizing that modern societies have abandoned many of the fundamental elements required for optimal human mental health. We can see the problem in the seemingly inexorable rise in depression rates around the world, which cannot be explained solely by better treatment and diagnosis. A person born in 1905 had only a 1 percent chance of suffering depression by age seventy-five, but by their twenty-fourth birthday, 6 percent of those born in 1955 had had an episode of serious depression. Other studies indicate that teen depression rates have increased by an incredible factor of ten in recent decades. We can also recognize this trend in changing patterns of marriage and divorce, in the difficulties people report in finding satisfying romantic relationships, in the constant struggle families across the economic spectrum have in attempting to find a balance between work and home life. The disconnect between what we need in order to be mentally healthy and what the modern world offers can also be seen in the constant unease felt by parents—about the Internet, the media, drugs, violent predators, pedophiles, economic inequality and above all, the values of our culture that shape our responses to these issues. From right to left, no one seems to believe that our current way of life is healthy, even as we disagree about exactly what's wrong and what should be done about it.

It's time for our leaders to step up and ask: "How do we build community in a modern world? How do you explore relationships in a world that is going to have television, that will include email, artificially extended days because of electric lights, and automobiles, airplanes, psychoactive drugs, plastic surgery and everything else that goes along with advancing technologies? How do we deal with the presence of all of those things and create a world that respects our biological needs, one that enhances our connections to others rather than ignores or disrupts them?"

I certainly don't have all the answers, but I do know that many of our current childcare practices are hurting our children. For example, in California, at a large center serving three- to five-year-olds, staff members are not allowed to touch the children. If they want to be hugged or held, the adults are supposed to push them away! This is a classic example of how a seemingly good idea—wanting to protect children from sexual predators—can have serious negative consequences. Children need healthy touch. As we've seen, infants can literally die without it. It's part of our biology.

Unfortunately, we've become so afraid of unhealthy touch that we may actually make it more likely by failing to meet the needs of children for healthy physical affection. This can make them more vulnerable to pedophiles, not less, as children will tend to seek out those who appear affectionate toward them. As we increase distrust of others by keeping children inside, by not allowing them to play spontaneously in their neighborhoods with their friends, by rigidly structuring their lives, we are also destroying the community bonds that keep all of us healthy.

I've seen the horrors that sexual molestation of children can cause. They are clear in the Gilmer case, in Tina's story and so many others. I know better than most people that worries about sexual abuse are grounded in a genuine and terrifying reality. But I also know that predators thrive by picking off the most vulnerable, by getting in where the fabric of the community is weakest. Any predator looks for the weakest prey; it's another aspect of biology. In order to keep our children safe, therefore, we need to form healthy relationships and connect with others; we need to hug our children. Protecting children needs to be done in ways that respect their needs by strengthening the community, not splintering it. To keep children safe in daycare, don't let lone adults touch children unobserved but, at the same time, don't ban physical affection and comfort. To create a safe neighborhood, get to know your neighbors. Don't keep your children locked away or only engaged in structured activities. We know enough about human nature to shape policies in ways that reflect and respect biology rather than ignoring it and then failing to recognize the consequences of doing so.

WHAT ELSE CAN WE DO TO PROTECT children from trauma, neglect and abuse? And how can we best help those who do get hurt? For one, we need to recognize that our current policies and practices do not put relationships first and that the current systems in place to help children don't work. We need to acknowledge that many of the "solutions" we currently have for social problems do not effectively address them and may exacerbate them in the long run. We need to understand what we evolved to need and then work on ways to provide those things in the modern world.

A good place to start is at the beginning, with the way we treat infants and new parents. As we've seen, in order to develop normally infants need the devoted attention of one or two primary, consistent caretakers, and those caretakers need the daily support of a loving community that recognizes and relieves the exhausting demands of new parenthood. When humans evolved they didn't live in a world where one woman spent her day alone with her offspring while her partner spent his day at the office. Both men and women worked hard to ensure survival, but women worked together with young children close at hand and older boys often accompanied men and were trained by them. An overwhelmed mother could hand her infant off to an aunt or a sister or a grandmother: there were, on average, four adolescents and adults for every young child. Today we think that a daycare center has an excellent adult/child ratio when there is one caregiver for every five children!

As primatologist and evolutionary theorist Sarah Blaffer Hrdy put it in an interview with *New Scientist* magazine, "Policy makers imagine that nuclear families epitomize the 'golden age' but in terms of the deep history of the human family, it is unusual for children to be reared only by their mothers and fathers. Children accustomed to nurturing from others view their social world as a benign place and act accordingly." Hrdy's book, *Mother Nature: Maternal Instincts and How They Shape the Human Species*, stresses the importance of extended family, whom she calls "alloparents." She notes, "For children at risk of

neglect, it is amazing how much difference alloparental interventions, say, from a grandparent, can make." We have seen that
throughout this book.

Further, when humans evolved, infants didn't have their
own room—they didn't even have their own bed. They were
usually never more than a few feet away from an adult or sibling at any time and most often were being held. Many of the
sleeping and crying problems seen in infancy today are likely
caused by the fact that a human infant left alone and out of
sight distance of adults for almost the entire evolutionary
history of humankind would have been facing near-certain
death. It's hardly surprising that babies find being left alone to
sleep distressing. In fact, what's startling (and what reflects the
adaptability of the human brain) is how quickly so many get
used to it. Infants might ultimately evolve such that being left
alone doesn't so easily set off their stress systems, but evolution
works over eons, not the timeline preferred by most parents.

We need to educate people about the needs of infants and
create better ways of addressing them. We need to have an infant-
and child-literate society, where everyone who has or works with
children knows what to expect. For example, if an infant doesn't
cry at all, like Connor, it's just as much of a cause for concern as
if he cries too much. Becoming more aware of age-appropriate
behavior will ensure that, when necessary, children can get help
as soon as possible.

Further, we need to call an immediate cease-fire in the
"Mommy wars" and recognize that everyone benefits when new
parents have the choice to spend more time with their children
and when they have community support and access to quality childcare. As Hrdy says, "We evolved in a context where
mothers had much more social support. Infants need this social
engagement to develop their full human potential." Many European countries—particularly the Scandinavian countries—have

managed to have both highly productive economies and provide high quality child care and lots of paid family leave. There's no reason that we can't develop similar policies.

To HELP CREATE A BIOLOGICALLY respectful home environment, parents can also do simple things like setting boundaries on media and technology—for example, having regular family meals when all phones, televisions and computers are off. In addition they can model behaviors that emphasize the importance of relationships, empathy and kindness in their interactions with people, whether they be relatives, neighbors, shopkeepers or others they encounter in their daily lives.

Schools, too, need to change. Our educational system has focused nearly obsessively on cognitive development and almost completely ignored children's emotional and physical needs. Only two decades ago elementary schools had both significant lunch periods and recess times, and gym class was mandatory several days a week. Homework rarely took more than an hour to complete each night and children were thought to be capable of remembering deadlines and meeting them on their own. Big projects that required parental assistance were undertaken only a few times each year.

All of those things were respectful to the biology of young children, particularly that of boys who mature more slowly than girls do. Schools recognized that a short attention span is characteristic of childhood, that children need free time to run and play and learn how to socialize with each other. My co-author Maia's nine-year-old nephew once told his mom that he didn't know who his friends were. His days in school were so structured that he didn't have enough free time to build real relationships. There was no recess. This is insane. In our rush to be sure our children have an environment as "enriched" as that of the neighbors' children, we are actually emotionally impoverishing them. A child's brain needs more than words and lessons and organized activities: it needs love and friendship and the freedom to play and daydream. Knowing this might allow more parents to resist social pressures and begin to push schools back in a more sensible direction.

In addition, our educational system and our society's general disrespect for the importance of relationships is undermining the development of empathy. Like language, empathy is a fundamental capacity of the human species, one that helps define what a human being is. But like language, empathy, too, must be learned. Ordinarily, we pick up both during early childhood, but as Connor and Leon's stories illustrate, the development of empathy and the relational skills that rely upon it require critical input from the environment. While fortunately very few babies are left on their own for long periods of time the way those two boys were, all too many young children are spending more and more of their lives in environments so structured and regimented that there is little time to build friendships and get the practice and repetition needed to support empathetic caring. Worse yet, time spent with their parents is often limited as well, and what remains is rapidly filled up with hours of homework or, alternatively, hours of television, computers, and video games.

Brain development is use-dependent: you use it or you lose it. If we don't give children time to learn how to be with others, to connect, to deal with conflict, and to negotiate complex social hierarchies, those areas of their brains will be underdeveloped. As Hrdy states: "One of the things we know about empathy is that the potential is expressed only under certain rearing conditions." If you don't provide these conditions through a caring, vibrant social network, it won't fully emerge.

We also need to recognize that not all stress is bad, that children require challenges and risk as well as safety. It is natural to want to protect our children, but we need to ask ourselves when the desire for risk-free childhoods has gone too far. The safest playground, after all, would have no swings, no steep slides, no rough surfaces, no trees, no other children—and no fun. Children's brains are shaped by what they do slowly and repeatedly over time. If they don't have the chance to practice coping with small risks and dealing with the consequences of those choices, they won't be well prepared for making larger and far more consequential decisions. In today's safety culture we seem to swing from strictly monitoring and guiding our children from infancy through high school, and then releasing them to the absolute freedom of college (though some parents are trying to encroach there as well). We have to remember that for most of human history adolescents took on adult roles earlier and rose admirably to the challenge. Many of the problems we have with teenagers result from failing to adequately challenge their growing brains. While we now know that the brain's decision-making areas aren't completely wired until at least their early twenties, it is experience making decisions that wires them, and it can't be done without taking some risks. We need to allow children to try and fail. And when they do make the stupid, shortsighted decisions that come from inexperience, we need to let them suffer the results. At the same time we also need to provide balance by not setting policies that will magnify one mistake, like drug use or fighting, into a life-derailing catastrophe. Unfortunately, this is exactly what our current "zero tolerance" policies—that expel children from school for just one rule violation—do.

We know that our biology predisposes us to mirror the actions of those we see around us. We know that what we repeat, we reinforce and ultimately incorporate. The more we do something, the stronger the system devoted to it becomes in our brain. These facts are wonderful when what we are considering repeating is loving and nurturing, but they are frankly terrifying when we think about violence and the increasing number of simulations of violence that surround us and our children.

Living in a pervasively violent community, being economically disadvantaged or witnessing or being victimized oneself by violent acts are far more important factors in determining which children will grow up violent than simple video game or television exposure. Reducing economic inequality and helping victims of domestic violence and child abuse are critical if we want to cut violence and crime. While most abused children do not grow up to become abusers themselves, the odds that a parent will be abusive or neglectful increase dramatically if he or she has had such experiences early in life. But this can be made even worse if such children live in frayed communities, are surrounded by simulations of violence and have few countervailing positive social interactions.

The American Psychiatric Association estimates that the average child views some 16,000 simulated murders and 200,000 acts of violence on television alone by the time she turns eighteen, although no research yet even documents the amount of exposure from violent video games or explores how it affects children's behavior. To build a society that emphasizes "the better angels" of our nature, limiting children's exposures to such violence is important. We've seen throughout this book how small influences and decisions can add up to big problems over time. As a result, changing many little negative influences could ultimately have a large effect.

FURTHER, HUMANS EVOLVED IN A situation in which cooperation was critical to survival. Although we have never been entirely peaceful, some societies have raised children and settled disputes in ways that tend to tone down our violent tendencies, while others have acted in ways that amp them up. One of the most difficult questions facing evolutionary theorists was understanding how cooperation evolved, because the "winners" in evolution are those animals that reproduce most successfully, and quite often selfish behavior maximizes the chances of survival and reproduction. Evolutionists had long emphasized "nature, red in tooth and claw," but a view that focused on the competition of the fittest for survival missed one of the most fascinating and important characteristics of humans and quite a few other species: the propensity for altruism.

Over time researchers discovered that in certain, delicately balanced situations, cooperation will arise in nature because those animals that do cooperate in these conditions are more likely to survive than those that always act on their own. In order for cooperation to persist, however, these favorable circumstances must also continue. In humans, the requirements for the maintenance of cooperation include a sense that others are likely to treat you fairly and the recognition and punishment (whether through legal systems or social rejection) of those who violate trust and cheat to benefit themselves at the expense of others.

Unfortunately, that basic sense of fairness and goodwill toward others is under threat in a society like ours that increasingly enriches the richest and abandons the rest to the vagaries of global competition. More and more our media and our school systems emphasize material success and the importance of triumphing over others both athletically and in the classroom. More and more, in an atmosphere of increased competitiveness, middle- and upper-class parents seem driven to greater and greater extremes to give their offspring whatever perceived "edge" they can find. This constant emphasis on competition drowns out the lessons of cooperation, empathy and altruism that are critical for human mental health and social cohesion.

I have often been asked to help develop a mental health

response following traumatic events that I believe are direct results of a fractured community and our unrelenting focus on competition. Some of the most distressing of these have been school shootings. What I've found time and again in these cases is a winner-takes-all school culture, where bullying is pervasive and accepted and where the "losers" are not considered people who need understanding and support, but utterly deserving of their alienation and exclusion. In these situations it is not only the teenagers who have built and enforced a strict social hierarchy that causes unmitigated misery for those on the bottom, but also the teachers, parents and school administrators. Humans have always been a hierarchical species, of course— that's another part of our biology—but when you emphasize merciless competition at the expense of all else, in a culture that glorifies violence, an occasional violent uprising by those who feel left out is hardly surprising. I don't believe we will be able to prevent these incidents unless we work much harder to ensure all students feel included in their school community.

THE BRAIN DEVELOPS OVER TIME, with a constant accretion of repetitions and exposures; each moment is a chance to reinforce either positive or negative patterns. Once a pattern is started, it becomes like a groove or a rut, making similar behavior easier, more likely to be repeated. The mirroring systems of our social brains make behaviors contagious. And again, this is wonderful when what you are practicing is sports or piano or kindness, but not so great when what's being repeated is impulsive, aggressive responses to threat. I think again about Leon and how, after he began to be neglected, repeated thousands of, in themselves, unimportant and small decisions, that came together and made bad behavior increasingly easy for him to choose and put good choices further and further out of his reach.

As a result of this property of the brain, earlier intervention is almost always better than later. But it has to be the right intervention. In Leon's case much of what was done to "help" him actually served to make things worse. When children start to misbehave our initial impulse to punish and deprive them often serves us poorly; we tend to see children who are whiny and demanding and aggressive as "spoiled" and "indulged," rather than recognizing that these qualities usually arise from unmet needs and unexplored potential, not from having too much or feeling too good. In order for a child to become kind, giving and empathetic, he needs to be treated that way. Punishment can't create or model those qualities. Although we do need to set limits, if we want our children to behave well, we have to treat them well. A child raised with love wants to make those around him happy because he sees that his happiness makes them happy, too; he doesn't simply comply to avoid punishment. These positive feedback loops are every bit as powerful as the negative ones, but they rely upon the sometimes counterintuitive response of first figuring out what drives misbehavior, then dealing with it, rather than acting first. I fully believe that if Leon had been reached early in his childhood, even if he'd already experienced some neglect by his mother, he would not have become the cold-hearted murderer I met.

However, working with children who have experienced the kind of early trauma that affected Connor, Peter, Justin, Leon and Laura requires two things that are often in short supply in our modern world: time and patience. Traumatized children tend to have overactive stress responses and, as we've seen, these can make them aggressive, impulsive and needy. These children are difficult, they are easy to upset and hard to calm, they may overreact to the slightest novelty or change and they often don't know how to think before they act. Before they can make any kind of lasting change at all in their behavior, they need to feel safe and loved. Unfortunately, however, many of the treatment programs and other interventions aimed at them get it backwards: they take a punitive approach and hope to lure children into good behavior by restoring love and safety only if the children first start acting "better." While such approaches may temporarily threaten children into doing what adults want, they can't provide the long-term, internal motivation that will ultimately help them control themselves better and become more loving toward others.

Troubled children are in some kind of pain—and pain makes people irritable, anxious and aggressive. Only patient, loving, consistent care works; there are no short-term miracle cures. This is as true for a child of three or four as it is for a teenager. Just because a child is older does not mean a punitive approach is more appropriate or effective. Unfortunately, again, the system doesn't tend to recognize this. It tends to provide "quick fixes," and when those fail, then there are long punishments. We need programs and resources that acknowledge that punishment, deprivation and force merely re-traumatize these children and exacerbate their problems.

One of the greatest lessons I've learned in my work is the importance of simply taking the time, before doing anything else, to pay attention and listen. Because of the mirroring neurobiology of our brains, one of the best ways to help someone else become calm and centered is to calm and center ourselves first—and then just pay attention.

When you approach a child from this perspective, the response you get is far different from when you simply assume you know what is going on and how to fix it. When I first approached Justin in his crib/cage, for example, I got a very different response than previous visitors had because I calmly recognized that underneath his frightening behavior was his own fear and hunger. Obviously it is difficult to have this kind of detachment when it is your own child who is misbehaving—especially when he's doing something that has made you angry or upset—but the more you try to see the world from the child's point of view and the safer you make him feel, the better his behavior is likely to be and the more likely you are to find ways of further improving it.

Another important implication of our mirrored biology is that concentrating children with aggressive or impulsive tendencies together is a bad idea, as they will tend to reflect and magnify this, rather than calm each other. Although research demonstrates the negative results of such grouping, we have unfortunately gotten into the habit of organizing therapy groups and residential programs in ways that concentrate such children. As we saw in Leon's case, it can actually serve to make problems worse.

I also cannot emphasize enough how important routine and repetition are to recovery. The brain changes in response to patterned, repetitive experiences: the more you repeat something, the more engrained it becomes. This means that, because it takes time to accumulate repetitions, recovery takes time and patience is called for as these repetitions continue. The longer the period of trauma, or the more extreme the trauma, the greater the number of repetitions required to regain balance. Also, because trauma at its core is an experience of utter powerlessness and loss of control, recovery requires that the patient be in charge of key aspects of the therapeutic interaction. Over and over again the research finds that if you use force, if you push people to open up when they aren't ready, if you require participation in therapy, if you don't respect individual differences, then your treatment can actually do serious harm. Because safety is critical to recovery and force creates fear, coercive therapies are dangerous and ineffective for victims of trauma. Trauma tends to drive other mental health problems like many teen behavior problems and an enormous percentage of addictions. Unfortunately, coercive forms of treatment are common in these areas, and this is yet another case in which our efforts to deal with a problem may actually exacerbate it. We need to educate both parents and professionals about these truths, and also work to ensure that the justice system, foster care system and child welfare and mental health care systems use evidence-based approaches that at the very least are informed by knowledge about trauma and reduce, rather than increase, harm.

OF COURSE MAKING OUR WORLD safer for children won't be easy. Efforts to do so must address some of the largest political controversies of our time: globalization, the "mommy wars," economic inequality, to name just a few. And the United States has historically done little more than give lip service to children's issues, with both parties raising the banner of "family values" while doing little to actually address the day-to-day problems affecting most parents and children. I don't have all the answers. But I do think that understanding ourselves as a social species, with a brain that evolved with certain unique capacities and weaknesses, a brain that becomes what it practices, will allow us at least to ask the right questions. And that is the best place to start when seeking to build a loving, caring community.

CHAPTER 12

A Picture, Not a Label

"A little learning is a dangerous thing;
Drink deep, or taste not the Pierian spring:
There shallow draughts intoxicate the brain,
And drinking largely sobers us again."
—"AN ESSAY ON CRITICISM" (1711) ALEXANDER POPE

A FEW YEARS AFTER WE WROTE *The Boy Who Was Raised as a Dog,* a Child Protective Services (CPS) supervisor from out of state called our clinic. He wanted to review a treatment approach that was being used by a private contractor who worked with abused and neglected children "in the system." Very few CPS agencies have internal clinical teams to provide therapeutic services, so these are often contracted out to private individuals or organizations in various ways.

Because the CPS system is essentially the legal guardian of the children involved, a caseworker is supposed to provide oversight of any treatment. In this particular instance, a supervisor had become aware that several young children with histories of sexual abuse were seeing a clinician who was using highly questionable therapeutic techniques. After providing a little context, he said, "Well, we want to know if what he is doing is in line with your theories."

"OK," I said, though I wasn't exactly sure which theories she meant. "What is he doing?"

"He has the children re-enact their sexual abuse."

"What do you mean?"

"Well he has them take sex toys and use them in reenacting anal and oral sex."

"Really?"

"Yes. And he has the kids pull their pants down when they are doing this and insert the dildo just like it happened—and he films it."

I was stunned. "That is not therapy. That is abuse."

"When we questioned what he was doing, he justified it by saying it was based on your work on how trauma and other experience changes the brain."

I took a deep breath. I said, "I have never, ever advocated that kind of behavior as part of a therapeutic approach. I would recommend you contact the police and report this. And certainly, do not allow these children to continue seeing this person. You can't use the veil of therapy to do acts that in any other context would be abuse. If you heard that any other adult did this, you wouldn't hesitate a second to call, well, CPS and the police"

The five-minute phone call was shocking to our clinical team: how could someone take what we had written and taught about our trauma and our therapeutic work and twist that into that kind of practice? What could they possibly have been thinking?

Not long after that incident we got another call, this time from a licensing board in another state. About six months earlier I had been in that state giving a "Grand Rounds" lecture at a medical school. I had an hour to provide an overview of our approach; as part of that presentation, I described our sequential treatment process with Connor, one of the boys whose stories was told in the chapter that gives this book its title. As you may recall, he had suffered from early life neglect and had a lifelong history of confusing and odd behaviors. In Connor's case, we had started with a focus on sensory integration and used therapeutic massage at the start of the therapeutic process.

The licensing board was calling to ask about our "neurodevelopmental model." A clinician who claimed to be using the "Perry neurodevelopmental model for trauma" had come to their attention. The distinguishing feature of this woman's approach was that *every* client who came to see her was getting a massage—"because that is where you need to start" according to her interpretation of our work. *Dr. Perry's Massage Parlor,* I thought. Not exactly the main message we had in mind for what we eventually came to call the Neurosequential Model of Therapeutics (NMT).

Again, our clinical team was surprised to hear this. It was such a misrepresentation of what we were doing or would ever intend to teach others to do. It became clear that we needed to create some way to ensure that individuals claiming to use the "Neurosequential Model" were adequately trained. The last thing I wanted to do was develop a "certification" process or unduly limit or censor the exportation of the core concepts that were the basis of the NMT, but I realized that the specific elements, the main ideas and our evolving "metrics" (a.k.a. measures), had to be exported properly so that they could be used with fidelity.

Basically, we had to develop a structured and well-controlled process to introduce clinicians to this model and ensure that they understood how to use our clinical practice tools and measurements in a responsible way. And so, for several years, we worked on the development of a formal NMT certification process and modifications to our NMT "Clinical Practice Tools"—the NMT metrics designed to help the clinician who is using the NMT approach. By 2008, about a year after *The Boy Who Was Raised as a Dog* was published, we started to offer "certification" in the NMT.

Even before Maia and I started writing this book, my colleagues and I at The ChildTrauma Academy had begun to systematize and then study the approach we described here. Our experiences with individuals like Connor gave us valuable insights that helped guide this process. By the time this book was published, 2007, our clinical team had already incorporated many of the core neurodevelopmental and clinical concepts presented in *The Boy Who Was Raised as a Dog* into our work.

The NMT clinical approach involves four key components:

1) Developmental History: Obtain a history of the timing, nature and severity of trauma, adversity and neglect, *as well as* relational experiences and "connectedness," which are associated with resilience.

2) Current Functioning: Assess current functioning with a focus on: a) the individual's strengths and vulnerabilities in multiple domains, such as sensory integration, regulation (the ability to manage stress, sensation, and emotion without becoming "overloaded" or shutting down), relational abilities (social skills and the general capacity to form relationships), and cognitive function. b) the individual's actual "connectedness" to family, friends, community, and culture: what we call their "therapeutic web."

3) Treatment Planning: Select and sequence educational, enrichment, and therapeutic experiences based upon the individual's developmental needs.

4) Implementation: Track the implementation and effectiveness of the plan and make appropriate modifications.

This process had been developed and refined over many years. A major challenge was to ensure that we included the most important elements of assessment and treatment, while avoiding redundant or unnecessary elements that can derail the treatment process. (For example, things like having the first visit to the clinic start with someone asking "How are you going to pay?"—and then sitting the overwhelmed and struggling parent down with a pile of forms for billing.)

We started doing much more work in the client's home and community. We worked to develop ways to get a better understanding of the child's developmental history—even when there were not reliable historians or many records. We developed ways to track the progress—or lack of progress—a child was making when the treatment plan was implemented. The results within our clinic were very promising.

We started by gathering a detailed history of the client's development, focusing on the nature, timing, and severity of trauma, neglect, and other adversities. This history also included the nature, timing, and quality of resilience-related factors, such as connection to family, community, and culture. Together, these findings gave us an estimate of the "developmental risk" that the individual had experienced at key times and developmental stages. This allowed us to "measure" the timing of developmental risk.

The evaluation of the current functioning of the client examines multiple capabilities that reflect different aspects of brain function—ranging from fine motor skills, to mood regulation, to speech and language. We assess a collection of these capabilities to give us some insight into how various areas of their brain are organized. For example, we measure heart rate regulation, respiration, the suck, swallow, and gag reflexes, and regulation of body temperature. All of these provide information about the organization and functioning of the brainstem. Similarly, measures of reading ability, the capacity to plan, delay gratification, and think in an abstract way give us insight into the workings of the cortex. By making some estimates of which brain areas have strengths and where deficits are found, we can develop a working model of the individual's brain that allows us to get a "picture" of the individual's current brain organization and functioning.

And I literally mean a picture: we use schematic diagrams of the brain, filled in with different colors to provide an easy way for clinicians and clients to visualize this data. These "brain maps" allow us to see which areas appear to be typical in development and organization and which areas seem underdeveloped or dysfunctional.

Once we have the client's brain map, we can then select and sequence therapeutic, educational, and enrichment experiences based upon his or her specific developmental strengths and challenges. Early on, when all of the clients were in our own clinic, we were able to follow up and determine whether or not the family, school, and other professionals working with the client followed our recommendations and if so, whether they had carried out the recommendations with adequate "dosing." The entire process required that the clinicians in our working group master core concepts from multiple disciplines that provide the theoretical underpinnings of the NMT approach.

Unfortunately, at this time, few social work, psychology, or even medical training programs had much teaching about the developmental neurosciences, trauma, attachment, neglect, and a range of related topics. Consequently, this meant that our clinical team was learning all the time—and that they needed to take an often unfamiliar, trans-disciplinary approach as a matter of course.

As we integrated these concepts and shifted our clinical model, we shared our experiences with colleagues in a variety of traditional academic ways. We presented on our findings at academic meetings. We did Grand Rounds at medical schools and consulted with other clinical teams. We published some of our work in academic books and journals. We had labeled our approach the "Neurosequential Model of Therapeutics" to capture some of the key concepts. Soon, other clinicians and clinical teams would adopt some of these ideas and use them in their work. A number of clinicians told us how helpful the shift in perspective had been for their work with any given challenging child; some organizations started to send us feedback about drops in "critical incidents" or the use of restraints when they started thinking in this developmentally-sensitive and trauma-informed way. This feedback was gratifying and mirrored our experiences with the utility of the approach.

Yet, we were soon to learn that "*a little learning is a dangerous thing*"—as I'd discovered to my horror from some of the phone calls I received.

Meanwhile, as our clinical team began to use this new approach, our research group struggled with a parallel and related set of problems. Simply stated, people are complex; families are complex; communities are complex; culture is complex. Development is complex; genetics is complex; the impact of trauma on the individual is complex; the developmental consequences of trauma and neglect are complex; the power of relationships to help protect and heal is complex.

And, yet, with all of this complexity, the research on trauma and children was often simplistic. Take a small number of subjects, look at them after a traumatic event, and then see if they meet DSM criteria for PTSD; there are literally hundreds of published reports like this. Rarely are multiple time points of evaluation considered—or even pre-existing adversity or trauma. Rarely is the timing of the trauma carefully examined. Outcome measures tend to measure only some functions—or are completely focused on diagnostic criteria for PTSD and whether people recover and no longer have symptoms. The few studies about clinical intervention were similarly simplistic: small numbers of very poorly characterized subjects, inadequate "comparators" ("control groups"), and very short durations of treatment (e.g., 12 weeks). To be fair, these exploratory and simple studies are important when an area of investigation is "young" and emerging. And the area of developmental trauma was—and still is—young.

But we knew we had to move beyond that research model, just as we had moved beyond the typical 50-minutes/week-in the-office therapeutic model. We had to have some way to understand, integrate, and better measure meaningful aspects of the complexity. Without doing so, we weren't going to make much progress in treating real, individual, complicated human beings. We now know much more about how trauma and neglect can change the course of brain development, and the importance of early childhood, bonding and attachment, community health factors, and culture. We also have more sophisticated ways to study therapies that can help manage these complexities.

Consequently, along with our new approach, we also needed to develop a better way of studying the people we treated. One immediate problem was how best to classify these children and the nature of their problems.

Sadly, most of the studies in traumatology still tend to classify people based on the kind of trauma they have experienced—but they don't recognize that the timing of trauma is at least as important. For example, few studies acknowledge the difference between the effects of sexual abuse experienced at age five and sexual abuse at age fifteen: a typical study on the effects of sexual abuse would put those two individuals in the same study group and then proceed to compare them to "controls."

Another problem of classification involves the nature of DSM diagnoses themselves. Take the case of "ADHD" and "Conduct Disorder." Many studies of children with these diagnoses never even assess whether they have been abused, neglected, exposed to violence, or otherwise suffered potentially traumatic experiences—even though, as we've seen, early life trauma exposure can profoundly influence both attention and behavior.

Indeed, I have often speculated that many of the studies of ADHD and conduct disorder are complicated by the fact that more than 30 percent of study participants are actually manifesting trauma-related symptoms, not just some sort of genetically-based problem with the development of the brain's attentional and executive control systems. Recent studies support this hypothesis.

For example, a retrospective study in a representative sample of 9,282 adults found that childhood adversities like trauma and neglect had strong correlations with thr onset of DSM-IV disorders. These connections were especially strong for children who experienced a host of different types of trauma linked to family dysfunction: for instance, having parents with both addiction and mental illness who are involved with the criminal justice system and experiencing family violence, neglect, and physical, emotional, and sexual abuse.

The study's authors used statistical techniques to tease out the role of childhood adversity in mental illness, finding that it is linked to 44.6 percent of all childhood-onset disorders and 25.9 percent to 32.0 percent of later-onset disorders. Clearly the researchers in our field—including our group—were not adequately addressing the complexity of development and the way that the same symptoms can be caused by genetic differences, environmental exposures, or more typically, a complicated combination of both that will vary depending on the age at which adversities are experienced.

But probably the most difficult and substantial problem with the DSM is that it is merely descriptive: it categorizes individuals based upon symptoms and signs, not based upon underlying physiological mechanisms, as is seen in the rest of medicine. It does not categorize based upon the mechanism by which a symptom is created. As the former head of the National Institute of Mental Health, Tom Insel, once put it, it would be as if physical medicine saw "chest pain" as a disease—whether it was caused by heartburn or a heart attack. Obviously, this would result in serious problems with treatment.

Moreover, there is no existing DSM category that captures developmental trauma adequately. As we have tried to show throughout this book, the multiple manifestations of trauma and neglect don't fit neatly into DSM diagnostic classes. As Insel wrote, "*a diagnostic system limited to clinical presentation could confer reliability and consistency but not validity. The strength of each of the editions of DSM has been 'reliability'—each edition has ensured that clinicians use the same terms in the same ways. The weakness is its lack of validity. Unlike our definitions of ischemic heart disease, lymphoma, or AIDS, the DSM diagnoses are based on a consensus about clusters of clinical symptoms, not any objective laboratory measure.*" (Insel, 2013).

We knew that we would never be able to get beyond simplistic study of these complex issues without a complete change in our frame of reference. Advancing research in developmental trauma will be impossible without addressing the complex interplay between genes, environment, and developmental timing. Much larger sample sizes are also required because there are so many different interacting factors—ranging from the complex biology and genetics of the brain to chemicals in the environment to social experiences, economic factors like employment, to culture, and, potentially, even to things like someone's grandparents' experiences of trauma, particularly in the context of multi-generational trauma like the colonization of indigenous peoples.

And so, in 2006, we decided we had no choice but to break away from the DSM framework. This was a daunting prospect for an academic psychiatrist: the DSM is referred to as the "Bible" for the mental health world—and, perhaps even more importantly, the entire medical economic reimbursement process in the United States is yoked to it. Fortunately, we did most of our clinical work pro bono—and got the majority of our clinical resources from other sources like private foundations, state-funded program development grants, and consultation work.

To begin, we intentionally stopped giving "labels" to individuals and started creating "pictures" of their developmental journey and their current brain organization and functioning. This immediately had a quite positive "side effect": it helped reduce stigma for our clients and made them feel less broken and alien. Further, the description of their journey to the present and the visual image of their current functioning helped them become more engaged participants in their own treatment planning process. They understood the rationale for certain recommendations; many of the older children could predict more about how the process might go and what kind of healing to realistically expect in a particular time frame. This gave them more control, more ownership, and more hope—all of which have been shown to help healing, in and of themselves.

With one foot in the clinical world and one foot in the research world, I realized that the need to create a "certification" process had been a blessing in disguise. If clinicians in multiple large systems began to use the same developmental and current functioning assessments, we might actually be able to collect useful information in a systematic way from thousands of clients. This way, we could actually get the large sample size we'd need to test our ideas properly. The clinical benefits of the model and the potential research benefits could seamlessly serve each other if we had an adequate export and fidelity model. The key was to make sure we could create a clinically-useful, affordable, and practical way to teach clinicians to use a modified, updated version of our Clinical Practice Tools (NMT metrics). And if we made the assessment components web-based, all of them could go into a common database.

Initially, I had been simply entering the data by hand and using Excel to create our "brain maps" within our clinic. As we started to teach other clinicians and organizations about the NMT, we started to use this beta-version of our metrics with their clients; the amount of data that I had to enter by hand to create these "brain maps" and NMT reports made it incredibly time consuming. We needed a way for each clinician to enter data on their own clients—we needed a web-based version of our NMT metrics.

The formal NMT certification process started in 2008. However, going back as far as 2002, I had hand-entered about 1,000 NMT assessments into this simple Excel version. It was a pain in the butt. But doing so had allowed me to really get a feel for which items were important, which were redundant, and how we could actually create something useful that we could standardize. In 2010, we launched our web-based version of the NMT Clinical Practice Tools, and the NMT Certification process took off.

Over the last ten years, The ChildTrauma Academy has been focusing on further refinement of the NMT, along with efforts to export it in responsible ways, mainly through our certification process. The results have been heartening. As I sit and write this chapter, over 1,500 clinicians from more than fifteen countries across the world have been fully certified—and each week more organizations and individual clinicians enroll in the certification process.

Over 90 large clinical organizations have incorporated NMT into their clinical practice model, including Casey Family Programs, University of California Davis Extension's Infant-Parent Mental Health Fellowship Program (California), Cal Farley's Ranch for Boys and Girls (Texas), NFI (Vermont), Alexander Youth Network (North Carolina), Mount St. Vincent Home (Colorado), Hull Services (a leader in child welfare and mental health in Alberta, CA), Take Two of Berry Street (a leader in child welfare in Australia), Kibble (a child welfare leader in Scotland), Palier (a specialized mental health facility in the Netherlands), the RVTS centers (specialized trauma treatment teams in Norway) among many others (see ChildTrauma.org for more).

In 2015 the Federally funded National Quality Improvement Center for Adoption/Guardianship Support and Preservation (QIC-AG: http://qic-ag.org) rated the NMT as Level 3 Promising Practice, and in 2016, NMT was selected as the emerging best-practice framework to include in a randomized controlled trial in one of the primary phases of this five-year program project dedicated to the development of best practices in child welfare.

In 2016, the Ministry of Human Services in Alberta, Canada (Alberta Human Services) formally announced that they would be using NMT as the practice framework to support therapeutic work with at-risk, maltreated, and traumatized children and youth. And in New Mexico, the NMT is a key part of their state-wide approach in the child welfare system.

Our adaptation of the model for schools, which is called the Neurosequential Model in Education (NME), has been an effective resource for teachers and others who work in schools.

When educators implement NME in a systematic fashion, many positive outcomes have been reported. One example comes from an inner-city school in the Midwest. This school serves a high poverty population, and most of the children who attend have significant academic and behavioral struggles. Before instituting NME, 498 students per year had been sent to a "punishment" classroom—one year later, after NME was implemented, this number was cut by more than half, to 161.

Moreover, the "punishment" room has now become more of a regulation area, where a teacher helps guide children to regulating activities—basically, whatever that particular child has previously found helpful—to help them calm down enough to return to class. Out of school suspensions decreased from 36 to 9 post-NME. There are now over 300 NME trainers across the world, who affect thousands of students in hundreds of classrooms.

Another variant of the Neurosequential Model has been created for caregivers like foster and adoptive parents. It is called NMC and so far it has been implemented with very positive results. This is a relatively new initiative and we are hopeful that this capacity-building project can help these carers—and, thereby, the children they nurture.

An international community of practice has also been created and is continuing to grow. Articles about the use of NMT have been published in several different languages and several books. Critically, NMT—a relatively young approach—has been established as an "evidence-based practice" and we continue to learn of positive outcomes. There have been two international Neurosequential Model Symposia; held in 2014 and 2016 with another planned for 2018. The exchange of ideas and experiences continues to teach us at The ChildTrauma Academy how to improve our work and our models.

Of course, not everything is positive. The NMT certification process is challenging. It includes over 130 hours of instruction, clinical case conferences, multimedia content, and practice with NMT metrics. Web-based and web archived learning modules make this process more convenient for the learners, but it is always a challenge to change your frame of reference and learn a new way of thinking.

Indeed, this neurodevelopmental perspective and the NMT are major conceptual shifts for some clinicians and clinical settings—and introducing any novelty to systems in which people are already feeling overloaded and distressed is likely to elicit pushback. So now we are learning about what's known as "implementation science." That is, how do you get large systems to change, not just individuals? Many of the core principles introduced in this book, and our second collaboration, *Born for Love: Why Empathy Is Essential—and Endangered* have helped us begin to understand this, but we have much more to learn.

In general, and not too surprisingly, we find that if people and organizations seek us out and want to become certified, things go well; if, however, there is some administrative mandate to become certified and the clinical site or clinician has had no prior introduction to these concepts and they are simply told to comply, the process is less efficient.

We are trying to use what we know about the brain and stress to ease the introduction of novel techniques and ideas like NMT into large systems. The NMT certification process includes a Train-the-Trainer component because we want the organization to be able to continue growing and training itself without dependence on us.

To date, this has worked well. We now have more individuals who have been certified in using NMT by our trainers than those who trained in a direct certification process with The ChildTrauma Academy. In fact, I personally want to get out of the training business and back to more research and writing. Now that the original vision of thousands of similarly evaluated individuals is coming to fruition, my research team has a unique opportunity.

So far, approximately 30,000 NMT assessments have been conducted and the data have been collected into a single data set. Each month, thousands more entries are added. Of these, at least 10,000 are high-quality assessments from users with good fidelity, making them suitable for research and outcomes evaluation. We have a team of researchers—including a big data statistical genius—and they are now able to learn from these thousands of children, youth, and adults.

The preliminary findings are exciting and powerful. We now have the infrastructure for a completely new way to understand and study motor, emotional, social, and cognitive functioning—and rather than give an imprecise and potentially stigmatizing diagnosis, we are able to describe each person in a dynamic and visual manner.

Without expensive equipment, we can literally create a picture of how their brains seem to be organized and use it for treatment planning. The core assumption of the NMT model is that each person has an individual developmental path and a unique combination of strengths and vulnerabilities. We are always best able to help someone if we first know them. We can help them better know themselves, too, if we give them a picture, not a label.

We continue to explore. The children and families we work with continue to teach us; our colleagues from multiple cultures and disciplines continue to teach us. And we hope to continue to "Drink deep" and share more than "a little learning"—and that you will join us on this path towards a better understanding of how our experiences shape us as we each weave our unique life story.

Appendix

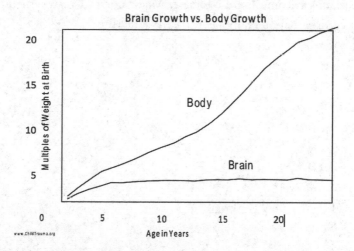

FIGURE 1. *Growth of the Body and the Brain.*

THE PHYSICAL GROWTH OF THE human body increases in a roughly linear manner from birth through adolescence. In contrast, the brain's physical growth follows a different pattern. The most rapid rate of growth takes place in utero, and from birth to age four the brain grows explosively. The brain of the four-year-old is 90 percent adult size! A majority of the physical growth of the brain's key neural networks takes place during this time. It is a time of great malleability and vulnerability as experiences are actively shaping the organizing brain. This is a time of great opportunity for the developing child: safe, predictable, nurturing and repetitive experiences can help express a full range of genetic potentials. Unfortunately, however, it is also when the organizing brain is most vulnerable to the destructive impact of threat, neglect and trauma.

However, this early pattern of brain growth does not mean that development or organization of the brain is finished. Indeed, important neurodevelopmental processes continue to take place throughout childhood and adolescence as the brain's systems become more complex. Major cortical restructuring and myelination continue into early adult life.

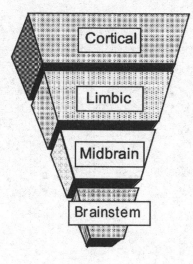

Abstract thought
Concrete Thought
Affiliation/reward
"Attachment"
Sexual Behavior
Emotional Reactivity
Motor Regulation
"Arousal"
Appetite/Satiety
Sleep
Blood Pressure
Heart Rate
Temperature

FIGURE 2. *Hierarchy of Brain Function.*

THE HUMAN BRAIN DEVELOPS sequentially in roughly the same order in which its regions evolved. The most primitive, central areas, starting with the brainstem, develop first. As a child grows, each successive brain region (moving out from the center toward the cortex), in turn, undergoes important changes and growth. But in order to develop properly each area requires appropriately timed, patterned, repetitive experiences. The neurosequential approach to helping traumatized and maltreated children first examines which regions and functions are underdeveloped or poorly functioning and then works to provide the missing stimulation to help the brain resume a more normal development.

Sense of Time	Extended Future	Days Hours	Hours Minutes	Minutes Seconds	No Sense of Time
Arousal Continuum	REST	VIGILANCE	RESISTANCE Crying	DEFIANCE Tantrums	AGGRESSION
Dissociative Continuum	REST	AVOIDANCE	COMPLIANCE Robotic	DISSOCIATION Fetal Rocking	FAINTING
Regulating Brain Region	NEOCORTEX Cortex	CORTEX Limbic	LIMBIC Midbrain	MIDBRAIN Brainstem	BRAINSTEM Autonomic
Cognitive Style	ABSTRACT	CONCRETE	EMOTIONAL	REACTIVE	REFLEXIVE
Internal State	CALM	ALERT	ALARM	FEAR	TERROR

FIGURE 3. *The Arousal Continuum, State-Dependent Learning and the Response to Threat.*

PEOPLE PROCESS, STORE, AND RETRIEVE information and then respond to the world in a manner that depends upon their current physiological state (in other words, their response is "state-dependent"). If a child has been exposed to extreme or pervasive threat or trauma, his stress system may become sensitized and he may respond to ordinary experiences as though they are threatening. Depending on his individual response to stress, he may move primarily along the dissociative or the arousal continuum, but either change will reduce his ability to learn cognitive information, such as schoolwork.

As a result his brain may be in a very different state than that of other children around him in a classroom. As the chart illustrates, a calm child will process information very differently from one who is in an "alarmed" state, whether he tends toward a dissociative or a hyperaroused response. Even if two children have identical IQs, the calmer child can more readily focus on the words of the teacher and, using her neocortex, engage in abstract thought and learning.

In contrast, the child who is alarmed will be less efficient at processing and storing the verbal information the teacher is providing. Subcortical and limbic areas will dominate this child's cognition. These areas focus on nonverbal information, such as the teacher's facial expressions, hand gestures, and perceived mood. Further, because the brain learns in a "use-dependent" fashion, this child will already have experienced more selective development of her nonverbal cognitive capacities. The child who has been traumatized or maltreated has learned that nonverbal information is more important than verbal—for example, "When Daddy smells like beer and walks funny, I know he will hurt Mommy."

As a child moves along the continuum of arousal, the part of the brain in control of his functioning shifts; the more distressed or threatened he is, the more primitive the behaviors and responses. During this state-related shift in cognition the child's sense of time is altered and the range of future planning is foreshortened. The threatened child is not thinking (nor should she think) about months from now: she is focused on the current threat.

This has profound implications for understanding the thoughts, reactions, and behavior of traumatized children. For these youth immediate reward is most reinforcing; delayed gratification is almost impossible. They are quite literally unable to consider the potential consequences of their behavior because of the physical arousal state of their brains.

As a result considered reflection about behavior—including violent behavior—is impossible for the child in an alarm state. Cut adrift from the internal regulating capabilities of the cortex, the brainstem acts reflexively, impulsively, and often aggressively to any perceived threat.

Due to this state-dependent processing, maltreated children may express a host of puzzling and seemingly insignificant "sensitivities." Eye contact for too long may be perceived as a life-threatening signal. A friendly touch to the shoulder may remind one child of sexual abuse by a stepfather. A well-intended, gentle tease to one may be a humiliating cut to another, similar to the endless sarcastic and degrading emotional abuse he experiences at home. A request to solve a problem on the board may terrify the girl living in a home where she can never do anything well enough. A slightly raised voice may feel like a shout to the little boy living in a violent home. To help traumatized children these responses must be taken into account and their stress response systems calmed so that they can feel safe enough to rely upon their higher brain functions and reduce the amount of time they spend higher on the arousal continuum.

Adapted from: Perry, B. D. "Fear and learning: trauma-related factors in education." *New Directions for Adult and Continuing Education, 110* (2006, Summer): 21–27.

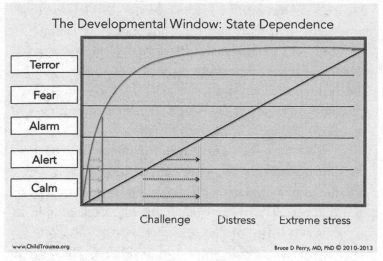

FIGURE 4. *The Developmental Window.*

THIS FIGURE ILLUSTRATES TWO stress-reactivity curves; the straight line is the reactivity curve of a "neurotypical" individual. This shows the linear relationship between the level of challenge, stress or threat and the appropriate proportional shift in internal state in the brain required to adapt and cope with the stressor. With minor stressors, there are minor shifts in the internal state—and with major stressors, a larger shift in internal state occurs. The top curved line illustrates the altered, sensitized stress-reactivity curve caused by patterns of extreme, unpredictable or prolonged stress activation. In this case, there is a significant over-activity at baseline and an overreaction even in the face of relatively minor challenges.

The major neural networks involved in the heterogeneous stress responses (see Chapters 2 and 3) can become 'sensitized' with patterns of activation that are unpredictable, extreme and prolonged. When this occurs, the major adaptive style used by the infant, toddler or child—either the hyperarousal (activate) or dissociation (shutdown) or, in some cases, both styles—becomes 'sensitized'—over active and overly reactive (see top curve).

The results are profoundly disruptive for subsequent development, as these over-reactions to novelty and stress will inhibit and distort the accurate processing of new experiences— even if the new experiences are predictable, consistent, nurturing, and enriching.

A major consequence of this sensitization is that it narrows the 'developmental' window (see hatched areas). Simply stated, in order to develop, learn or heal (i.e., make new associations in neural networks), the individual has to be exposed to novel experiences that, in turn, create novel patterns of neural activity.

For optimal development (or learning or therapeutic change), this novelty has to have a "Goldilocks" effect—enough novelty to challenge and expand the existing comfort zone (the set of previously acquired and mastered capabilities) but not so much novelty (or demand) that the capacity of the individual to process and assimilate is overwhelmed.

When someone has sensitized stress-response system(s), exposure to any novelty or unpredictability can rapidly move the person from active-alert to a state of fear, thereby interfering with the process of learning. The more sensitized the stress response, the narrower this therapeutic or learning "window" is, the smaller the dose of novelty that can be tolerated, and the less likely it will be that the child can benefit from typical developmental experiences. The end result is a profound frustration in parents and educators, resulting from the seemingly endless number of repetitions required for a child to master a concept or learn a behavior.

The key is to somehow shift this overly-reactive stress response either temporarily, by using some regulatory activity or, ideally, chronically by providing regular opportunities to experience controllable, predicable and moderate (for the individual) activations of their stress response systems.

Organizational Pressures	Resource-surplus Predictable Stable/Safe	Resource-limited Unpredictable Novel	Resource-poor Inconsistent Threatening
Prevailing Cognitive Capacity	Abstract Creative ("Group" IQ = 120)	Concrete Superstitious/Defensive ("Group" IQ = 100)	Reactive Regressive ("Group" IQ = 80)
Prevailing Affective 'Tone'	CALM	ANXIETY	FEAR
Systemic Solutions	Reflective INNOVATIVE	Concrete SIMPLISTIC	Fear-based REACTIONARY
Focus of Solution	FUTURE Intentional Inflection	SHORT-TERM Serendipitous Inflection	PRESENT Forced Inflection
Policies and Practices	Abstract Conceptual	Concrete Superstitious Intrusive	Restrictive Punitive
Staff & Supervisory Practices	Nurturing Flexible Enriching	Ambivalent Obsessive Controlling	Apathetic Oppressive Harsh

TABLE 1. *State-Dependence in Organizations.*

JUST AS THREAT ALTERS THE functioning of the individual (see Appendix, Table 1), it also changes functioning in an organization. Organizations—and the leaders in the organization who often set the emotional or affective "tone" within the organization—can experience a range of challenges. The cognitive capacity (Group IQ) of the group shifts as the affective tone in the organization shifts.

When there are no external threats and resources are plentiful and predictable (Column 1), individuals within the group have the luxury of thinking in abstract ways to solve problems (e.g., Bell Labs from 1940 to 1965). This is a very rare condition for an entire organization; some organizations are able to "protect" a small group (e.g. an R & D division) within the organization to do their "abstract" and creative thinking but even this is very rare. When it does happen, the innovations and problem-solving focus on the future, changes within the organization are intentional (inflections), and the least powerful members of the organization (e.g., front line case workers) can be treated with flexible, nurturing, and enriching approaches.

When resources become limited and there are economic, environmental, or social threats (Column 2), the organization becomes less capable of complex, abstract problem solving. Any "inflections"—major changes in organizational—direction tend to be serendipitous or accidental. All government systems are usually in this state; they stumble into the future, with a focus on self-preservation. The practices and programs are responsive to the immediate future (e.g., the next funding cycle, the next election cycle) and all aspects of functioning in the group regress. The least powerful are ignored or controlled to minimize any excessive drain on the most powerful.

In the organization under direct threat (Column 3), the focus of all problem solving becomes the moment. Organizational inflections are "forced" (e.g., consent decrees, bankruptcy). The solutions to current problems tend to be reactive and regressive. The more out of control the external situation is, the more controlling, reactive, and oppressive the internally focused actions of this group will become. In each of these situations, the supervisory styles will create employees that will reinforce the organization's structure: in a safe and abstract-thinking group the staff will be more likely to receive and benefit from enrichment and education, thereby optimizing their potential for creativity, abstraction, and productivity. In contrast, staff in organizations under threat will be more likely to reflect their impulsive, concrete, and reactive supervision—and be so dysregulated that their interactions with clients, students, parents, and children will be incapable of helping any of them regulate. They will be ineffective—and sometimes actually destructive, further creating distress and unpredictability for the very people they are charged to engage, respect, help, and heal.

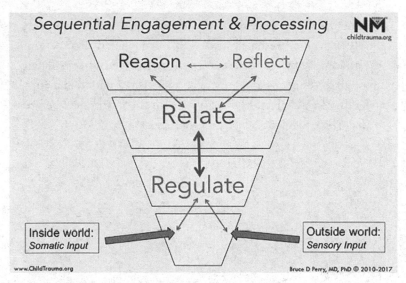

FIGURE 5. *Sequence of Engagement.*

ALL INCOMING SENSORY SIGNALS from the outside world and from our body (the inside world) are first processed in lower areas of the brain. These lower areas of the brain can act on that information and pass it "up" to higher areas of the brain for more complex sorting, integration, and interpretation. If the nature of the incoming neural activity is "familiar" and neutral or familiar and previously categorized as "safe" these lower areas of the brain pass the information up without activating and significant "stress" response. If, however, the incoming information is unfamiliar (novel), or familiar and previously associated with threat, pain, or fear, these lower areas of the brain will activate a stress response—even before the fully integrated and accurately interpreted information can get to the "smart" parts of the brain. This activation will also interfere with the accurate cortical processing by "shutting down" certain areas of the cortex. The result is that the activated stress response will create a host of "state-dependent" shifts in thinking, feeling, and behaving. The sequential nature of processing all sensory experience means that if we want to "get to the cortex" and reason with another person, we must adhere to a sequence of interaction; we and the individual we are interacting with must be regulated enough to connect—and only once there is regulation and connection can we effectively "reason" with them. Connect before you correct; regulate, relate, and then, reason.

Chapter Commentaries for the 2017 Edition

Chapter One: Tina's World

Ten years is a long time in a child's life—but a mere instant in the development of a discipline like child psychiatry or the neurosciences. During the decade since the first edition of this book was released, much progress has been made in these fields. Yet systems—and the ideas within them that frame policies, practices, and programs—change far more slowly.

It is estimated, for example, that once a new concept or principle of practice is well established by research, it takes between twenty and thirty years for the "new" ideas to become standard practice. And, as we all know, by that time there is often newer research that suggests modifications and improvements on this "innovation"—and it will take years before these become standard practice, too. The bottom line is that the rate of discovery is faster than the rate at which an organization or system can adapt and incorporate these changes.

We see evidence of this "innovation gap" in all aspects of our life. An important example related to the main challenges that faced Tina and her family is in the early childhood area. For decades, there has been overwhelming economic and developmental research demonstrating the value of high-quality early childhood interventions for "at risk" young families like hers. For every one dollar invested in high-quality early childhood programs like preschool and support for new parents, nine are returned in terms of improved academic performance, better employment, and reduced addiction, mental illness, and crime—yet we still do not provide high-quality, affordable preschool, paid family leave, and adequate support for vulnerable families. Sadly, if anything our public systems like child mental health, child welfare, juvenile justice, and education are slower to change than other organizations such as those in the corporate sector.

Over these last ten years, The ChildTrauma Academy has been working to close its "innovation gap" in several areas. One of the most important relates to the conceptualization of "therapy." In the twenty-five years since I worked with Tina, my understanding of therapy and the therapeutic interaction has changed dramatically.

During our work, as we challenged ourselves to better understand these children, we kept asking: what is a meaningful therapeutic interaction? How long should that interaction be? Fifty minutes? Ten minutes? Two seconds? Does the "dosing schedule" of therapy—and the supposed therapeutic interactions—have to be once a week for fifty minutes? Could it be twice a week for thirty minutes or some other variant? What is an effective dose of therapy? Who provides that therapeutic experience? Only a "trained" professional? Or can a parent, coach, friend—or the client herself, in an inner process—provide a therapeutic moment?

And how much time do you need between therapeutic interactions to optimize positive change? How do you "space" the therapeutic doses? Are there specific patterns that lead to more effective change—or is simple regularity enough? And are there specific environments or experiences that interfere with—or enhance—a therapeutic interaction?

Over the last ten years our interest and understanding of these issues has matured. In the last paragraph of "Tina's World," we note that an hour a week of therapy was unable to "undo that set of associations," which were related to her history of being abused. It is more accurate now to re-phrase that comment; therapy does not undo associations. Instead, it creates new associations which, over time, can become the new "default" or "template" for guiding responses to future experiences.

In Tina's case, if she had been given enough time and opportunity to interact with healthy and attuned men and boys who provided sufficient positive or neutral interactions for a long enough time and in a clear enough pattern, she could have created new default associations about men—and male attributes. The associations created by her early history of sexual abuse would remain, although hopefully over time they would be much less "activated" and their intensity would fade.

The major challenge here is that we know so little about how to dose and schedule therapeutic experiences in order to create this therapeutic change. But study of the brain and how it changes may provide us some clues. These days, the buzzword in neuroscience is "neuroplasticity," which refers to the capacity of neurons and their networks to be altered by experience.

There are some promising clues to the concept of therapeutic dosing in the study of how new synapses—those connections between neurons that link them into networks—are formed and altered to create or change memories. One of the most studied and most important areas of the neurosciences has to do with what is called Long-term Potentiation (LTP). Basically, this refers to the strengthening of synaptic connections, which occurs in response to a brief pattern of intense stimulation. The resulting cascade of cellular changes following this intense stimulation leads to enduring neuronal changes all the way to the chromosome, altering gene expression. It is widely believed that LTP is an important factor in learning and memory formation.

This has important implications for the dosing of therapy: it suggests that even really short experiences can have a big impact. Indeed, long-term and enduring changes in neural networks can be created by an intense period of stimulation that lasts less than a minute. Synaptic splitting, which is one way these connections can change, can occur in mere seconds of intense stimulation—and if the intense experience is repeated four times within an hour, the change will be maintained long term.

Just as a traumatic experience can alter a life in an instant, so too can a therapeutic encounter. Unfortunately, in order for positive "doses" of interaction to lead to long-term change, much more repetition is needed. Consequently, the pattern and spacing required to ensure long-term maintenance of any therapeutic change is going to require a density of therapeutic interactions that our current mental health model of fifty minutes once a week cannot provide. For children like Tina to truly benefit from therapy, it needs to be embedded in a context of safe and positive interactions.

The good news is that anyone can help with this part of "therapy"—it merely requires being present in social settings and being, well, basically, kind. An attentive, attuned, and responsive person will help create opportunities for a traumatized child to control the dose and pattern of rewiring their trauma-related associations. For people who have been sexually abused, like Tina, just being acknowledged in a supportive, respectful, and non-threatening way aids healing. The more we can provide each other these moments of simple, human connection—even a brief nod or moment of eye contact—the more we'll be able to help heal those who have suffered traumatic experience.

Chapter Two: For Your Own Good

Today, no one would argue that a three-year-old who witnessed the death of her mother, was slashed and left for dead, then placed in foster care is not at risk for suffering lasting psychological damage. While, thankfully, most children have the capacity to recover, the data suggesting that severe early life stress can have a lifelong impact has only continued to accumulate since this book was first published.

So too has our understanding of the role of sensitization and tolerance in trauma and healing. These are two key processes that alter critical stress response networks in the brain. Sensitization amps up the baseline activity and reactivity of these systems, while tolerance dampens down stress response reactivity. (See Figure 6 at the end of this commentary.) Importantly, there are certain patterns of activation that lead to sensitization and can cause problems, while other patterns lead to tolerance and can build resilience.

Neuroscientists have been studying these phenomena for over 50 years. Their relevance to experiences like drug use, addiction, and pain management have long been obvious, but ten years ago, their importance in understanding the effects of childhood trauma was only beginning to be recognized.

Today, the neurobiology of sensitization and tolerance has taught us a great deal about the crucial roles of pattern and predictability in the development and regulation of our stress response systems. Early life experience sets the template for later life responses—this is true of our stress responses, not just our memories. Changing the average level of activity in stress systems and their responsiveness or reactivity during development can have profound and lingering effects.

The key point here is that some patterns of experience make these systems become more easily activated and more prone to reacting even to small changes—while other patterns help allow these systems to respond more smoothly and with less likelihood of over-reaction. Thus, the decades of neuroscience research that suggest how these mechanisms work can account not only for how and why symptoms can result from potentially traumatic experiences but can also give us essential clues to the healing process.

One of the major advances in the clinical arena over the last ten years is the understanding that some forms of developmental experience—for instance, food and housing insecurity, racial or cultural marginalization, and other stresses often associated with poverty—can result in physiological, emotional, social, and cognitive symptoms similar to those seen following extreme traumatic events, including physical or sexual abuse or exposure to domestic violence.

This has led some in the field to refer to big "T" trauma versus little "t" trauma; we don't use that language but appreciate the point being made. We prefer to think of both capital "T" and small "t" as examples of "sensitizing" patterns of stress response activation that would result in predictable changes throughout the brain and body.

In neuroscience studies, you can create a sensitized stress response by simply creating uncontrollable, unpredictable exposure to small stressors, which, if experienced only once or twice or if their timing was known in advance, would not be likely to be traumatic for typical people. Many of us have had real-life experience with this, for example, in a workplace where a supervisor is unpredictably shaming, then supportive, then angry. Over time, in this situation, many employees become will become sensitized to the boss's moods and experience anxiety, intrusive thoughts and worries, particularly a desire to avoid dealing with the person. These are all classic PTSD symptoms, though a bad boss rarely will be awful enough to cause a full-fledged case in an adult with no history of developmental adversity.

This same sensitization—often described as "walking on eggshells"—can happen with foster or adoptive parents when the behaviors of the child are, to the carers, completely unpredictable. Obviously, a child's tantrum is not considered a "traumatic" event on the scale of witnessing a shooting, yet over time the physiological and psychological effects of many small, uncontrollable stresses can be very similar to those we associate with more extreme experiences.

The pattern and context of stress system activation—i.e., whether it is controllable or not, whether it occurs predictably or not—is as important as the intensity of the activation, and can sometimes be more so. In the real world, this means that a child of color living in poverty with no exposure to abuse, domestic violence, or other overt "trauma" can develop "trauma-related" problems that look just like those seen in a child who witnessed a shooting or lived through a natural disaster. And, if children like this also have exposure to overt major trauma such as community violence, their problems will be compounded.

To explore this further, let's briefly review the features of the patterns of stress activation that can lead to a less sensitive, less reactive stress response capacity. As we've seen, the majority of physical, emotional, behavioral, social, and cognitive problems related to developmental trauma can be linked to changes in the pervasive, widely-distributed neural networks involved in responding to stressors. We've seen as well that neural networks are "plastic"—capable of changing. So what does research in the area of neuroplasticity tell us about how to change these systems?

The first and primary principle of neuroplasticity is that in order to intentionally modify—in any way—a specific neural network, we must first "activate" (or, in some cases "deactivate") that _specific_ neural network. This of course seems obvious; in order to learn how to play the piano, one must sit at the piano and play. Reading a book or watching a YouTube video about playing piano won't change the _specific_ neural networks responsible for piano playing. Your time at the piano may benefit from what you can learn in a book or video, but you will not create or modify the widely-distributed neural network that allows "piano playing" unless you activate it fully by actually tickling the ivories.

The same is true for traumatic memory and the sensitized stress response networks that are yoked to the complex, widely-distributed trauma reaction that follows the traumatic event. For Sandy, her set of trauma memories were reinforced and strengthened each time an evocative cue activated this chain: for example, when she did something as simple as drink milk. The vast majority of these activations for the first years following her mother's murder were unpredictable to her because she didn't know when to expect them. As a result, her stress response systems became more and more sensitized, and she often experienced an extreme and prolonged response. And as a result of that, she got worse.

A major challenge of doing therapy when trauma and sensitized stress responses are involved is that the principle of specificity has to be applied in order to change the sensitized stress response systems; healing involves the process of "revisiting" and "reactivating" very painful experiences in some way. The key to effective healing and therapeutic work is paying attention to the three essential elements of the resilience-building and healing pattern of stress activation. These are predictability, controllability, and moderation.

What we've learned about these factors since we first wrote this book relates back to the concept of "dosing." What is a moderate dose of revisiting a trauma and reactivating a chain of traumatic memory? Who determines what is moderate? Should it be the clinician who asks the child to recount the traumatic event— or the child?

When we ask a child to come to our office once a week for a 50-minute dose of revisiting, doesn't that, in itself, take control away from him or her? Can we create safe and regulated settings for children to control the dose, space, and pattern of their healing journeys? In Sandy's case, during our therapy, she could go back to these dark times, spend some moments living with the pain of the reactivated trauma memory—but she also could control her own disengagement, so she could regulate herself before revisiting the experience.

She controlled what parts of that experience she would reactivate and reenact—this provided controllability. She also decided for herself how long she would stay there—this controlled the dosage. She determined how much time would pass before she would revisit those experiences, which controlled the spacing of the experience. In our sessions, she allowed herself to activate some component of her pervasive trauma memory, and then created controllable, predictable, and moderate activation of her sensitized stress response systems. Over time, this led to a less reactive system, a shift in symptoms, and some degree of healing.

We cannot emphasize enough how important it is for traumatized children to be given the most possible control, predictability, and ability to moderate the timing, duration, and intensity of their experiences. They need these elements to be maximized, not just in therapy—but in the rest of their lives, particularly places where they spend a lot of time, like school. To become resilient, children need environments where they feel safe and comfortable, and know what to expect so that their sensitized, overreactive stress systems can gradually become calmer, and more "smoothly" regulated.

(The chart below illustrates the key principles here).

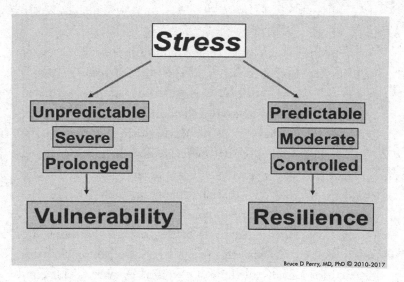

Bruce D Perry, MD, PhD © 2010-2017

Chapter Three: Stairway to Heaven

Almost twenty-five years have passed since the disastrous raid on David Koresh's Ranch Apocalypse in Waco, Texas, and in that time, our understanding of how threat and fear affect both groups and individuals has evolved.

Specifically, we have learned much more about the importance of relationships *within a group* to create opportunities for development and healing—or to do the opposite. Increasingly, we're realizing that the health of the group can have a large effect on the health of an individual.

As we've seen, perceived threat and fear will change the way the brain works in any given situation. In general, when people feel threatened, key networks in the cortex will shut down: specifically, the regions involved in reasoning, planning, and other complex thinking. This allows rapid action in emergencies, but is obviously not the state of mind you want to have when you are in class or studying for a test (see Appendix, Figure 3).

In fact, all of the functions of the brain—learning, thinking, feeling, moving, regulating hormones and other chemicals—are "state-dependent." This means they will change with our physical, and importantly here, emotional states and experiences.

The consequences are profound: a child in a state of fear will have a difficult time learning anything, even physical activities, like sports. And children's behaviors will reflect their emotional state: during fear, they are primed to fight, freeze, or flee, as we have seen.

But as we discuss in much greater depth in our second book, *Born for Love*, groups also respond to situations in a state-dependent manner (see Appendix, Figure 5). Human beings are social creatures, and our individual neurobiology and body physiology are influenced by those around us. The moods and actions of those around us are contagious—especially those of the perceived "leader" of the group. This has countless implications: the most relevant of these for working with traumatized, maltreated, and fearful children is that the "helping" adults cannot teach children to regulate their emotions and behaviors unless they themselves are in an emotionally calm and reasonably well-regulated state.

Just like dogs, all humans, especially traumatized children, can sense fear and anxiety—so self-care for those who work with maltreated children is essential for effective therapy. Front line workers—or parents, teachers, or caregivers—who are themselves being poorly treated by supervisors or others in power can inadvertently pass their distress down to these vulnerable children.

This means that a demoralized, disrespected, and overworked clinician will have a hard time being effective. An underpaid, micro-managed teacher will be less likely to inspire learning, and an overwhelmed, anxious and exhausted foster carer will be less capable of being present, nurturing, and regulating. (Sandra Bloom's Sanctuary Model, which helps organizations prioritize this insight, is among the best I've seen. For those who would like to help leadership implement relevant changes, see Sanctuaryweb.com for more information.)

Another major change in the field in the past decade is the increased awareness of the "Adverse Childhood Experiences (ACEs)" epidemiological studies. As we mention throughout the book, developmental adversity impacts the entire body—not just the brain. The first ACE study, which looked at the current health of 17,000 adults, was led by Robert Anda of the Centers for Disease Control and Vince Felitti of Kaiser Permanente in California. They began publishing results in 1998. The basic findings were stunning: as the number of ACEs increased, so did the risk for everything from heart disease, stroke, and obesity to addictions and depression in adult life. (We discuss this work throughout the book; for more on the specifics of this research, see Chapter Seven in *Born for Love*). Despite the importance and power of these findings, a twenty-year "innovation gap" followed. Only within the past five years have these important studies begun to have widespread impact on practice and policy.

These and similar findings have led to an explosion of "trauma-informed" practices in education, juvenile justice, mental health, child protection, and even in neighborhoods. This has been heartening and there are many programs that have truly made a difference in children's lives.

At the same time, unfortunately, as with all large-scale shifts of focus in society, especially when people recognize that there is money to be made, there is a lot of chaff with the wheat. Self-declared experts arise with packages of programs allowing systems to "check the box" about being "trauma-informed." Over time, this will settle out, and we remain hopeful that the ultimate result will be positive.

In the meantime, appreciating how state-dependence plays out in organizations can be useful in understanding some of the challenges we face when attempting to make positive changes in practice, programs, and policy in any organization or system (see Appendix, Figure 5).

Chapter Four: Skin Hunger

Over the years, I have been asked about almost all of the individual children we discuss in the book. Sometimes people want an update; often someone will identify closely with one of these children; some people describe sharing similar symptoms and feel relieved to understand a bit more about themselves. Clinicians, too, will share that they had similar challenges or point out where I neglected to mention a key issue, which was frequent, owing to both my own limitations and those inherent in writing about very complex clinical situations. And some people even have offered to foster or adopt one of these children.

The comments and queries vary; by far, however, the most frequent questions are about Mama P. *Can I just meet Mama P. ? Does she live in Texas? Does she still take in children? I think I know Mama P.*

We all should have a Mama P. in our lives. The wonderful qualities of Mama P.—her patience, strength, wisdom, and capacity for love—made her a special and powerful healer, and as a longtime leader in the foster care community, a key part of the child welfare system where she lives. Nonetheless, I must keep her personal information private.

I started my adult psychiatry residency at Yale in 1984. Since then, the nature of child welfare in the United States has shifted dramatically. One major change has been in the way children and families are served by the child welfare system. With a new emphasis on finding "forever families" for children, the system has focused increasingly on getting children into permanent guardianship—often with someone in their extended family, like an aunt or grandparent—or adoption. From the perspective of child trauma, this is a positive trend, but, as with everything else involving human systems, the shift has not occurred without raising a different set of problems.

In the US, the responsibility for funding and carrying out child welfare services such as investigation, removing children from homes deemed unsafe, placing children in foster homes, shelters, kinship homes, and funding some level of evaluation and needed medical and mental health services falls to the state. Each individual state will choose how to do this: some states delegate the majority of these responsibilities to counties and provide some organizational oversight and funding, while other states have a system that is unified at the state level.

In all cases, the federal government provides some funding for these agencies. Title IV-E is a federal program that will reimburse states for some of the cost of providing foster care, adoption assistance, and kinship guardianship assistance on behalf of each child who meets federal eligibility criteria. Not all children who require care from Child Protective Services do meet these criteria, so generally speaking IV-E-funded cases are an underestimate of the actual numbers of children served by the states. Nonetheless, the shifts in Title IV-E-funded cases from 1984 through to 2013 indicate the dramatic change in the focus of child welfare resources.

In 1984, there were 102,100 children in "out of home" or substitute care—in other words, foster care or kinship care—

funded by Federal IV-E funding. There were 11,600 children in IV-E adoption or guardianship homes. Thus, just 10% of the total funded cases were in permanent placements. But by 2001, 49%—and by 2013 74%—of the IV-E-funded children were adopted or with permanent guardians. In 2015, roughly 430,000 children were in foster care (both IV-E- and non-IV-E-supported), and at least 500,000 were in IV-E-supported permanent adoptive or guardianship homes.

So why does this shift in IV-E-funded cases matter? This entire book is about the impact that developmental trauma, neglect, attachment disruptions, and related childhood adversity can have on the child. And we know that the rates of significant emotional, behavioral, social, and cognitive problems in children removed from their homes can reach up to 70%, if not more, over time. The number of children in need grows; the problems related to their developmental trauma don't disappear when they enter a "forever home."

Over time, the burden of dealing with these children's complex problems has shifted to the families providing elements of permanence for these children: kin and adoptive carers. But the child welfare system has not caught up enough (remember the "innovation gap") to develop high quality "developmentally-informed" and "trauma-sensitive" resources for these families or for the foster families that care for hundreds of thousands of these children each year. We are simply shifting the problems from one system to another.

If only there were 430,000 Mama P.'s available to provide the individualized, nurturing care that the 430,000 children in foster care require—and deserve. If only the half a million children in permanent or adoptive care had caregivers who understood the complexities of developmental trauma. Unfortunately, the foster care systems in most states struggle to get qualified homes—and when they do recruit a family, the amount of education provided about development, trauma, attachment, and the various challenges these children face is minimal. Most carers are self-taught with all of the potential benefits and pitfalls that can bring. In general, many of our foster and adoptive carers are overwhelmed by the needs and challenges of these children, and many tend to be poorly equipped or supported to deal with the range of complex problems that these children often have.

On top of that, schools are even less capable of being supportive of the foster family's efforts, often ignoring good input from the foster or adoptive parent and implementing practices such as suspension, expulsion, seclusion, and restraint. All of these measures simply make things worse for the child and the family.

Then, there is the medical community—who should know more about all of these issues—who are viewed as the experts by schools, families, and, all too often, themselves. The medical community—including psychiatry—can be as trauma-and-development-ignorant as any other. Over the last ten years, this has not changed much, unfortunately.

And one area where this ignorance is especially tragic is in the inappropriate and harmful use of medications. If anything, this has become worse over the last ten years. Irrational psychopharmacology—where doctors prescribe medications for which there is no evidence of effectiveness or actual evidence that the medication does *not* work—has exploded. So has the use of multiple medications, or poly-pharmacy, even though there is rarely any evidence related to whether or not it helps.

Foster children are much more likely than other children with similar problems to be prescribed multiple medications that will have no impact on their symptoms. These medications, particularly the so-called atypical antipsychotics (medications like Risperdal, Abilify, and Seroquel) can shorten life and have severe side effects, like weight gain great enough to increase risk for diabetes.

The over prescribing and inappropriate prescribing of such

medications to children in foster care has been so dramatic that the Government Accountability Office has issued a special report condemning it. Both the federal government and several states have sued Big Pharma for targeting foster care children, resulting in multi-million-dollar settlements.

In the last few years, attention to these issues by legal groups, such as the National Center for Youth Law in Oakland, the press (an excellent example can be seen in the online series from the Mercury News by Karen de Sa), and advocacy groups such as Foster Youth in Action, has increased awareness of this problem. These investigations and advocacy are leading to some positive changes. For example, California passed legislation to monitor prescribing to children in foster care.

But sadly, rather than joining in or even leading efforts to improve the quality of care for foster and adopted youth, most medical and psychiatric groups have resisted or even openly opposed these efforts. Change is hard, and it is hardest for those with the most to lose. As Annette Jackson and I wrote in 2014, "the academic or interest group most threatened by the innovations which challenge their existing frame of reference or perspective, will be the most vocal and hostile to the new ideas." Nevertheless, we persist.

Chapter Five: The Coldest Heart

Looking back at this chapter, I laughed—and blushed—at the arrogance of our last sentence. We are still nowhere near unlocking the secrets of the brain, and, if anything, advances in the developmental and social neurosciences have added complexities that we didn't even know about ten years ago. It's that "the more we learn, the less we know" thing. We are still far from understanding complex cases of sociopathy like Leon's.

In addition, we are learning that the quality of the genetics, neurochemistry, and neuroimaging studies that have examined human psychiatric conditions like sociopathy are woefully inadequate and may be essentially uninterpretable: too often, they have inadequate sample sizes, poor characterizations of the population studied—and of course, they use DSM labels, which, as we've seen, are deeply problematic.

As a field, we have spent a lot of time and money getting, well, not too far, in understanding the complexities of brain development and its effect on behavior. With all of that said, we are still actually making progress.

As we slowly increase our understanding of development, the brain, and humankind, there will always be a gap between what we are learning and what we can actually apply. Right now, that chasm seems especially large—but it is often darkest just before dawn.

Sometimes, of course, we create practices, programs, and policy based on "what we know" only to learn later that this "understanding" was immature or even wrong. Psychiatry has far too many examples of this: the frontal lobotomy, ice-cold baths, and insulin-induced shock are only the low lights. The area of what is now known as "translational medicine" is intended to take what is being discovered in basic sciences and develop practical applications of those discoveries. The concept is good; the application part has been challenging, and this occurs at least in part both because of the "innovation gap" and the tendency of those who benefit from the existing approaches to push back when "translational" innovations emerge.

Our working group has always been at the interface between discovery and application; we have attempted to bring advances in the neurosciences—and related disciplines—into clinical practice, education, and caregiving. This requires "translating" complex facts, principles, and concepts into a language that is clear and understandable. A key problem is that things really do get lost in translation. Due to the abundance of facts in the neurosciences, we often choose to teach concepts or general principles when we communicate to non-neuroscientists; we use shorthand and teaching devices to illustrate the key concepts, such as the images and tables included in the Appendix.

But for each principle, there are often important exceptions to the rule.

And simplification often includes hidden distortions that can lead to false conclusions when people try to generalize from it. An attempt to teach about the explosive rate of development in utero and in the first years of life, for example, can get turned into "Dr. Perry says it's too late to change the brain after age three."

Another example of this over the last ten years has been seen in the emerging "trauma-informed" world. The phrases "the amygdala hijacks the brain" and "an amygdala storm" have become common language amongst the "trauma-informed." The attempt to teach a little about the neurobiology of threat interpretation and how fear alters the way we process and act on information gets turned into a distorting buzz phrase.

Unfortunately, people like simple explanations such as "The amygdala is the 'fear center'" and a child's meltdown is an "amygdala hijacking." Misunderstandings and distortion about the complex functioning of the amygdala in processing and interpreting fear-related cues became so pervasive that Joseph LeDoux, the pioneer in study of the amygdala and fear, and the person typically cited when the "amygdala storm" language is used, finally wrote a blog entry about it. It was titled *"The Amygdala Is NOT the Brain's Fear Center."* Indeed, this region is involved in many different emotions and the complexity of the brain means that phrases like "hijacking" often incorrectly reduce complex human behaviors into the actions of will-less zombies.

Translational work has implications for policy and practice outside of clinical settings. The legal system, for example, has been using neuroscience and developmental trauma research in a variety of ways. Cognitive impairment and obvious mental illnesses—both neurobiological conditions—have always been taken into consideration in determining guilt and sentencing. In recent landmark cases, including two Supreme Court cases, the role of the "immature adolescent cortex" in judgment and impulsivity has been cited in modifying sentencing guidelines related to the death penalty and life without parole; neither sentence can now be used with adolescents. The ChildTrauma Academy has been involved in educating the courts and the juvenile justice system about the neurobiology of trauma, the role of trauma in the development of violent behaviors, the impact of seclusion and solitary confinement, the effects of indiscriminate use of shackles on youth in court, and especially, the creation of trauma-aware and trauma-sensitive practices in juvenile justice settings.

Unfortunately, the legal system is also vulnerable to the "mistranslations" or distorted interpretations of work on trauma and development. On numerous occasions, I have been asked to become an expert witness to give testimony about the impact that a given experience has had on a person; this is a significant area in civil (not criminal) litigation, seeking to prove "damages" following some event or injury. Sometimes the event is clearly traumatic. For example, an employee is seriously injured in an explosion at a factory that also kills several co-workers and the effects are obvious: sleep problems, anxiety, cue-specific panic, avoidant behaviors.

In other cases, the legal team will try to convince me that an adolescent living in a household with documented history of domestic violence was instead "traumatized" by a hostile teacher and that his impulsive and aggressive behaviors all stem from this teacher's "abusive" practices, such as giving him a "0" on a homework assignment that he forgot to bring in.

I don't do very much forensic work, and when I do, I try to pick cases where I think I can learn something—and Leon's case was, in fact, one of these. Over the last ten years, research has confirmed that people convicted of violent crimes, like Leon, have astoundingly high rates of early life attachment disruption and chronic developmental trauma, especially exposure to violence. These findings have lead to efforts to create a "trauma-aware" judiciary and "trauma-informed" juvenile justice and criminal justice programs—in prisons and probation. True rehabilitation will not be possible without awareness of the multiple complex effects of trauma, neglect, poverty, racism, and other developmental adversities. Addressing recidivism and successful re-entry to the community is impossible without a respectful, humane, *and* developmentally-informed, trauma-aware perspective.

"Translation" matters. It does help the people in these systems better understand these children, youth, and families, and this can truly help improve our systems. And, no matter how often our efforts at translation get twisted, we can't give up. Connect, correct, clarify, and carry on.

Chapter Six: The Boy Who Was Raised as a Dog

Both Justin and Connor experienced severe early neglect, as well as other traumatic stressors that profoundly affected their development. For Justin, having been raised in a kennel with much canine, but little human contact, was obviously not a normal upbringing; Connor, who was simply left alone all day during the work week for his first 18 months by a negligent nanny also suffered enduring problems.

It's pretty much inevitable for people who are trained to be doctors—and psychiatrists particularly—to focus on pathology when we meet children like Justin and Connor. How do we identify and measure their deficits? What can we do to understand the causes of their problems? What are the mechanisms that led to these specific difficulties, and bearing these in mind, what can we do to try to help?

This chapter was written with that general frame of reference. Ten years on, however, I have become much more focused on the strength and resilience demonstrated by children like Connor and Justin in the face of such dramatic and devastating experiences. Most importantly, I want to know why they were able to make such rapid progress while other children with similar symptoms and seemingly similar abuse and neglect do not. The key word here turns out to be "seemingly."

If the children in this book tell us anything, it is: "Listen closely and look carefully at my life story." Unfortunately, in medicine, we are notoriously "bad listeners" and are often poor observers. It takes time to gather a complete and thorough developmental history—certainly much more time than a typical initial assessment visit to most clinics allows. Multiple sources of "patient history" are required to fill in the gaps. These include medical and educational records, conversations with parents, teachers, previous mental health providers, and more. All of these take time and money to gather. And even if you do all of this, if you don't ask and don't look for the presence of critical experiences that influence development, you won't find them.

Systematic evaluation for a history of developmental trauma (or adverse childhood experience, ACE) is only now becoming a routine component of a mental health evaluation—and this is a significant advance. Still, it is rarely included in typical pediatric visits—despite the fact that we know this is a major risk factor for physical health problems such as asthma, diabetes, and cardiovascular risk. As discussed throughout the book, the timing and nature of developmental trauma matters. As we developed our NMT assessment process, we realized it was essential to quantify the nature, severity, and timing of an individual's developmental trauma. But does this allow us to "look carefully" enough?

As we mention in this chapter, these two boys had two things in common: early neglect and a good response to developmentally-appropriate intervention. Closer examination of their histories gives us some clues to why they were so responsive to treatment. Despite his years of neglect, Justin did have positive relational connections in his first year of life, before his primary caregiver, his grandmother, died. Once he started living in the kennel, he also did have the warm physical contact and unconditional love that so many of us get from dogs, albeit in more typical situations.

In Connor's case, he had normal and healthy loving parenting for the first eight weeks of his life—along with ongoing "booster" touch and connection in the evenings and weekends throughout the time he was neglected. Both of these boys had an abnormal but partial history of positive relational interactions in the first years of life. Even fragmented positive interactions were protective.

"Listening closely and looking carefully" means that we need to quantify children's "relational health"—in other words, the nature, number, quality, and timing of their relational connections, what we might call their overall "social connectedness." Social connectedness refers to the quality and number of connections an individual has with family, friends, and acquaintances: it is a key component of community and cultural cohesiveness. As we discuss in depth in our second book, *Born for Love*, this connectedness is a major factor in both individual and community health.

As we worked to develop the NMT, we created a process to measure the timing and severity of adversity such as abuse and neglect—as well as the timing and intensity of "social connectedness," which includes the strength of the child's connection to healthy aspects of family, community, and culture.

The "balance" between the scores on the adversity measure and the relational health measure gives us a more accurate estimate of true "developmental risk"—in other words, a child with a strong network of social connectedness is at far less risk from a potentially traumatic experience than a child without such support would be.

Over the last six years, The ChildTrauma Academy's network of clinical partners has systematically evaluated over 30,000 children, youth, and adults using these adversity and relational health measures. We also looked at the current emotional, social, behavioral, and cognitive functioning of these 30,000 individuals.

What we learned included some significant surprises. The first and most important of these is that relational health measures are more predictive of outcomes than adverse developmental experiences are. In other words, having a strong social network with many, high quality relational interactions over time predicts good mental health and other positive outcomes better than traumatic experiences predict poor prospects. Relational connectedness buffers current distress and helps heal past trauma.

That's not to say that developmental adversity doesn't do serious harm—it certainly can. But strong relational health can help protect children from lasting damage connected to these experiences and is essential to their resilience. Consequently, if you want to predict someone's mental health and functioning based on their childhood experiences, looking at positive social factors will actually tell you more than focusing exclusively on trauma. If there is trauma, good social supports can actually counteract the harm that has occurred.

This observation has profound implications. For one, it's consistent with data on population and community health, which shows that social support is critical for health and that communities lacking healthy social ties tend to be wracked by problems like diabetes, heart disease, obesity, and addictions. These findings are also in line with research on resilience, which again, links it to social ties and healthy support. Finally, it suggests important and practical intervention and prevention strategies, such as measures that aid school and community connection, programs to support and connect parents, and basically anything that helps people make friends and nurture families.

Our research also confirmed that the timing of developmental risk does make a significant difference in outcomes. In twelve-year-old children, for example, having been maltreated in the absence of social buffering during the first year of life—and then being in a much healthier and safer environment for the next eleven years—led to worse outcomes than the reverse; i.e., where the child was healthy and safe in the first year, but not for the next eleven! In this case, the first year of good experience helped "inoculate" against the eleven years of adversity—but unfortunately, a bad first year was really tough to overcome, even with eleven years of safe and positive experience.

This pattern is consistent with what we know about brain development, so much of which occurs in the first few years. It's also consistent with the large impact of high quality home visitation models like Healthy Families America and Nurse-Family Partnership, which involves nurses visiting and regularly supporting first-time moms during pregnancy and the first year of a child's life. These programs have been shown to improve academic achievement and cut crime and addiction later in life.

Nonetheless, seeing these large effects of early experience come out so strongly in our data is sobering.

Currently the public systems we have to identify and help the most isolated, marginalized, struggling young families—and their infants—are under-resourced and ill-equipped to meet the demands. As our society struggles with the myriad problems related to childhood trauma, developmental adversity, and relational poverty, it will be essential to infuse the problem-solving process with well-interpreted, quality data. If we don't learn from these children and families—if we don't systematically "listen closely and look carefully"—we will all lose out.

Chapter Seven: Satanic Panic

Starting with our work treating the children of the Branch Davidians in 1993, The ChildTrauma Academy has had a good relationship with the Texas agency that oversees Child Protective Services (CPS) in that state.

The leadership knew me, they had come to trust our work, and they frequently asked for input about ongoing program or practice issues. We, in turn, learned more about the challenges facing individual caseworkers and the CPS system as a whole. It was very tough work; individual workers and supervisors faced high workloads, emotionally wrenching situations, frequent high-conflict interactions with family members or attorneys, and, all too often, not a lot of support or clinical supervision.

Furthermore, the natural emotional contagion that occurs between humans makes proximity to continuous traumatic situations a perfect setup for "secondary" traumatic stress, with all of the anxiety, sleep problems, depression, irritability, and demoralization that can go with it. This combination leads to a depleted and burned out CPS workforce.

Unfortunately, the solution for many caseworkers is to quit. During the time we worked with CPS in Texas, it was typical for one third of the new caseworkers to quit within the first year. Those who stay have to try to stay regulated—and keep good control over how they manage stress. Of course, there are healthy and unhealthy ways to regulate yourself. Healthy ways include working out, keeping good boundaries between work and home, connecting with colleagues and friends on a regular basis for support and just for fun, taking adequate time away from work, and more.

Unhealthy ways, of course, include disengaging or even dissociating and sleep walking through the work, or trying to self-regulate with food, cigarettes, alcohol, or other drugs. This continues to be one of the major challenges of most CPS systems; adequate training, ongoing support and quality clinical supervision are needed to help all staff manage this important but often distressing work.

In the case of Texas, CPS responded to these problems, in part, by issuing a grant for crisis intervention and debriefing to follow obviously severe incidents like what happened in Waco, in Gilmer as described in this chapter, and other cases of severe child injuries or deaths. Each year for over ten years, The ChildTrauma Academy was awarded this grant; our program proposal was always called "Crisis Intervention and Secondary Trauma Prevention."

It involved a _reactive_ set of program activities, such as going into Gilmer to meet with the caseworkers, children, families, and other personnel involved and providing consultation and recommendations. It also included a set of _proactive_ program activities, like providing a curriculum on trauma, neglect, and secondary trauma for caseworker training and ongoing professional development. We felt very strongly that if the caseworkers were better trained about trauma and related issues, they would be less vulnerable to secondary trauma and more effective in their work.

In other words, we would have less need to have expensive after-the-fact interventions if we had more proactive program elements ahead of time. And yet, every year we had that grant, the Crisis Intervention component was funded and the preventative proactive component was defunded. Following event after event, we would give feedback about the practice, program, and policy actions that would prevent such events—such as the panic that occurred in Gilmer and the resulting custody cases and trauma—and every year our recommendations were disregarded and tucked away in someone's file cabinet. It was frustrating.

The importance of self-care in effective child welfare work was just getting lip-service. Further, the crucial insight and support that frontline workers need to better understand these children—and themselves—was not being provided. Texas officials would listen to us when they were in the midst of a crisis—like in April 2008, when they asked us to lead the mental health and assessment process after the removal of 439 children from the Yearning for Zion (YFZ) Ranch run by the Fundamentalist Church of Jesus Christ of Latter-Day Saints (FLDS) in Central Texas. The FLDS is a polygamist sect led by "prophet" Warren Jeffs. Claims had been made that children being raised in the group were being sexually abused.

That was a pretty complex—and often surreal—situation, but that's a whole other book. Seriously, it is. Maia wrote a book with one of the key witnesses in that situation, Brent Jeffs, who is the nephew of Warren and whose account of having been sexually abused in the church by his uncle set off the series of events that led to the raid. (It's called *Lost Boy.*)

In any case, Texas CPS leadership changed, and I started to feel that we were becoming part of the problem by simply rolling over every year when the proactive part of the grant was defunded. They wanted our help in crisis but didn't want to listen to our input about how to prevent these catastrophes. By 2009, we were actively involved with child welfare systems in other states; when the call for proposals for the Texas grant came along, we didn't apply. We were learning more about systemic change—and despite our best efforts, that Crisis Intervention and Secondary Trauma Prevention project wasn't changing the child welfare system in Texas.

So how could we help change systems? All of these extreme and complex situations in the child welfare and mental health system where we were consulted were, to some degree, preventable. Think of each of the children described in this book and their life stories. Whether it is the parent, foster parent, therapist, case-worker, judge, FBI tactical team, pediatrician, teacher, or child psychiatrist, an awareness of the fundamentals of the brain, development, attachment, trauma, and neglect could have diverted or minimized the tragic trajectories of these children. Thus, the relentless focus of The ChildTrauma Academy has been on translation and dissemination of this content over the last thirty years.

We have much to be hopeful about in this area. We have been actively involved in the development and implementation of training and other "capacity building" projects that teach and implement the core concepts of our Neurosequential Model in multiple settings (clinical, school, juvenile justice) and for non-professional caregivers (parents, foster and adoptive parents). Over the last ten years we have developed curricula and related activities to teach these concepts to just about any profession you can think of—physicians and psychologists of all sub-specialties, social workers, nurses, occupational therapists, physical therapists, teachers, judges, parole officers, law enforcement, all the way up to the corporate and business community.

We have developed training, practice, and program elements suitable for dozens of organizations and systems: early childhood settings, schools at all levels, jails (juvenile and adult), courts (family and criminal), and the child welfare, mental health, and juvenile justice systems. As we will describe later, these efforts have exploded over that last ten years.

The most promising projects involve actually embedding these concepts into schools of social work, education, and medical school. When we engage professionals after they have been trained, we are asking them to shift or change their perspective: a big ask. However, when we teach the social work, education, or medical student these concepts up front, this becomes their primary frame of reference; it is much easier for them to immediately understand and implement developmentally-informed and trauma sensitive practices when they enter the field. As we've seen over and over, it's better to start early whenever possible.

Chapter Eight: The Raven

The young woman stood patiently in the background as the group of people slowly dispersed. We had a brief moment of eye contact, both of us smiling. She looked familiar. But I meet so many people—and I'm terrible at remembering names, so I couldn't place her.

I had just given a public lecture focused on the importance of relationships in shaping our physical and mental health. A small group of people approached me. This woman, however, stood apart, letting everyone else go first. Soon the auditorium was empty, aside from a few members of the organizing committee cleaning up—and an older woman in the very back of the auditorium with two young children.

She stepped forward, clearly anxious. "Do you remember me?"

"You look familiar but you'll have to remind me. . . I'm getting old and my memory is shot." I tried to use humor to hide my embarrassment.

"Funny. You always did joke around." She rolled up her sleeve and I immediately recognized the raven tattoo.

"Amber. Oh wow. So great to see you."

And it was. She looked different; older, no obvious piercings and her hair was light brown, almost blonde. She smiled as I asked her to catch me up on her life. We spent the next ten minutes talking and as we did, the older woman and the children walked from the back of the auditorium up to where we were sitting. I could soon see that the woman was Jill, Amber's mom. When she approached, Jill smiled and we exchanged a few words about how they ended up in this city, which was far from Texas. Amber corralled her children, hugging one in each arm.

"I want you to meet my children," she said, "This is Tori*. She is seven, and Thomas* is three." She turned to speak to her children. "This is my friend Dr. Perry. We met a long time ago when I was just a little girl."

Not so little, I thought. *Interesting that she said that—maybe she felt smaller than she was at the time.* The children had a moment of obligatory stillness, looked at me—probably trying to imagine "Mom" as a little girl—then wiggled out of Amber's hug and continued exploring the auditorium under the watchful eyes of Grandma Jill.

It was one of those rare moments in a clinician's life when you have the opportunity to see how things played out for a patient. She'd had had her ups and downs, but for now, was in a healthy relationship with the children's father. They lived together, but had decided to not marry. Jill lived nearby and often helped out with the children. Amber had decided initially to become a social worker and had a brief spell working in child welfare, but she found it "too triggering." She now worked with a non-profit faith-based organization supporting refugee families.

This clinical "rupture" of the treatment process with Amber described in this chapter is characteristic of the discontinuity of most therapeutic work with maltreated or traumatized children. In most public mental health clinics, the average number of consecutive clinical visits before there is an unplanned break in treatment is about three. The family moves, or wears out, or the crisis that brought the child in passes. If the child is in foster care, he may end up going home, or to the hospital, or a residential setting, or another foster home. The fragmentation of therapeutic contact is complicated by the medical economic model, which tends to approve and pay for ten or maybe twenty visits.

Ten years of abuse, neglect, humiliation, marginalization—twenty placements—two grade-levels behind in school, speech and language problems, sensory integration issues, no friends, no family, no social skills, impulsive, inattentive, dysregulated, attachment problems, hundreds of evocative cues from years of maltreatment, now in a new foster home. *We approve twenty sessions of Trauma Focused-Cognitive Behavioral Therapy* for all of that.

The caseworker checks the "therapy" box and we all move on. Any wonder the long-term outcomes for children in the child welfare system—despite the millions of dollars and person-hours spent trying to help them—are so bad? Maybe part of us doesn't want to see how things play out for our patients; maybe part of us wants to believe the magic of our twenty sessions: one hour a week actually built in a new "template" for relationships, re-organized the stress response networks in the brain, created a new set of "default" associations to bypass the evocative cues, taught the child social and cognitive strategies, built in new executive functioning capabilities in the cortex, and jumped the child two grade levels in school. (Oh, I forgot—that is not our job—that is for the schools to fix.)

Ok, maybe I'm a little too harsh. Important and enduring things can happen in those sessions; you can reach a child and make a difference, but I hope you get the point. Our current models cannot conceivably meet the overwhelming needs of these children. Knowing this, we must change the models. And we have some very good insights—and research—to help us make changes. Probably, the most important clue we have has to do with the remarkable power of relationships.

Indeed, one of the most important and recurring findings regarding health—in all domains of life—is the powerful role of relational continuity, enduring connectedness with others. The key role for relationships in resilience and healing has been described for decades; yet we continue to develop educational and therapeutic models that pretend that people are interchangeable. Each year in elementary school we get a new teacher: the special bond that can form has a shelf-life, the academic year. Then, in middle and high school, each year, we have many more new teachers.

Certainly, these relationships are important, but what about the power of continuity? If a mentor starts with an at-risk child in middle school, has lunch with that child once a week for the school year, and mentors the same child all the way through high school, there are multiple benefits to the child—including a significantly higher rate of graduation. The duration of the mentoring relationship appears to be one of the major factors in effectiveness. Having a series of mentors over the same time period has fewer benefits, and for some children, these ruptured relationships make things worse. Healing relationships are not interchangeable: we recognize this with marriage and family, and we don't expect people to simply substitute in a new spouse or new siblings when the school year changes. We recognize it with our own adult friendships, but we have a hard time appreciating the need for this kind of permanence in children's lives.

Another great example of the importance of enduring relationships is a remarkably effective organization called A Home Within, founded by Dr. Toni Heineman in the Bay Area in 1994. She was tired of working with foster children that came into her practice and then disappeared when they were moved. She made the commitment to create an enduring therapeutic relationship with the foster children she worked with no matter where they went—other foster homes, hospitals, residential centers or back home. She stayed with these kids; and they flourished. Soon, Dr. Heineman got other therapists to volunteer to do the same for one or two foster children.

Over the years, hundreds of clinicians across the United States have been providing high quality ongoing therapeutic services with children in foster care. The outcomes are excellent; in fact they are far superior to the typical outcomes of youth in the foster care system. Relationships help buffer present stressors and heal from past trauma. And so, the heart of any reinvention of therapeutic models has to be the number, nature, and permanence of relationships in the child's life: the enduring therapeutic web. After all, the key characteristic of a relationship that buffers stress is that it is lasting: the person is known to be safe, familiar, and at least reasonably predictable. This cannot be built in a day: viewing people as interchangeable simply creates a repetitive cycle of grief and loss. To break it, we have to stick around.

Chapter Nine: "Mom Is Lying. Mom Is Hurting Me. Please Call the Police."

Merle, James's adoptive mother, clearly had problems with attachment. She had a desperate need to be needed—but unfortunately, there was a lot of toxic stuff mixed in with it. In general, however, foster and adoptive parents tend to have big hearts. While each family makes the choice to parent and adopt for a range of personal reasons, by and large such people are comfortable as "helpers" and they usually have the best possible intentions.

And this is a good thing, because these children and youth need help. But it can be *not* so good when "the well runs dry." Living with and caring for children affected by trauma and neglect can be very challenging, to put it mildly. It can often rapidly lead to exhausted, demoralized, disengaged, and burned-out caregivers. The very qualities that make a foster parent capable of connecting, empathizing, and nurturing can make her vulnerable to the emotional turmoil these children carry and can create. Secondary trauma can affect these families, just as it does caseworkers or clinicians working in the child welfare system. And of course, as noted earlier, the system is not great at providing support, training, or supervision for foster and adoptive families.

While it is getting better, the vast majority of situations leave these families with challenging children and minimal support. Add to this the tendency to overload the best foster families with too many challenging children at one time and you set up a perfect storm: a higher probability of child-on-child bullying and abuse, a higher probability of very symptomatic, dysregulated children, and a higher probability of disrupted placement. And that, of course, is simply another relational discontinuity, and this failure further reinforces the child's distorted view of himself and the world. All of this contributes to poor outcomes for the children and youth. It is not unusual for us to work with a child who has had dozens of failed placements.

Now, shift your focus from the challenges in a foster family to the challenges that a young, often marginally-capable parent faces during reunification with three, or four, or seven of her challenging children. Several years ago, I was consulting with a well-known and highly respected national organization; I believe they do really good work. The caseworkers were presenting the details of a high-needs child who had been stabilized in foster care. I asked about how long this child would be able to be in the home with the current treatment plan in place. My focus was on relational continuity.

But they were working on reunification within a few months. Previously, the child's mother had been in an abusive relationship and she'd been using multiple drugs. After her children were removed, though, she got out of that relationship, completed rehab, and was now back in school learning a trade. I envisioned a fragile young mother just getting her life together so I asked more.

It turns out that she had seven children in three different placements—and all of them were struggling and having difficulties in their placements and in school. The plan was to reunite them all in her custody. I could see clearly that this would fail. One single parent, with minimal extended family or community connection, was expected to care for seven extremely troubled and traumatized children, all while dealing with her own trauma issues and recovery from addiction.

This, and similar situations, prompted me to develop a new "metric"—in this case, a measure of the strengths of a particular caregiver and home, balanced against the challenges posed by the specific children in the home. Simply subtracting the challenge score from the strengths score gives us a "caregiving reserve" score. Anything below -200 is pretty challenging; the family described above scored -860 on this measure. We have added this "Caregiving Challenge Estimator" (CCE) to our online set of Clinical Practice Tools and it helps treatment teams and families see when they are either setting up a foster family to "burn out"—or creating a situation in which a biological family reunification will likely fail.

Like our other metrics, we hope that the "picture" that the CCE generates will lead to better decision making. If a "helper" or caregiver sees that she is overloaded, she is more likely to be open to better "self-care" planning and to accepting additional help when it is available. If a case-worker sees that a foster family is stretched too thin, he won't push to place another child there; if a judge sees an impending disaster—like the one described above—in a reunification, possibly she will be open to a better transitional plan with more supports for the biological family.

Would a metric like the CCE have helped anyone see Merle more clearly? Could it have helped child protective workers recognize that James was in a potentially dangerous situation? In this case, probably not. The metric would have shown that the caregiving challenge in Merle's home was well beyond her capacity to provide—but she had what is thankfully a rare pathological need. When we try to understand the behaviors of someone like Merle, it always takes us back to their personal history. What happened to her during her own childhood, when she was growing up? We tend to parent the way we were parented. We speak the language spoken to us when we were young. We mirror the gestures and facial expressions of our parents, family, and culture. Humans pass both good and bad things down from generation to generation. How does that happen?

As you might expect, it's complicated—but this is another area where we have learned a great deal more than we knew when we originally published this book. There are multiple mechanisms that shape us. The most obvious of these factors is genes, but there is a new wrinkle in our understanding of genetics that makes understanding the way genes work even more complex. It's called "epigenetics" and the research here shows that the environment into which a child is born helps determine which genes become active and which remain silent. For example, in a calm, safe environment, certain genes will be highly active—but in a chaotic and unpredictable situation, different genes will dominate. This is part of how the environment in the womb and in children's first few years of life affects development.

And genetic, epigenetic, prenatal, early childhood interactions, and our whole lifetime of experiences in turn are influenced by community and culture. The exact mixture of which ingredients are most powerful for any given feature will vary: genetics is pretty important when it comes to the color of your eyes, for example, while your family, community, and culture are pretty important in determining what language you speak and your style of dress. And this complexity matters when we look at the degree to which trauma in one generation impacts the next generation. It is highly likely that Merle reflected her own experiences of childhood in how she herself parented—and before her, her caregivers had reflected their own. With each generation, there are additions, subtractions, twists, and turns in how we are influenced by the generation that raised us, but the momentum of transgenerational mirroring is powerful.

Transgenerational trauma—which is passed down from one generation to the next—is an important aspect of the emerging field of traumatology. There are several lenses that can be used to look at the transgenerational impact of trauma; one of the most important of these is socio-cultural. Over the years we have worked with multiple groups that have been affected by relatively recent histories of genocide, ethnic cleansing, or cultural genocide. These include First Nations communities in Canada, Aboriginal communities in Australia, multiple Native American tribes in the United States, and several tribal or ethnic groups in Africa and central Europe. The complex impact of their large-scale multidimensional traumatic experiences is rarely appreciated and has not yet been studied nearly enough.

It is clear however that large-scale systematic abuse of a people will have a transgenerational impact that will echo down a family's history. Whether this involves the centuries of genocidal policies and practices targeting Native American groups in the United States, the history of slavery of African American people, or policies like the removal of indigenous children in many countries to brutal residential schools, so-called "historical trauma" doesn't stay in the past.

I believe that systematic analysis and study of these experiences is extremely important: what we learn here will not only enable us to help trauma survivors overcome their symptoms, but will also move us towards a more just society, which doesn't have to replicate oppression and pass its scars on to our children and our children's children.

Chapter Ten: The Kindness of Children

Peter's teacher—and his school—demonstrated remarkable flexibility and tolerance by allowing me to visit his class to discuss the brain and neglect. If I hadn't had some stature in this area, I suspect the response might have been, "We have worked with children like this for years. We know what to do."

Indeed, for the last thirty years, a major frustration for trauma-aware parents has been the experience of finally figuring out what works to help their child stay regulated and learn, and then trying unsuccessfully to share it with the school. For example, one mom might tell a teacher, "I know it seems silly but he likes to keep this small toy in his pocket," or, "If you see him start to get really quiet and withdraw, you might want to let him just walk around a little," or, "You have to give him a couple of warnings before you make a transition." Sometimes a teacher or principal will listen, but often not. And, of course, if the fourth-grade teacher listens and makes accommodations, it is no guarantee that the fifth-grade teacher will do the same. Again, relational discontinuities disrupt progress for these children.

Typically, the way educators have viewed, taught, and disciplined maltreated and traumatized children is through a "behaviorist" lens. Behaviorism is a field of psychology which, historically, has been focused on the observable behaviors the individual exhibits and ignores—or has less focus on—emotions or underlying internal mechanisms that drive people to act. This perspective fits well with the DSM model of assigning diagnoses based upon observable behaviors. For instance, Billy is inattentive, impulsive, and has difficulties with age-appropriate social skills. He meets diagnostic criteria for ADHD. Therefore, he "has" ADHD. But we all know that those very behaviors and skill deficits can also be caused by developmental trauma and adversity.

The perspective of behaviorism can be useful in many situations, but, like all models, it has shortcomings. A huge shortcoming for children and youth with trauma-related sensitization of their stress response networks is in the use of "operant" (also called "contingent") strategies. This is the "reward and punishment" view you probably learned in Psych 101; one common example is the "point and level" system often used in residential programs in which children advance to "higher" levels with greater privileges if they behave as expected—or are "set back" to lower levels where they lose privileges if they do not comply.

The idea, of course, is that this will increase desirable behaviors through "reward" and minimize or extinguish undesirable behaviors using "consequences," which, let's face it, everyone knows means punishment. This model cannot and never was intended to help children develop complex capabilities such as social skills, which require a child to perceive subtle signals that often vary and cannot be taught through simple compliance. Nor can it help people learn to regulate their stress responses.

Sadly, when a child with a history of trauma struggles in school and has behavior problems as well, he will often be put into a "behavioral" program. And when the teacher gives the consequences attached to this approach, it will not calm him down or allow him to get control over his behavior; rather, it will escalate the child, increasing the probability of more disruptive behavior or even a critical incident, such as running away or becoming aggressive, which can lead to being physically restrained. Basically, what happens in these cases is that a "flight or fight" response is elicited from the child. The effect in the classroom is the opposite of what is desired: these children then get put into seclusion, or are suspended, or even expelled from school. Our schools, due to well-intended, but trauma-ignorant, practices, often make the lives of our maltreated and traumatized children worse. But it doesn't have to be that way.

In 2010, Steve Graner—a lifelong friend of mine who happens to be an English teacher and coach—heard me speak at a daylong conference in our hometown, Bismarck, North Dakota. He and one of his teaching colleagues, Crystal Halseth, a science teacher, immediately saw the benefits of applying the concepts I was teaching about the brain, stress, and development to better reach children in their classrooms.

They talked with me and other colleagues at The ChildTrauma Academy, and we sent them the material we use for clinical training. We had always worked with schools to help them better understand children affected by trauma; we had hoped to develop a version of the Neurosequential Model for Education (NME). We were working to modify our training process and metrics so that they could be used in educational settings. But we were all so busy that the process of developing the model was slow. And so, we were happy to let Steve pick up the ball.

Steve and Crystal started by having a completely voluntary book group, in which they met with other teachers and discussed *The Boy Who Was Raised as a Dog*. They went chapter by chapter, and participants told them that they found the group stimulating and productive. Then, Steve, Crystal, and a number of other teachers started to think about how to bring rhythm into the classroom, both to help regulate children by giving them brief sensory "breaks" and also to teach content. For example, they started using rhyme more often in their curriculum. Word of mouth within their school led to another round of book study, and then another for other schools in the school district. (Steve ultimately wrote the majority of an older version of the book study guide included in this edition of the book.) Steve and Crystal went through and selected and modified some of our teaching content; we worked together to make sure it would be able to reach teachers without distorting the neuroscience or core clinical concepts.

With their energy and time, we finally had a way to develop the beta-version of the NME. In 2012, Steve retired from teaching, and we convinced him to come out of retirement to lead the ongoing development and dissemination of this program. As we will explore a bit further in the last chapter of the book, the growth and effectiveness of the NME has been impressive.

Over the last ten years, other clinicians and educators have been addressing the need to have a trauma-informed educational system. In our experience, Collaborative Problem Solving (CPS) is the most flexible and effective. CPS has been around for over twenty years and incorporates the key principles we teach in the NMT. It was co-developed by Dr. Stuart Ablon. CPS can teach parents, educators, children, and clinicians practical and effective ways to understand and address behavioral problems in the school setting; this includes trauma-related behaviors.

Most important, CPS has a sequence of implementation that understands the fundamental reality that, in order to "get to the cortex" and prepare children to learn abstract and cognitively challenging material, we have to first relationally connect with them. And, before we can effectively connect, the child has to be regulated—at least to a certain degree. The sequence of effective engagement, therefore is (1) regulate (2) relate, and then (3) reason with the child (see Appendix, Figure 7). Getting out of sequence will result in ineffective communication, frustration for both parties, and sometimes flight or fight or "shut down" dissociative behaviors. In any human interaction, the only way to the cortex is through the brainstem/diencephalon and then the limbic system (see Appendix, Figure 2).

While conventionally viewed as a cognitive intervention, CPS is also fundamentally a relational intervention and uses a variety of sequenced, effective, and rhythmic interactions to promote regulation, connection and, ultimately, the cognitive process of defining and solving a specific problem in a collaborative way. The Neurosequential Model and CPS can help embed all of the six Rs that are key to an optimal learning environment. These are: Relevant (developmentally appropriate) content, Regulating rhythm, Repetition (in the correct patterns of dose and spacing), Relational (safe and predictable), Rewarding (pleasurable), and Respectful (of child, family, and culture). (For more on CPS, see the website ThinkKids.org; to learn more about other trauma-sensitive practices in education see TraumaAndLearning.org.)

Study Guide and Comments for Group Leaders

IN THE TEN YEARS SINCE THE original publication of this book, we've been delighted to learn that it has become part of the curriculum in a wide range of classes—including those covering psychology, psychiatry, social work, neuroscience and training for attorneys, other court officials, and educators. This study guide is intended to aid those who wish to use the book in a systematic way to improve their understanding of development, attachment, the brain and the effects of adversity, such as trauma and neglect, on children. This understanding can help us interact with all children in a way that is both neurodevelopmentally informed and sensitive to the possibility of trauma exposure.

To that end, we've included some questions and answers related to the key themes of each chapter. The answers here aren't the only "correct" responses—we include them only to help instructors and readers understand the main points and how they relate to helping trauma-exposed children. The questions appear first, and the main points to explore when answering them are at end of this guide.

Chapter One: Tina's World

1. A critical part of working with traumatized children is recognizing that, in order to produce long-term changes in the brain and behavior, patterned, repetitive experience is required. What kinds of experiences would be healing or "therapeutic" with Tina—and did the clinical work with Dr. Perry provide those? What role did the "dosing" of therapeutic interactions play in Tina's therapy?

2. Brain development occurs in a specific sequence: some regions mature earlier than others, and the successful maturation of later regions relies on sufficient development in areas that mature earlier. What does this suggest about why early trauma will have a different impact compared to later trauma?

3. What brain regions develop first, and how does this matter in terms of what kinds of problems will be associated with trauma that occurs at particular times?

4. What happens to the brain when a child like Tina experiences an aberrant early pattern, in her case, ongoing sexual abuse?

5. How does the stress of poverty affect brain development?

6. On pages 4–8, Dr. Perry interacts with two of his mentors, Dr. Stine and Dr. Dyrud. Contrast the two men's styles and conclusions about Tina and the behavior of her mother. Then contrast two schools of thought that may exist among people working with traumatized kids: one that uses the Neurosequential Model and one that is more traditional.

7. Why is the patterning of experience so important and how can you help create more predictability for the children you work with?

8. Why does frequent repetition matter, and how do you find a balance between repeating something enough for learning to occur but not too much as to become boring?

9. What was Dr. Perry's therapeutic approach in his work with

Tina, and what techniques seemed to be most important in helping her make initial progress? How can you use these ideas in your own work with children?

10. On pages 25–27, Dr. Perry discusses how brains can have either a negative or positive response to novelty. What are some ways that traumatized children might respond to novelty that might lead adults to misinterpret their behavior?

11. How does their style of response to novelty affect children who have experienced trauma at home when they enter a new setting like a preschool, kindergarten, court, or therapist's office?

12. Tina's sexualized reactions to men and boys was often seen as evidence that she was a "bad" girl who was "acting out"—and responses to these behaviors by schools and other organizations tend to be punitive. What are some better ways of helping young children like Tina who replay sexual trauma? How can your organization be sensitive to the possibility that early sexual trauma is involved in children's behavior?

13. As Tina's impulse control improved, she learned to be ashamed about and hide her sexual acts rather than discontinue them. How can we help victims avoid this path?

14. After careful reading of the last paragraph of the chapter, describe how schools or other institutions which have regular, frequent contact with children could be game changers in their lives.

Chapter Two: For Your Own Good

1. "Resilient children are made, not born," (p. 38). How does the "right" amount and pattern of stress help children develop resilience?

2. How is building resilience similar to building muscle? How

can facing appropriate amounts of stress aid learning and the development of self control?

3. What are the "arousal continuum" and the "dissociative continuum," and why is understanding where a child is on these spectrums at any given time important in being able to communicate effectively with him or her?

4. What is tolerance, and how does providing slowly-increasing and predictable "doses" of stress build it?

5. What is sensitization and how does unpredictable, erratic, and sometimes large "doses" of stressful experience create it?

6. What is hyperarousal, and how might a child who is experiencing it behave? How can you avoid behavior and academic problems with children prone to hyperarousal?

7. What is dissociation, and what does this look like in children? How can you avoid behavior and academic problems in children who are prone to dissociation?

8. Why might a traumatized child who is experiencing hyperarousal and/or dissociation be mistaken for a child with ADHD? How can we ensure that these symptoms of trauma are not inappropriately understood and medicated?

9. Why do some traumatized children seem to deliberately antagonize new caregivers and create chaos, and what is the best way to deal with this?

10. Children like Sandy often reenact their traumatic experiences in play. How did Dr. Perry help her when she reenacted witnessing her mother's killing? How important is it to let the child have control over these reenactment experiences?

11. What is "learned helplessness," and how important is a sense of control to people who have to cope with large amounts of unpredictable stress?

Chapter Three: Stairway to Heaven

1. Why was the original plan for placing the Branch Davidian children into separate foster care homes less than optimal?

2. On page 64, Dr. Perry advises the mental health agencies caring for the children to "create consistency, routine, and familiarity." For the professionals, this meant "establishing order, setting up clear boundaries, and improving cross-organizational communication."

   Why are routine and predictability so important after a traumatic experience has completely disrupted the usual pattern of a child's life? Why is it especially important that familiar and supportive people be involved, rather than a set of new professional helpers who may be better trained?

3. How can you ensure that during an emergency or disaster, the children you are working with have a stable, predictable, and relationally supportive environment?

4. On pages 76–77, Dr. Perry discusses the creation of a "therapeutic web" among those who were working to treat the Branch Davidian children. How can your school or organization create such a web for the children you work with and work to maintain and improve it?

5. Dr. Perry identified a particular Texas Ranger who had been assigned to guard the children—one who was initially highly skeptical of his expertise—as a very positive influence because he was calm, supportive, and non-intrusive. What individual strengths do you see in people in your team that could be useful as part of a therapeutic web of support? In yourself?

6. On page 85, Dr. Perry says, "The research on the most effective treatments to help child trauma victims might be accurately summed up this way: what works best is anything that increases the quality and number of relationships in the child's life."

What is your staff doing now or what can you do in future to help build a variety of high-quality relationships in the lives of the children you work with? Record some practical steps to take that will make this possible.

7. Humans mirror each other's moods and behavior and this can lead to "emotional contagion" of feelings like fear and anger. Moods tend to travel down the status hierarchy—so a parent's bad mood is more likely to be echoed by a child and a boss's fear is more likely to be picked up by her employees (p. 71). How can you use this principle to help calm children? When you are stressed out, what do you do in order to avoid spreading it to the children you work with?

8. The Branch Davidian children who had the best outcomes were not those who got the most therapy, were the least stressed, or were removed from relatives who continued to follow David Koresh's religion. Instead, they were the ones who had the strongest, healthiest support systems, regardless of their religious beliefs. What does this suggest about how we should work with troubled children?

Chapter Four: Skin Hunger

1. "When two patterns of neural activity occur simultaneously with sufficient repetitions, an association is made between the two patterns" (p. 91). How does this typically allow parents and children to interact positively? How can this principle be used in your work with children?

2. We often think of cuteness as silly and trivial—however, it plays an important evolutionary role. What is it and how can we use cuteness for self soothing?

3. What is "use-dependent" development, and how does this affect the way children's brains respond to trauma?

4. What is a "sensitive period" in brain development, and how does life experience during these periods affect development?

5. Why might a child who has missed critical input during a sensitive period have behavioral and emotional needs that are similar to a much younger child, and how should this be handled?

6. How does nurturing touch and a pattern of mutual interaction between child and caregiver help the child learn to manage stress?

7. Why is being held and touched literally necessary in order for children to grow?

8. How does your own experience of being parented affect the way you parent? How can you use this insight to help children whose parents may have had their own experiences of trauma and neglect?

9. Some theories of mental illness and developmental disorders—infamously, with regard to autism, schizophrenia, and anorexia—have historically blamed parents and labeled the children's behavior as "attention seeking," "aberrant," and "manipulative." How can this perspective harm children and why is it better to try to first understand the child's and parents' histories and how they may shape the way they interact with the world?

10. Discuss and detail the therapeutic style of Mama P. Find at least five key ingredients of her intimate and effective work with Virginia and Laura. Then, draw as many parallels as possible with how your staff members could provide similar therapy for the troubled children with whom you work.

11. Why is it traumatic for babies and children to transition from one loving set of caregivers to another, and why is it harmful to children not to have one or two consistent, loving caregivers as they grow up? What can we do for children who have had many transitions between foster homes?

Chapter Five: The Coldest Heart

1. Compare and contrast the personalities and early experiences of Leon and his brother Frank. How did early experience affect each brother differently?
2. Discuss Leon's aberrant sense of pleasure. Detail the wide-ranging effects this had on his behavior—from his reaction to discipline to his inability to feel compassion for others.
3. Is a child like Leon salvageable? What kind of interventions might have worked if caregivers had understood what had gone wrong in his early childhood?
4. What is "cognitive empathy" or "theory of mind," and what is emotional empathy?
5. How do the different problems related to empathy seen in autism and sociopathy lead to very different types of behavior? How can we avoid stigmatizing autistic people as "lacking empathy?"
6. How can small, apparently-insignificant events combine over the course of development to produce large differences in outcome, and what does this mean for working with troubled children?
7. Whose fault was it that Leon turned out the way he did, and how much responsibility should be given to genes, parenting, the environment in which he grew up, and his own choices?
8. What are the legal and social implications of the complexity of the way sociopathy develops?

Chapter Six: The Boy Who Was Raised as a Dog

1. Why is it important to understand the sensory environment— and the sensory sensitivities of particular children—before trying to communicate with them? How might the environ-

ment where you work affect people with sensory differences—and what are some ways you might make it easier for them?

2. Why is it a bad idea to surprise or suddenly interact with traumatized and neglected children? How can you use awareness of this in order to improve the environment and approach you take to working with these kids?

3. Why is taking a good case history so important in working with children with behavior problems? How can you learn more about the children you work with in order to understand their behavior?

4. How can brain changes associated with neglect be misunderstood as pre-existing brain damage and what implications does this have for traumatized children?

5. Detail the steps Dr. Perry and other staff took as they began Justin's therapy. How was each area of the brain given attention?

6. How might living with dogs actually have provided some of the social stimulation Justin needed as a young child? How can animals and interactions with animals be used to help similar children?

7. How did Dr. Perry use what he'd learned from Justin to help Connor, and what parts of the brain did he target in sequence?

8. How can nonverbal approaches like music and movement classes or massage reach parts of the brain that talk therapies cannot?

9. Why is it critical when working with traumatized children to let them control the pace and intensity of the therapy?

10. Why can helping children understand brain development help their recovery?

Chapter Seven: Satanic Panic

1. Researchers used to believe that memory was stable and that recall was like mentally looking at an old video or

photograph. Now we know that every time a memory is recalled, it can be mentally "edited" and changed, like a file that's open on a computer. What does this mean for how we should approach therapies based on childhood memories?

2. Child sexual abuse is real and not uncommon—but children are also suggestible if they are questioned repeatedly and believe that they have to give the answer that their interrogators (whether parents, teachers, therapists, or police) want to hear from them. How do you strike the best balance when dealing with potential cases of sexual abuse?

3. During the 1980s and 1990s, many Americans became convinced that there were networks of Satanic cults whose members sexually abused and ritually sacrificed children taken from nursery schools and daycare programs. Although dozens of people were convicted of perpetrating such abuse, no physical evidence (such as the bodies of children who were sacrificed) was ever found, and these convictions were eventually overturned.

4. What is "emotional contagion" and what does it tell us about why even modern societies can fall prey to such panics? How did Dr. Perry try to avoid getting wrapped up in the panic in Gilmer, Texas, and how can you protect yourself from being taken in when these sorts of fears are being spread?

5. Why are coercive methods like "holding therapy" dangerous to children, particularly those who have already been traumatized?

6. Therapists used to believe that everyone who had certain conditions like eating disorders or addictions had suffered childhood trauma but many couldn't recall it—and consequently, attempting to find these hidden memories would solve their current problems. What's wrong with this approach and why can attempting to find "repressed" memories actually sometimes do harm?

7. Should children who have been through a traumatic experience be pressed to discuss it if they don't show symptoms? Why or why not?

Chapter Eight: The Raven

1. What are traumatic memory "triggers," and how do they affect survivors?
2. After examining Amber's case, detail the signs of a dissociative threat response that you might be able to recognize in children you work with.
3. Why do trauma survivors sometimes turn to "cutting" or other forms of self-mutilation? What effects does this have on the brain?
4. Why did Dr. Perry tell Amber that she didn't have to meet with him and she shouldn't trust him until she knew him better?
5. Why did Amber try to get her abuser to drink alcohol and sometimes appear to "encourage" the abuse? What does this tell us about the importance of control to coping with trauma?
6. Should "triggers" always be avoided, or should survivors gradually learn to cope with them? Why?
7. What types of drugs produce experiences similar to dissociation? To hyperarousal? Why might these similarities put trauma survivors at increased risk for addiction?
8. What gender differences are there in the dissociative response, and how might these affect your efforts to calm students and help them be prepared to learn?

Chapter Nine: "Mom Is Lying. Mom Is Hurting Me. Please Call the Police."

1. What is Reactive Attachment Disorder (RAD), and which children are at risk?

2. Why do children with RAD tend to act indiscriminately affectionate?

3. Why is it important *not* to "hear hoofbeats and think of zebras" as physicians say, when considering whether a child has a rare condition like RAD or a mother has a rare condition like Munchausen by proxy?

4. How does examining records and information from multiple sources in a child's life help in figuring out complex cases like this?

Chapter Ten: The Kindness of Children

1. What is "splintered development" and what makes it so frustrating for parents and teachers?

2. What is the best way to help a child who may act appropriately in some situations, but revert to the behaviors of a much younger child in other cases?

3. Why does stress in particular tend to push children to act in less mature ways?

4. Why was it so important to get peer support for Peter, and why was teaching the whole class—and not just Peter himself— a better approach?

Chapter Eleven: Healing Communities

1. Why are supportive relationships so critical to mental and physical health, and how does this reflect the way our stress systems are wired during childhood?

2. What can you do to increase the number and quality of the relationships that the children in your life have?

3. How can your community become more supportive of traumatized children? List concrete changes that can be made in order to support relational health.

Group Leader Comments for Discussion Questions

NOTE: WE ARE RESPONDING TO our own questions in this section, but not because we are afraid that people who are leading discussions of this book will provide the "wrong" answers. We hope you'll be willing to field and respectfully appreciate the wide variety of responses you get and that this will stimulate many different types of conversations. However, we do want to include a few talking points that we hope these questions generate. These can help those who want to apply relevant insights from the Neurosequential Model to their interactions with children.

The points included here relate to the question numbers given above. The numbers link back to the numbers of the original questions in the first part of this guide—some have several numbers because the associated discussion is linked to more than one question.

Chapter One: Key Points

1) One principle of the neurosequential approach that can't be overemphasized is that changing the brain requires patterned,

repetitive experience. This is true at home, in the classroom, in therapy, and everywhere else we'd like to see behavior change.

People feel safe when they feel in control and the environment is predictable: this matters even for adults, but it is especially important for children and even more so for those who have experienced trauma or who have trouble self-regulating.

Sometimes people who work with children worry about being too repetitive. In an attempt to be innovative, they forget that balancing the novel and the predictable is the best way to teach. In Dr. Perry's work with Tina, he used routine and warmth to make her feel safe, stuck to an established pattern in their interactions, and introduced novelty only when he could see she was ready for it. The trauma-sensitive rationale for this approach should be emphasized in discussing this chapter.

2–3) Discussion of this chapter should also focus on how the order in which brain regions develop determines which kinds of experiences can best reach a child. The lower brain regions that come on-line first—like the brainstem and diencephalon— are especially responsive to rhythm and routine. Children who have been neglected or otherwise traumatized very early in life when these regions most need calming touch and responsive care will often not be able to make progress until such needs are met. To build a foundation for higher cognitive skills, delays or disorganization in these areas must first be addressed.

4, 12, 13) Sexual abuse is obviously a highly difficult and uncomfortable issue. But it is, unfortunately, common, and many survivors are deeply affected by it, as Tina was. Be gentle and careful when broaching this topic, as many survivors remain sensitive even decades later, particularly to accounts of cases like the one in this chapter. Focus here should be on how to increase empathy and support for sexual abuse survivors, how to reduce shame, and how to deal effectively with inappropriate sexual behavior by children who have been victimized in a nonjudgmental, non-punitive, but also protective, manner.

5) Tina grew up in a poor neighborhood that is isolated from public transit, with high rates of violent crime and few support services for families. Discussion of how and why poverty increases the probability of "sensitizing" patterns of stress activation (for example: more unpredictability, chaotic living situations, food and housing insecurity) and makes recovery more difficult can help readers reflect on how to work with children from lower socioeconomic backgrounds and the extra challenges this can raise. Practical concerns, like childcare arrangements, costs (even ones that seem small to people with decent jobs), and transportation issues, need to be kept front and center when working with these children.

6) The differences between Dr. Stine and Dr. Dyrud (pp. 5–7) reflect two different ways of working with children. Dr. Stine's was heavily reliant on medication, on brief weekly therapy, and on keeping therapy separate from the realities of day-to-day life. This distance is seen as important to the therapy, with failure blamed on the patient's "resistance" or lack of resolve.

Dr. Dyrud's approach was more personal and recognized how conditions like poverty can affect a child's development. He sought to understand how aberrant behavior may reflect traumatic experience and attempts to cope with it and help patients change by learning better ways to self-regulate.

In discussing these differences, consider the nature of professional boundaries and how understanding children's social and emotional environments can help the people in their lives make sense of their behavior and respond to it more productively.

7–9) Dr. Perry's approach to therapy with Tina has several important lessons for those who work with children. Most importantly, it takes many repetitions of positive experiences—often many, many more than you would expect—in order for traumatized children to trust again and change. When neural networks are not exposed to the appropriate stimulation at the right time, helping them develop properly requires many more repetitions than would have been needed initially. This can be frustrating, but patience is essential. These children can learn and change—but it takes time.

Continual re-enforcement of the need for patience—and, particularly, the likelihood of setbacks and the fact that people do not change in a linear fashion—is critical. Also, it might be helpful to look at practices in your area that may inadvertently harm children because they do not change rapidly or all at once. For example, consider "level systems" in discipline that punish setbacks or any other kind of disciplinary practice that does not recognize the time and process of trial and error that it can take to learn different behavior.

10, 11) Novelty can be perceived either as exciting or threatening, and the way it is perceived will influence how children act. The conversation here can highlight how understanding different responses to novelty can help adults who work with traumatized children be more sensitive to their needs. Again, stress the importance of routine, repetition, and a sense of control and safety.

12) Unlike weekly therapy or other brief forms of contact, schools have contact with children at least six hours a day, five days a week. This gives them a unique opportunity to create a safe environment in which to provide structure and repeated positive interactions. Of course, it also means that schools have a huge responsibility to minimize bullying and reduce the number of negative social contacts children experience. If your discussion primarily involves educators, focusing directly on how to improve schools' social and emotional climate makes sense here—but if your work with children is outside of school, finding ways to impact school climate for the children you see also matters.

Chapter Two: Key Points

1, 2, 4, 5) Stress itself is neither positive nor negative: the context and the dose matter tremendously in whether stress will be a force for resilience or harm. Too much, and a child will be overwhelmed and unable to learn; too little, and she'll be bored and tuned out. Children's individual level of development and their own sensitivity to stress also matter.

This means that, when working with youth, it's critical to have a sense of their particular comfort zones, just like a good trainer has a sense of the amount of weight each individual can lift safely at a specific point in a workout. The analogy to working out with weights is extremely useful here because the amount of weight a muscle can bear before training is many times smaller than it can lift after training—but lifting too much, too quickly, and too soon can cause serious injury. This can help ground the discussion in real world experience and help frame ways to individualize work with children.

Discussion here should explore key ideas, like tolerance (reacting less intensely as an experience becomes familiar) and sensitization (reacting more quickly and more strongly to situations associated with past negative experience), and how they affect the response to stress.

3) The concepts of the arousal and dissociative continuums can help predict when traumatized children will "melt down," "space out," or just have difficulty taking in new information. Depending on the children and the particular circumstances, stress can move them further along these spectrums and into mental states where they cannot learn or take in new abstract information. The questions here are aimed at eliciting discussion of these ideas.

A child who tends towards hyperarousal will move under stress towards increasing vigilance, then to resistance, defiance, and sometimes aggression; a child who tends towards dissociation will move from avoidance, to compliance, to dissociative behaviors like sitting and rocking. (See chart on p. 296.)

Consider here how stress can be modulated to avoid moving children into the more troubling parts of these continuums and, particularly, how Dr. Perry worked with Sandy by making himself appear small and safe, demanding nothing from her until she seemed ready to respond. Appearing big and scary would have pushed her towards hyperarousal, which was her way of coping with threatening experiences with men.

Whether you are a teacher, a social worker, a law enforcement officer, or a parent, you can use your understanding of these ideas in interactions with traumatized children. These children can move rapidly along these continuums if they frequently witness or engage in conflict with adults. Standing over them, raising your voice, and threatening them with dire consequences may be what they are familiar with from having lived with abuse, and they can go into survival mode quickly when faced with this template. Crouching down to their size, speaking softly but firmly, and making children aware that they are in a safe space can help keep children from becoming too aroused or dissociated to learn. Over time, they will be better able to deal with more intense experience.

6, 7) Understanding the differences between hyperarousal and dissociative responses is also important to working with these children. Here, discuss your own experiences of what these responses look like.

For example, hyper-aroused children tend to act out. They fidget, make noise, and talk out of turn. You can easily tell that they are not on task. Dissociative children, however, tend to blend in. They are seen as "good" children, even if they don't get good grades, because they cause no trouble.

Both cases can be difficult to manage. Hyper-aroused kids can get our own adrenaline flowing—but we need to remain as calm as possible, keep our voices quiet, kneel down if needed, get close, and speak firmly. We must resist the temptation to make examples of these kids and embarrass them in front of their peers. That will only escalate the fear response. Still, you must also let them know that you have responsibility for setting the tone for everyone and you are not going to allow them to agitate or upset others. Be calm, present, fair—but not afraid.

Chapter Three: Key Points

1, 2, 3) As noted above, the Neurosequential approach emphasizes creating consistency, routine, and familiarity. Discussion here should center on how this can be engendered in the particular setting where you work with children and how keeping children in contact with familiar people and places is more important than many agencies tend to consider. Also, consider how to help re-establish routine when an unusual event has disrupted it.

4) A "therapeutic web" or healthy, supportive social network is critical to the recovery of traumatized children. Discuss here how to create this within your organization, and elicit comments about what kinds of issues may interfere with it and how to reduce them.

5) When creating a socially supportive setting, it's important to recognize people's individual strengths and weaknesses and place people in positions that take advantage of the first and minimize the second. Consider how the same trait can be a weakness in one setting, but a strength in another. Discussion leaders may want to give examples of such strengths and weaknesses in their own personality and have others share their experience.

It's also important for people who work with traumatized children to take care of themselves and one another. Helping each other with physical, emotional, and psychological health concerns makes for a staff that has energy and spirit. The more you can foster a "family" environment among your group, the better you will be at handling the most difficult cases.

Remember that it can be a pleasure both to help and be helped: don't be an island of excellence, be a stream that flows freely to everyone who needs support. Celebrate the diversity of your staff, and make the variety of personalities a source of strength.

6, 7, 8) The number and quality of children's relationships is a critical determinant of their ability to be resilient. However, working with troubled children can be difficult: many are cold, unfriendly, defiant, and seem hard to like. The mirroring qualities of our brains will automatically reflect this negativity and make us want to step away.

It's our job, however, to give them a positive emotion to mirror and to be positive when they cannot be. They will often need many, many positive interactions before they can begin to reciprocate. If every staff member—from cleaner to CEO—makes it a point to greet at least one of the toughest kids every day, that child will ultimately have a hard time resisting feeling better. Numbers matter—and this discussion should stress this point.

But quality does, too. So, while saying "Hi" is good, saying, "Hi, how are you?" and taking time to really hear the response is much better. The more we can be calm and compassionate, the better we will be at helping children reflect this back at us and the better we will be at helping them ultimately learn to self-regulate.

Chapter Four: Key Points

1) Repeated, co-occurring or simultaneous patterns of neural activity create associations between these patterns. When these associations are pleasant, a virtuous cycle can begin in which, for example, learning becomes associated with success and people are seen as sources of support.

When learning is paired with a stable, predictable relationship, teachers—or anyone else who wants to help children change—can become a source of affirmation and joy. The brain makes an association between learning, connection, and pleasure.

It's important to realize that, in many systems dealing with children—schools, juvenile justice, child welfare—an underlying assumption is that children learn best through punishment and failure, by picking themselves up by their bootstraps and learning to just "get it done." But this is not how most kids are actually motivated: in fact, traumatized children are often triggered by failure itself, and this creates a stress response that can prevent them from learning from any "consequences." This doesn't mean that those who work with troubled children should have low standards or make everything easy—it's just that we always need to keep in mind the particular child and what level of stress he or she can handle at that specific time.

2) Cuteness is the signal nature sends to us that says that a creature is young, vulnerable, and needs nurturing. Seeing cuteness is usually pleasurable and cues us to interact positively with

children and young animals. Because cuteness can be such a great source of pleasure—hence the popularity of internet kittens and puppies—it can be used to help children (and adults!) manage stress and soothe themselves.

3, 4, 5) The concepts of "use dependence" and that of "sensitive periods" are interrelated and critical to understanding brain development. Both should be emphasized in discussion of this chapter. As noted on page 39, "use dependence" means that a neural network will only develop properly if its functionality is used—again, just like a muscle. During development, certain networks have "sensitive periods" during which particular experiences must occur in order for normal maturation to take place.

Some examples are language, which requires appropriate input during the first years of life in order to be learned easily, and vision, which will not be as sharp as possible if a baby doesn't get normal input from the eyes in infancy (i.e., has her eyes obstructed physically for some reason or is only kept in the dark). Children who have not gotten the sensory or physical experiences required for development during sensitive periods may seem far younger than their actual age and may need much more repetition to learn missed skills because the brain's sensitive period has passed.

6, 7, 10) These are five key ingredients of Mama P's therapeutic style, which should be included in discussions of these questions:

1. Need to be loved: troubled children tend to have experienced a great deal of conflict, anger, and demonstrations of dominance in their lives. They need a "new normal" and people who are patient enough to deliver the repetitions it will require to develop trust and a sense of safety. When children feel loved, they feel safer, and this allows them to learn much more effectively.

2. Appropriate touch: in Mama P's case, she was able to hold Laura and hug her and, over time, start to build in

associations between physical touch and safety and pleasure. In some settings, this isn't possible, and adults have to learn to "touch without touching," by doing things like getting closer, sitting with children and lowering stature, rather than towering over them, speaking softly, and laughing together. Using music and rhythm can also help support appropriate contact.

3. Sense of humor: adults need to laugh as much as children do. It is a stress release, an infusion of pleasure, and creates a positive association between learning and fun. Adults who can laugh at themselves also make a healthy statement to the children around them: I'm not perfect, I don't need to be, and I like being here with you.

4. Rocking / rhythmic movement: sensory breaks that involve walking, balancing, dancing, or rhythmic hand movements can be regulating for everyone, especially children who struggle with self-regulation.

5. Developmental awareness: Even children who are the same chronological age are often at highly different stages of development. To grow intellectually, all of them need to have both hope for success and some personal experience of success to motivate further progress. They need to feel accepted and then challenged. They can only move towards new ideas and experiences when they have a foundation of acceptance and safety.

9, 11) Emphasize here that focusing on child trauma does not necessarily mean that parents are at fault: many traumatic experiences are not caused by parents at all or are the result of ignorance, not deliberate abuse or neglect. In Laura and Virginia's case, Laura's eating problems resulted from a lack of healthy touch—but Virginia was in no way trying to harm her child. Virginia's early experience of being "raised by the system" interfered with her ability to parent effectively. Babies need to be cared for by one or two consistent people: every time they are moved to a new set of caregivers and lose the old ones, it is traumatic, and this can affect mental and physical health for a lifetime.

Chapter Five: The Coldest Heart

1) The key points here are that Leon's early life was marked by neglect and abandonment—while Frank had not only the support of both of his parents, but also their extended family during times when Maria became overwhelmed and wasn't able to care for him. For Frank, human connection was consistent and available, which connected relationships with pleasure and relief; for Leon, his cries for help often went unanswered or were actually punished.

2) The ability to take pleasure in human relationships is critical to healthy development because proper socialization relies on children finding connecting with others to be rewarding. The implications here are profound: in cases like Leon's, where, instead, relationships are seen as unreliable or painful, a distorted view of humanity can develop. For one, if human connection itself isn't pleasant, children won't aim to please parents or teachers, which will make discipline and education difficult: if the child doesn't care what adults think, he has little incentive to seek their praise or comply with their demands.

Secondly, such children will only value others as objects: possible sources of money, food, casual sex, or other pleasures that don't rely on connection. This means that they will also view others as seeing the world in the same way: that, for example, love is just a word you say to get sex, and compassion is just a pretense people make in order to look good or a ruse used by the weak. Consider what the social world would look like if you had this perspective.

3) Whether or not Leon could have been saved by early intervention is, of course, unknowable, but there are points in his story when it could have really mattered that should be discussed here. For example, he was in an "at risk" preschool program—but it was not well-staffed enough to meet the needs of a child who had suffered such severe neglect. He needed significant one-on-one attention, not being one in a group of six or more.

A neurosequential approach would have also recognized that he had missed out on the touch, talk, and interplay as an infant that are needed to develop healthy self-regulation and sensory regulation. This approach could have provided opportunities, like animal-assisted therapy and repetitive, simple, supportive interactions with adults, in order to make up for what was missed.

A responsive school would have allowed a child like him sensory breaks to move around and help regulate himself, and once he started to do well in any of these settings, he could have started to have more positive relationships with teachers and peers, which could begin to create a virtuous, positive cycle. Of course, the best remedy would have been having parents who did not neglect him in the first place—but children who have suffered similar neglect have been helped by these approaches and had much better outcomes.

4, 5) Cognitive empathy or "theory of mind" is understanding intellectually what it is like to take someone else's perspective, while "emotional empathy" is understanding what it feels like emotionally from that point of view. The distinction is important because those who struggle with cognitive empathy—like some people with autism—can be caring and supportive once they realize what the other person is feeling, while those who lack emotional empathy—like sociopaths—are much harder to reach.

7, 8) These will tend to be a matter of spirited discussion: no right answers here!

Chapter Six: The Boy Who Was Raised as a Dog

1, 2) These questions deal with the importance of understanding a child's sensory experiences and previous environment in order to help. Sensory differences can make new or overwhelming environments (noisy, bright, crowded, etc.) difficult for many children: discussion should focus on how to reduce surprise, minimize intensity, and allow for individual differences in sensory tolerance.

3) There can never be too much emphasis on the importance of understanding a child's history from as many perspectives as possible, in our view.

4) While "neuroplasticity" has only recently become a buzzword, the reality is that every experience, memory, and sensation reflects a change in the brain. In Justin's case, doctors overlooked the power of a deprived environment to change the developing brain. It's important to realize that environment, emotional trauma, and stimulation (or lack of stimulation) can cause big changes to the brain, not just obvious forces like injury or birth defect.

5) Dr. Perry first began by trying to make Justin feel as safe and comfortable as possible. He did everything he could think of to reduce his fear and to try to feed him in a way that would create positive associations and pleasure. He didn't attempt to question him, just spoke rhythmically and used calming body language. These efforts were intended to help Justin "regulate" first. The sequence of engagement should always be "regulate, relate, then reason."

Then, he removed Justin from the overwhelming sensory overload of the NICU and kept human contact limited to small doses at first. New experiences, like physical therapy, were introduced slowly, with speech therapy added once he began to respond to that. These treatments followed the course of typical brain development, moving up from the brainstem and limbic system, then to the cortex. Once Justin felt safe and knew he would be cared for, he was able to catch up quickly in foster care. Regulate, relate, reason.

6) Dogs are highly social and tactile animals, and their warmth and contact probably helped Justin survive, providing at least some stimulation for his developing brain while he lived in the kennel. Interacting with animals can be very healing for traumatized children because it is often simpler and more predictable than dealing with people.

7, 8) Connor's therapy followed a similar sequence to that of Justin. His early neglect had left him with touch defensiveness. So Dr. Perry started by using a slow, safe, systematic, and rhythmic massage therapy. Connor's mom was present to soothe him and learn the technique herself. Connor's heart rate was monitored to keep stress manageable.

Next, Connor started a music and movement class to improve his sense of rhythm. This targeted both the brainstem and the midbrain, but it also helped him with social skills. It improved his gait and reduced his need to rock and hum. Nonverbal therapies helped address problems with areas in the brain that are not reached by language.

As these lower brain regions began to strengthen, Dr. Perry added parallel play therapy to improve the limbic system. He allowed Connor to dictate the terms of the interaction, reducing the power differential. He only used talk therapy if Connor initiated it and, otherwise, simply quietly shared space with him, building trust. Soon, Connor became more ready to move outside his comfort zone and learn to socialize.

At this point, Connor was ready to make friends his own age, and he soon bonded with a boy he'd met in the music and movement class. They enjoyed Pokémon cards together, dealt with some teasing at school, and, gradually, became more functional socially.

9) Different brain regions respond to different types of stimulation, so reaching areas that are not involved in experiences that can be verbalized requires other approaches. Music and movement are especially helpful because they reach deep emotional parts of the brain, which may need healing before verbal therapy can even be effective.

10) It is always important in treating trauma to understand that, because traumatic experience is at its essence a feeling of powerlessness and helplessness, control over one's current experience is crucial for recovery. Discussion should center here on how allowing children to set their own pace and responding sensitively to their reaction to intensity can make the difference between re-traumatizing someone and helping him or her to recover. Remember the importance of dosing and spacing. An acceptable "dose" for one person may be overwhelming for another.

11) Often times, understanding how things work can help people step out of their own experience and look at the situation more effectively and compassionately. Teaching kids about their brains is one way to do this. It allows them to become "co-therapists" and collaborate in the process of selecting and sequencing educational and regulatory activities that best fit their interests and needs.

Chapter Seven: Satanic Panic

1, 5) Memory is complex and highly influenced by cues and other aspects of recall in the present moment. Discussion here should center on the ways in which memory can be unreliable and the way that the emotions related to them can, nonetheless, shape our lives. Searching for "repressed memories" as an answer to psychological problems can do harm because these problems are caused by many different factors and "memories" revealed under such pressure can be inaccurate.

2) The key point is that sexual abuse cases require exquisitely sensitive handling: avoid the extremes of seeing it everywhere and using interrogation techniques that can create false reports—but at the same time, don't refuse to believe that it may have occurred. If there is any doubt, genuine expert advice should be sought.

3) "Emotional contagion" is the basis of empathy—it's when you "catch feelings" from people around you, and it's useful in connecting people to each other. However, it can also lead to political overreaction and bad policy. Recognizing the signs of moral panics—like believing incredible claims without sufficient evidence, being caught up in a group that refuses to question any of its beliefs when presented with legitimate conflicting evidence, and feeling pushed by fear to act without thinking—can help restore rationality.

4, 6) Coercive methods are dangerous because they repeat a key element of trauma—the person involved has no choice and no way out. This is also why children should never be forced to discuss traumatic experience: some people cope best by not verbalizing.

Chapter Eight: The Raven

1) "Triggers," or cues that evoke traumatic experiences, can be anything from a sight, smell, or sound, to a word or even just the slant of light at certain times of year. It's important to discuss

the wide range of these cues for memory as well as how they can prompt dissociation or hyper-vigilance and other idiosyncratic reactions related to the experience and the survivor.

2) Both Amber and Ted had dissociative responses to reminders of their trauma, and at their most extreme, these led to loss of consciousness. If you have experience with traumatized or at-risk children, discuss what dissociative responses—most of which are far less extreme—might look like. For example, some children simply appear to be "not present" and inattentive.

3) "Cutting" and other types of self-mutilation can be attractive to trauma survivors, especially those who have "sensitized" dissociative responses because they stimulate the release of the brain's natural heroin-like chemicals, the endogenous opioids, which include endorphins. This can produce both a "high" and a dissociative state, which can allow relief from traumatic memories and experiences.

4, 5) Dr. Perry's invitation to Amber to interact with him only at her discretion and to trust him if he seemed trustworthy is another example of how important it is for trauma survivors to have control over key elements of a therapeutic process if it is to be effective. Amber's attempt to get her abuser to drink so that she could control the timing of the abuse was one of her ways of coping: it is important to understand that this did not mean she desired or consented to the abuse.

6) Triggers and "trigger warnings" have become a source of controversy on college campuses, which makes them important to discuss here. Triggers should not always be avoided: in fact, when trauma survivors are in a safe place and feel ready, facing triggers and moving past fear and avoidance can be critical to recovery. Remember dosing—when survivors can control their exposure and the level of intensity, working with triggering

stimuli can help them become de-sensitized and, eventually, to no longer respond at all. All of this needs to be individualized and involve the guidance of the person who has been traumatized: it's perfectly appropriate to warn people about disturbing violent and / or potentially offensive content, but trauma survivors can be triggered by many other things, and their recovery ultimately depends on learning to manage them.

7) Stimulants, like cocaine and methamphetamine, produce experiences that are similar to hyper-vigilance, while depressants, like alcohol, opioids, and benzodiazepines, produce feelings that are more distancing, like dissociation. Because these drugs have these properties, this can be one way that trauma increases addiction risk.

8) In general, females have a higher risk for and are more prone to dissociative responses to threat, while males are more likely to have a hyper-vigilant response. The hyper-vigilant response can lead to aggression, which is also more common in males. Understanding these differences—and recognizing that people of both genders often have both types of responses—can help tailor our approach to these children.

It's also important to note that, since dissociative responses are basically aimed at being invisible, traumatized girls are less likely to come to the attention of teachers or other authorities, while boys will be more likely to get in trouble through visible, aggressive reactions. We need to look out for both responses—and offer these children ways to work through them in order to ensure that all children who have been traumatized can maximize their potential.

Also note: being able to move around when feeling threatened—and, particularly, being given opportunities to do helpful things like running errands or other tasks that require getting up and being physical—can be especially important for these kids and, counter-intuitively, can actually allow them to focus better by giving them a chance to restore and re-regulate themselves. Incorporating opportunities to play, move, dance, and just run around is good for both mental and physical health.

Chapter Nine: "Mom Is Lying. Mom Is Hurting Me. Please Call the Police."

1) The most important things to recognize about reactive attachment disorder is that it is rare; it is caused by extremely aberrant early environments, like orphanages or multiple early loss of parent figures; and it involves cold, antisocial, manipulative behavior, often alternating with apparently indiscriminate affectionate responses to strangers. Further, remember that you can't get an accurate understanding of the relational or cognitive capacities of someone who is very dysregulated. Frequently, "attachment" and cognitive problems improve dramatically when the child's stress response systems are calmed.

2) The seemingly affectionate behavior these children exhibit around strangers is less of a genuine emotional response and more a "submission" type reaction aimed at placating those who might, for all the child knows, be his or her next caregivers.

3) Rare conditions, like RAD and Munchausen's-by-proxy, are easy to mistake for more common syndromes, and because misdiagnosis of these conditions can lead to severe consequences for families, it is absolutely critical to first rule out more likely potential explanations.

4) Once again, taking good histories / knowing as much as possible about a child's life from multiple sources needs to be emphasized!

Chapter Ten: The Kindness of Children

1) "Splintered development" refers to the idea that one area of functioning will develop normally while others may not. For example, a child may exhibit significant age-appropriate strengths in one domain—like large-motor functioning (sports)—and be four years behind in social skills and two years behind peers in academics. State-dependent functioning refers to the shift in functioning that occurs when we move from one brain state—like being calm—to another state, such as fear. We all experience these shifts; an example is the less mature and irritable way we are when we are tired, sleep-deprived, or sick. But, for traumatized children and those with developmental disorders, these shifts can be rapid and extreme: one minute, the child will be perfectly able to function in class, and the next he will be on the floor, screaming.

Understanding what triggers these shifts and being able to "meet the child where he's at" can help—but learning how to manage this can be challenging and frustrating because the outbursts may appear random and can look like all progress has been lost. This is another reason to be sure that systems recognize that progress is not linear and change takes time. Remember—know the "stage" (i.e., where the child is developmentally in motor, social, emotional, and cognitive domains) and the "state" of arousal (i.e., calm, alert, alarm, fear, terror).

2, 3) The most important thing to understand about helping these children is that stress is the most likely trigger for regression. Since they are so reactive, small stressors can set them off; as they activate their stress response systems, they shut down key cortical networks. The more dysregulated they become, the less access they have to more mature networks in their brain; by the time they are in "panic" mode, their functioning is more similar to a frustrated toddler than a fifteen-year-old adolescent.

Compassion, routine, structure, and predictability can all help reduce problems. Becoming attuned to the child's developmental capacities at particular times and when doing certain activities—and providing appropriate input for that stage with numerous repetitions—will help the lagging regions catch up and will help prevent kids from being pushed into the "panic zone" as frequently.

4) While we often think about children being naturally and carelessly cruel—and have historically seen bullying as inevitable—the reality is far more complex. The bullying of children who are seen as "different," like Peter, occurs in context: some schools and societies look the other way, while others work actively on inclusion and tolerance.

Dr. Perry's visit to Peter's school helped his peers understand his strange behavior—and, by doing so, defused the fear and rejection that often occur when kids are faced with a child who seems extremely unlike them. Teaching the whole class about brain development helped make what was weird and frightening about Peter explicable—and this helped him get the social support he needed.

More generally, students who begin to understand the brain begin to recognize why differences among peers exist and why those differences do not have to be feared. They begin to recognize that different temperaments and personalities exist and that other people may experience the world in very different ways, some of which can lead to unusual behavior. They also start to understand their own fear responses and how they can use things like strong relationships, exercise, music, better sleep, and diet to cope.

Understanding our own brains also leads towards empathy, a greater understanding of others and how helping others can not only improve the world, but is also a source of pleasure and joy.

One additional note: any institution that works with children needs to recognize how important adult approval is in children's "natural" behavior. Children do "naturally" fear what's different—but they can be taught to overcome this through experiences like the one Dr. Perry provided for Peter and his class.

And, importantly, schools and communities that do not tolerate bullying and that model inclusion see reductions in not only childhood behavior problems, but also in teen drug use, crime, and adult mental health issues.

Chapter Eleven: Healing Communities

1) This is a good place to re-iterate how important relationships are to good health and to reducing the impact of overwhelming stress. Our brains are wired to rely on support from others for comfort and healing: the fact that social brain regions modulate stress systems is fundamental to understanding these connections. Babies are initially dependent on their parents to modulate stress: the development of the brain's stress systems relies on nurturing, responsive parenting.

Further, uncontrollable stress affects the body via the brain: it will impact mental health through many of the brain's circuits, and it can increase diabetes, heart disease, and other physical health problems directly via the autonomic nervous system, neuroendocrine, and neuroimmune systems as well as by increasing the probability of unhealthy high-risk behavior, like smoking and overeating.

2, 3) There are obviously myriad ways to increase relational health for children. These range from small (but important!) things, like having adults—everyone from principals, administrative staff, and teachers to bus drivers, cafeteria workers, etc.—greet them personally, trying to make even the briefest interactions pleasant and fun. It's also important for everyone to recognize how their own mood and anxiety level can affect the children's. Innovative ways to increase the number and quality of children's relationships are definitely needed— and we'd love to hear about your best ideas and strategies for achieving this.

Acknowledgments

Bruce D. Perry acknowledgments:
The greatest contributors to this book are those I cannot acknowledge by name: the hundreds of maltreated and traumatized children who continue to shape my evolving understanding of their condition and therapeutic needs. I am honored to have worked with each of them—and I thank them for their grace, for their courage, and for their willingness to share their pain so that others might benefit. I hope their strength and spirit comes through on these pages and that we have done justice to their stories.

I would also like to thank a series of brilliant scientists and gifted clinician-researchers for the wisdom and guidance they provided throughout my professional career. These include Drs. Seymour Levine, Charles Sorenson, David U'Prichard, Jon Stolk, Earl Giller, and Steve Southwick. I thank my insightful clinician-mentors, especially Drs. Jarl Dyrud and Richard Kaufman. In addition, I was fortunate to have a series of administrative mentors who provided time, lab space, resources, and guidance, most notably Drs. Bennett Leventhal and Stuart Yudofsky. My primary neuroscience collaborators, Drs. Lewis Seiden, Al Heller, and Bill Woolverton, also deserve mention. Further, I am deeply indebted to Drs. Lenore Terr, Robert Pynoos, and Frank Putnam—and many other pioneer clinicians and researchers who inspired me. Space does not permit me to list them all.

I also wish to acknowledge here the work and ongoing inspiration of author and attorney Andrew Vachss. Over the years, he has been generous with his wisdom and guidance in shaping my work. He has helped me ask the right questions. He is true north in a murky world.

In addition, I am grateful to the current and former Fellows and staff of The ChildTrauma Academy. The compassion these clinicians show for troubled children has always been inspiring, and the intellectual stimulation they provide is priceless. First among equals is Dr. Robin Fancourt, a remarkable and selfless pediatrician who has transformed an entire country by her efforts. Special thanks are due to the present ChildTrauma Academy leadership, Jana Rosenfelt, Dr. Chris Dobson, and Stephanie Schick, and to my current primary clinical research collaborators in the CTA, Drs. Rick Gaskill and Gizane Indart.

Our work over the years has been supported by many generous and compassionate individuals. I especially wish to thank here Irving Harris, Jeffery Jacobs, Maconda Brown O'Connor, and Richard and Meg Weekley. Further gratitude is due to Jo Ann Miller, editorial director of Basic Books, for her editorial sculpting and support and to Andrew Stuart, our agent, for his hard work and encouragement during this project.

My greatest thanks, however, must go to my family. My father, Duncan, and mother, Donna, have many gifts: curiosity, humor, compassion, industry. My own gifts reflect the world they gave me as a child. For that and so much more, I am profoundly grateful. But of all my family, my utmost gratitude must be reserved for my wife, Barbara. She has tolerated moves, time away from home, too much time working at home, and me, in general. Our children are my greatest joy and my greatest teachers. My family continues to provide the love, strength, support and inspiration that sustains me.

Finally, this book exists because of Maia Szalavitz. I am extremely grateful that we have started this collaboration. She is a hard-working and superb writer with a remarkable capacity to digest scientific concepts across many disciplines and translate these concepts for general readers. Most importantly, she has a big heart. I hope you have enjoyed reading this book as much as we have enjoyed writing it.

2017—

All I wrote earlier is so very true, and I continue to be a lucky and grateful man. Over the last ten years, I have continued to benefit from the courage and insights of the children and families we work with. It is inspiring and humbling to see the resilience and grace with which so many carry the burdens of loss, pain, and trauma. My professional growth has been aided by friendships with colleagues, including Drs. Kristie Brandt, Gene Griffin, Stuart Ablon, Sandy Bloom, Nelba Marquez-Greene, and Ed Tronick. The work of The ChildTrauma Academy has expanded, and I am grateful for the hard work and leadership of Jana Rosenfelt, Emily Perry, Diane Vines and Steve Graner. Drs. Erin Hambrick and Thomas Brawner (the big data genius) have helped lead our research efforts. Our web-based assessment model has been possible because of the brilliance and hard work of Rob Smith. Finally, I am grateful for the work of The ChildTrauma Academy Fellows, associates, and all of our NMT and NME learning network – too many to name, but visit ChildTrauma.org to see the remarkable collaborative of caring professionals I am fortunate to work with.

Maia Szalavitz acknowledgments:
It has been a real honor to work with one of my scientific heroes, Bruce D. Perry, and I couldn't have asked for a better collaborator. I thank him first and foremost for his kindness, wisdom, generosity, support, and inspiration and for allowing me to help this book come into being. As a science writer, my idea of heaven is being paid to ask important questions of great minds—and this project involved just that. Kudos are due as well from me to our agent Andrew Stuart for his guidance and help in shaping this book from proposal onwards and to Jo Ann Miller for elegant editing and support. Special thanks to Lisa Rae Coleman for her fine transcription, friendship, and sharp wit, and to Trevor Butterworth and stats.org for their ongoing support. My mom, Nora Staffanell, and my Dad, Miklos Szalavitz, my siblings Kira Smith (and her children, Aaron, Celeste, and Eliana), Sarah, and Ari Szalavitz also deserve credit. As ever, my gratitude also goes to Peter McDermott for making both my work and my life better.

Notes

Introduction

xxiv *affect at least 7 percent of all Americans:* Kessler, R. C., Berglund, P., Demler, O., Jin, R., Merikangas, K. R., & Walters, E. E. (2005, June). Lifetime prevalence and age-of-onset distributions of DSM-IV disorders in the National Comorbidity Survey Replication. *Archives of General Psychiatry, 62(6),* 593–602. See also: Kessler, R. C., et al. (1995, December). Posttraumatic Stress Disorder in the National Comorbidity Survey. *Archives of General Psychiatry, 52(12),* 1048–1060.

xxv *about 40 percent of American children:* Franey, K., Geffner, R., & Falconer, R. (Eds.). (2001). *The Cost of Maltreatment: Who Pays? We All Do* (pp. 15–37). San Diego, CA: Family Violence and Sexual Assault Institute. See also: Anda, R. F., Felitti, V. J., Bremner J. D., Walker, J. D., Whitfield, C. H., Perry, B. D., Dube, S. R., & Giles, W. H. (2006, April). The enduring effects of abuse and related adverse experiences in childhood: A convergence of evidence from neurobiology and epidemiology. *European Archives of Psychiatry and Clinical Neuroscience, 256(3),* 174–186. Epub 2005, November 29.

xxv *around 872,000 of these cases were confirmed:* http://www.acf.hhs.gov/programs/cb/ pubs/cm04/index.htm

xxv *one in eight children under the age of seventeen :* Finkelhor, D., Ormrod, R., Turner, H., & Hamby, S. L. (2005, February). The victimization of children and youth: A comprehensive, national survey. *Child*

389

Maltreatment, 10(1), 5–25.

xxv   *about 27 percent of women and 16 percent of men*: Finkelhor, D., Hotaling, G., Lewis, I. A., & Smith, C. (1990). Sexual abuse in a national survey of adult men and women: Prevalence, characteristics, and risk factors. *Child Abuse & Neglect, 14*, 19–28.

xxv   *6 percent of mothers and 3 percent of fathers: A statistical portrait of fathers and mothers in America.* (2002). (p. 24). Washington, D.C.: ChildTrends. Survey results from 1995 Gallup Survey on Disciplining Children in America.

xxv   *up to ten million American children*: Strauss, M. A. (1991). *Children as witnesses to marital violence: A risk factor for lifelong problems among a nationally representative sample of American men and women.* [Paper presented at the Ross Roundtable on "Children and Violence."] Washington, D.C.

xxv   *4 percent of American children under the age of fifteen*: Strauss, M. A. (1991). Ibid.

xxv   *some 800,000 children will spend time in foster care*: Child Welfare League of America. (2005, June 5). Statement of the Child Welfare League of America for House Subcommittee on Human Resources of the Committee on Ways and Means for the hearing on federal foster care financing. http://www.cwla.org/advocacy/fostercare050609.htm

xxvi *more than eight million American children suffer from serious, diagnosable, trauma-related psychiatric problems*: Perry, B. D. & Pollard, R. (1998, January). Homeostasis, Stress, Trauma and Adaptation. *Child and Adolescent Psychiatric Clinics of North America, (7)1*, 33–51.

xxvi *one-third of children who are abused*: Perry, B. D. & Azad, I. (1999, Aug). Posttraumatic stress disorders in children and adolescents. *Current Opinion in Pediatrics, 11(4)*, 310–316.

Chapter One: Tina's World

17   *eighty-six billion neurons (brain cells), and for each*: von Bartheld, C. S., Bahney, J. and Herculano-Houzel, S. (2016), The search for true numbers of neurons and glial cells in the human brain: A review of 150 years of cell counting. J. Comp. Neurol., 524: 3865–3895.

20   *respond properly to stress for a lifetime*: Perry, B. D., Stolk, J. M., Vantini, G., Guchhait, R. B., & U'Prichard, D. C. (1983). Strain differences in rat brain epinephrine synthesis and alpha-adrenergic receptor number: Apparent in vivo regulation of brain alphaadrenergic receptors by epinephrine. *Science, 221*, 1297–1299.

21   *change a rat's stress response forever*: Reviewed in Levine, S. (2005, November). Developmental determinants of sensitivity and resistance to stress. *Psychoneuroendocrinology*, 30(10), 939–946. See also generally: Terr, L. (1990). *Too scared to cry: How trauma affects children and ultimately, us all*. New York: Basic Books.

Chapter Two: For Your Own Good

35   *stress-response systems in vets with PTSD*: Perry, B. D., Giller, E. L., & Southwick, S. (1987). Altered platelet alpha2-adrenergic binding sites in post-traumatic stress disorder. *American Journal of Psychiatry, 144(11)*, 1511–1512; Perry, B. D., Southwick, S. W., Yehuda, R., & Giller, E. L. (1990). Adrenergic receptor regulation in post-traumatic stress disorder. In Ebi . L. Giller, (Ed.), *Advances in psychiatry: Biological assessment and treatment of post traumatic stress disorder* (pp. 87–115). Washington, D.C.: American Psychiatric Press; Giller, E. L., Perry, B. D., Southwick, S. M., Yehuda, R., Wahby, V., Kosten, T. R., & Mason, J. W. (1990). Psychoendocrinology of posttraumatic stress disorder. In M. E. Wolf & A. D. Mosnaim (Eds.), *PTSD: Biological mechanisms and clinical aspects* (pp. 158–170). Washington, DC: American Psychiatric Press.

36   *improve their schoolwork and interpersonal skills*: Perry, B. D. (1994). Neurobiological sequelae of childhood trauma: Post traumatic stress disorders in children. In M. Murburg (Ed.), *Catecholamine function in post traumatic stress disorder: Emerging concepts* (pp. 253–276). Washington, D.C.: American Psychiatric Press.

39   *pattern of drug use is different*: Kleven, M., Perry, B. D., Woolverton, W., & Seiden, L. (1990). Effects of repeated injections of cocaine on D1 and D2 dopamine receptors in rat brain. *Brain Research, 532*, 265–270; Farfel, G., Kleven, M. S., Woolverton, W. L., Seiden, L. S., & Perry, B. D. (1992). Effects of repeated injections of cocaine on catecholamine receptor binding sites, dopamine transporter binding sites and behavior in Rhesus monkeys. *Brain Res, 578*, 235–243.

Chapter Three: Stairway to Heaven

60   *violated to those of hunted animals*: Breault, M. & King, M. (1993). Inside the cult: a member's chilling, exclusive account of madness and depravity in David Koresh's compound. New York: Signet Nonfiction.

76   *post-traumatic stress disorder following such "treatment."*: Rose,

S., Bisson, J., Churchill, R., & Wessely, S. (2002). Psychological debriefing for preventing post traumatic stress disorder (PTSD). The Cochrane Database of Systematic Reviews, 2.

81   *in response to the event itself*: Perry, B. D., Pollard, R., Blakely, T., Baker, W., & Vigilante, D. (1995). Childhood trauma, the neurobiology of adaptation and 'use-dependent' development of the brain: How "states" become "traits." Infant Mental Health Journal, 16(4), 271–291.

Chapter Four: Skin Hunger

92   *sight and depth perception is lost*: Hubel D. H. and Wiesel, T. N. (1959, October). Receptive fields of single neurons in the cat's striate cortex. *Journal of Physiology, 148*, 574–591.

92   *speak or understand speech normally*: Rymer, R. (1994). *Genie: A scientific tragedy.* New York: Harper Paperbacks.

92   *language he does learn with an accent*: Pinker, S. (2000). *The language instinct: How the mind creates language* (pp. 295–296). New York: Harper Perennial Modern Classics.

95   *by age two—an extraordinarily high death rate*: Iwaniec, D. (2004). *Children who fail to thrive: A practice guide.* Chichester, UK: Wiley.

99   *reduced levels of growth hormone*: Stanhope, R., Wilks, Z., Hamill, G. (1994, November-December). Failure to grow: Lack of food or lack of love? *Professional Care of the Mother and Child, 4(8)*, 234–7; Albanese, A., Hamill, G., Jones, J., Skuse, D., Matthews, D. R., Stanhope, R. (1994, May). Reversibility of physiological growth hormone secretion in children with psychosocial dwarfism. *Clinical Endocrinology, (Oxf), 40(5)*, 687–692.

Chapter Five: The Coldest Heart

113   *often seen in abused or traumatized children*: Perry, B. D. (1999). Memories of fear: How the brain stores and retrieves physiologic states, feelings, behaviors and thoughts from traumatic events. In J. M. Goodwin and R. Attias (Eds.), *Splintered reflections: Images of the body in trauma* (pp. 26–47). New York: Basic Books; Perry, B. D. (2001). The neurodevelopmental impact of violence in childhood. In D. Schetky & E. P. Benedek (Eds.), *Textbook of Child and Adolescent Forensic Psychiatry* (pp. 221–238). Washington, D.C.: American Psychiatric Press.

114   *proportion rises to over 35 percent*: Yeudall, L. T. (1977). Neuropsychological assessment of forensic disorder. *Canada's Mental Health,*

25, 7–15; Gillen, R. & Hesselbrock, V. (1992, April). Cognitive functioning, ASP, and family history of alcoholism in young men at risk for alcoholism. *Alcoholism: Clinical and Experimental Research, 16(2)*, 206.

125 *tends to escalate bad behavior*: Dishion, T. J.; McCord, J., & Poulin, F. (1999). When interventions harm: Peer groups and problem behavior. *American Psychologist, 54(9)*, 755–764; Poulin, F.; Dishion, T. J. & Burraston, B. (2001). 3-year iatrogenic effects associated with aggregating high-risk adolescents in cognitive-behavioral preventive interventions. *Applied Development Science, 5(4)*, 214–224.

126 *frontal cortex, just over the eyes*: Frith, U. (1998). What autism teaches us about communication. *Logopedics, Phoniatrics Vocology, 23*, 51–58.

128 *(which can be measured in a saliva test)*: Susman, E. J. (2006). Psychobiology of persistent antisocial behavior: Stress, early vulnerabilities and the attenuation hypothesis. *Neuroscience Biobehavior Review, 30(3)*, 376–89. Loney, B. R., Butler, M. A., Lima, E. N., Counts, C. A., & Eckel, L. A. (2006, January). The relation between salivary cortisol, callous-unemotional traits, and conduct problems in an adolescent non-referred sample. *Journal of Child Psychology and Psychiatry and Allied Disciplines, 47(1)*, 30–36. van Bokhoven, I., Van Goozen, S. H., van Engeland, H., Schaal, B., Arseneault, L., Seguin, J. R., Nagin, D. S., Vitaro, F., & Tremblay, R. E. (2005, August). Salivary cortisol and aggression in a population-based longitudinal study of adolescent males. *Journal of Neural Transmission, 112(8)*, 1083–1096.

128 *anything except extreme stimulation*: Unis, A. S., Cook, E. H., Vincent, J. G., Gjerde, D. K., Perry, B. D., & Mitchell, J. (1997). Peripheral serotonergic measures correlate with aggression and impulsivity in juvenile offenders. *Biological Psychiatry, (42)7*, 553–560; Perry, B. D. (1997). Incubated in terror: Neurodevelopmental factors in the 'cycle of violence.' In J. Osofsky (Ed.), *Children in a violent society* (pp. 124–148). New York: Guilford Press.

128 *the brain alone has 86 billion nerve cells (and supporting glial cells for each of those)*: von Bartheld, C. S., Bahney, J. and Herculano-Houzel, S. (2016), The search for true numbers of neurons and glial cells in the human brain: A review of 150 years of cell counting. *J. Comp. Neurol., 524*: 3865–3895.

133 *by the time they reach the pros*: Dubner, S. J. and Levitt, S. D. (2006, May 7). A star is made. *New York Times Magazine*.

Chapter Six: The Boy Who Was Raised as a Dog

137 *services for maltreated and traumatized children*: Perry, B. D. (2001). The neuroarcheology of childhood maltreatment: The neurodevelopmental costs of adverse childhood events. In K. Franey, R. Geffner, & R. Falconer (Eds.), *The Cost of Maltreatment: Who Pays? We All Do* (pp. 15–37). San Diego, CA: Family Violence and Sexual Assault Institute; Perry, B. D. (2006). Applying principles of neuroscience to clinical work with traumatized and maltreated children: The neurosequential model of therapeutics. In N. B. Webb (Ed.), *Working with traumatized youth in child welfare* (pp. 27–52). New York: The Guilford Press.

137 *neglect far, far worse than what had been done to Leon*: Research supporting treatment used in neurosequential approach: Jones, N. A. & Field, T. (1999, Fall). Massage and music therapies attenuate frontal EEG asymmetry in depressed adolescents. *Adolescence, 34(135),* 529–534; Field, T. (1998, March-April). Maternal depression effects on infants and early interventions. *Preventive Medicine, 27(2),* 200–203; Diego, M. A., Field, T., Hart, S., Hernandez-Reif, M., Jones, N., Cullen, C., Schanberg, S., & Kuhn, C. (2002). Facial expressions and EEG in infants of intrusive and withdrawn mothers with depressive symptoms. *Depress Anxiety, 15(1),* 10–17; Field, T., Martinez, A., Nawrocki, T., Pickens, J., Fox, N. A., Schanberg, S. (1998, Spring). Music shifts frontal EEG in depressed adolescents. *Adolescence, 33(129),* 109–116; Khilnani, S., Field, T., Hernandez-Reif, M., & Schanberg, S. (2003, Winter). Massage therapy improves mood and behavior of students with attention-deficit/hyperactivity disorder. *Adolescence, 38(152),* 623–638.

141 *visibly smaller head sizes and tinier brains*: Perry, B. D. (2002). Childhood experience and the expression of genetic potential: What childhood neglect tells us about nature and nurture. *Brain and Mind, 3,* 79–100; Johnson, R., Browne, K., & HamiltonGiachritsis, C. (2006, January). Young children in institutional care at risk of harm. *Trauma Violence Abuse, (1),* 34–60; Anda, R. F., Felitti, V. J., Bremner, J. D., Walker, J. D., Whitfield, C. H., Perry, B. D., Dube, S. R., & Giles, W. H. (2006, Apr). The enduring effects of abuse and related adverse experiences in childhood: A convergence of evidence from neurobiology and epidemiology. *European Archives of Psychiatry and Clinical Neuroscience, 256(3),* 174–186. Epub 2005, November 29. Additional background on effects of neglect: Smith, M. G. & Fong, R. (2004). *The children of neglect: When no one cares.* New York: Brunner-Routledge.

154   *compared to sight, smell, taste, and hearing*: Weiss, S. J. (2005). Haptic perception and the psychosocial functioning of preterm, low birth weight infants. *Infant Behavior and Development, 28*, 329–359.

154   *almost a week earlier on average*: Field, T. (2002, December). Preterm infant massage therapy studies: an American approach. *Seminars in Neonatology, 7(6)*, 487–494.

154   *stress hormones released by the brain*: Field, T., Hernandez-Reif, M., Diego, M., Schanberg, S., Kuhn, C. (2005, October). Cortisol decreases and serotonin and dopamine increase following massage therapy. *International Journal of Neuroscience, 115(10)*, 1397–1413.

154   *escalate the parents' commitment to therapy*: Cullen-Powell, L. A., Barlow, J. H., Cushway, D. (2005, December). Exploring a massage intervention for parents and their children with autism: The implications for bonding and attachment. *Journal of Child Health Care, 9(4)*, 245–255.

158   *important role in infant development*: Mithen, S. (2005). *The singing neanderthals: The origins of music, language, mind and body.* London: Weidenfeld and Nicholson.

166   *genetics and intrauterine environment is one*: Cowen, E. L., Wyman, P. A., & Work, W. C. (1996, Winter). Resilience in highly stressed urban children: Concepts and findings. *Bulletin of the New York Academy of Medicine, 73(2)*, 267–284.

166   *Intelligence is another critical factor*: Masten, A. S., Hubbard, J. J., Gest, S. D., Tellegen, A., Garmezy, N., & Ramirez, M. (1999, Winter). Competence in the context of adversity: Pathways to resilience and maladaptation from childhood to late adolescence. *Development and Psychopathology, 11(1)*, 143–169.

Chapter Seven: Satanic Panic

173   *seeing someone possessed by a demon*: Elizabeth Loftus, award for distinguished scientific applications of psychology. (2003, November). *American Psychologist, 58(11)*, 864–867; Loftus, E. F. (2005, July-August). Planting misinformation in the human mind: A 30-year investigation of the malleability of memory. *Learning and Memory, 12(4)*, 361–366. Epub 2005, July 18.

173   *until the back of his head "was mushy."*: Loe, V. (1993, December 3). Satanic Cult Scare Takes Massive Human Toll on Texas Town. *Dallas Morning News.*

176   *one in four adult residents cannot read*: Wade, R. M. (1999). When Satan Came to Texas. *The Skeptic, 7(4)*.

179   *events they recall are literally true*: Loftus, E. (2003, November). Make believe memories. *American Psychologist*; Pendergrast, M. (1996). *Victims of Memory: Sex Abuse Accusations and Shattered Lives*. Vermont: Upper Access Books; Ofshe, R. J. (1992, July). Inadvertent hypnosis during interrogation: False confession due to dissociative state; mis-identified multiple personality and the Satanic cult hypothesis. *International Journal of Clinical and Experimental Hypnosis, 40(3)*, 125–156. Ofshe, R. and Watters, E. (1996). *Making Monsters: False Memories, Psychotherapy and Sexual Hysteria*. Berkeley & Los Angeles: University of California Press.

180   *deaths associated with their "therapy."*: Bowers, K. (2000, July 27). Suffer the children. *Westword (New Times)*.

182   *the devil would get us.*: Wade, R. M. (1999). When Satan came to Texas. *The Skeptic, 7(4)*.

184   *ruminating on past negative events*: Nolen-Hoeksema, S., Morrow, J., Fredrickson, B. L. (1993, February). Response styles and the duration of episodes of depressed mood. *Journal of Abnormal Psychology, 102(1)*, 20–28; Lyubomirsky, S. & Nolen-Hoeksema, S. (1993, August). Self-perpetuating properties of dysphoric rumination. *Journal of Personality and Social Psychology, 65(2)*, 339–349.

188   *financially, and in every other way*: Vaughn, V. (1995, February). Witch hunt. *North Texas Skeptic*.

Chapter Eight: The Raven

203   *sense of distance from one's troubles*: Perry, B. D. (1994). Neurobiological sequelae of childhood trauma: Post traumatic stress disorders in children. In M. Murburg (Ed.), *Catecholamine function in post traumatic stress disorder: Emerging concepts* (pp. 253–276). Washington, D.C.: American Psychiatric Press.

203   *known as endorphins and enkephalins*: van der Kolk, B., Greenberg, M., Boyd, H., & Krystal, J. (1985, March). Inescapable shock, neurotransmitters, and addiction to trauma: Toward a psychobiology of post traumatic stress. *Biological Psychiatry, 20(3)*, 314–325.

210   *becoming a Goth didn't increase self-harm*: Young, R., Sweeting, H., & West, P. (2006, April 13). Prevalence of deliberate self harm and attempted suicide within contemporary Goth youth subculture: Longitudinal cohort study. *British Medical Journal*.

211   *Research on addicts and alcoholics*: Felitti, V.J. (2003, October). The origins of addiction: Evidence from the adverse childhood experiences study. *Prax Kinderpsychology and Kinderpsychiatry, 52(8)*, 547–559;

Dube, S. R., Felitti, V. J., Dong, M., Chapman, D. P., Giles, W. H., & Anda, R. F. (2003, March). Childhood abuse, neglect, and household dysfunction and the risk of illicit drug use: The adverse childhood experiences study. *Pediatrics, 111(3),* 564–572; Clark, H. W., Masson, C. L., Delucchi, K. L., Hall, S. M., & Sees, K. L. (2001, March). Violent traumatic events and drug abuse severity. *Journal of Substance Abuse Treatment, 20(2),* 121–127.

211 *physical abuse and neglect, and other trauma:* Dansky, B. S., Byrne, C. A., & Brady, K. T. (1999, May). Intimate violence and post-traumatic stress disorder among individuals with cocaine dependence. *American Journal of Drug and Alcohol Abuse, 25(2),* 257–268; Palacios, W. R., Urmann, C. F., Newel, R., & Hamilton, N. (1999, July-September). Developing a sociological framework for dually diagnosed women. *Journal of Substance Abuse Treatment, 17(1–2),* 91–102.

211 *show changes during addiction:* Daglish, M. R., Weinstein, A., Malizia, A. L., Wilson, S., Melichar, J. K., Lingford-Hughes, A., Myles, J. S., Grasby, P., & Nutt, D. J. (2003, December). Functional connectivity analysis of the neural circuits of opiate craving: "More" rather than "different"? *Neuroimage, 20(1);* Carey, P. D., Warwick, J., Niehaus, D. J., van der Linden, G., van Heerden, B. B., Harvey, B. H., Seedat, S., Stein, D. J. (2004, October 14). Single photon emission computed tomography (SPECT) of anxiety disorders before and after treatment with citalopram. *BMC Psychiatry, 4,* 30; Carlezon, W. A. Jr., Duman, R. S., & Nestler, E. J. (2005, August). The many faces of CREB. *Trends in Neuroscience, 28(8),* 436–445; Astur, R. S., St. Germain, S. A., Tolin, D., Ford, J., Russell, D., & Stevens, M. (2006, April). Hippocampus function predicts severity of post-traumatic stress disorder. *Cyberpsychology and Behavior, 9(2),* 234–240.

211 *found relief in dissociation:* Winchel, R. M. & Stanley, M. (1991, March). Self-injurious behavior: A review of the behavior and biology of self-mutilation. *American Journal of Psychiatry, 148(3),* 306–317.

211 *do not find them overwhelmingly blissful:* Conley, K. M., Toledano, A. Y., Apfelbaum, J. L., & Zacny, J. P. (1997). The modulating effects of a cold water stimulus on opioid effects in volunteers. *Psychopharmacology, 131,* 313–320.

Chapter Nine: "Mom Is Lying. Mom Is Hurting Me. Please Call the Police."

232 *Please call the police:* Hanson, E. (2000, April 14). Jurors are asked to terminate parental rights in abuse case. *Houston Chronicle.*

235   be *affected by the environment*: Read, J., Perry, B. D., Moskowitz, A., & Connolly, J. (2001). The contribution of early traumatic events to schizophrenia in some patients: A traumagenic neurodevelopmental model. *Psychiatry, 64(4)*, 319–345; Anda, R. F., Felitti, R. F., Walker, J., Whitfield, C., Bremner, D. J., Perry, B. D., Dube, S. R., & Giles, W. G. (2006). The enduring effects of childhood abuse and related experiences: A convergence of evidence from neurobiology and epidemiology. *European Archives of Psychiatric and Clinical Neuroscience, 256(3)*, 174–186.

237   *ultimately convicted of the murders*: Talan, J. & Firstman, R. (1998). *The death of innocents: A true story of murder, medicine, and high-stake science*. New York: Bantam.

237   *killed eight of the babies*: Southall, D. P., Plunkett, M. C., Banks, M. W., Falkov, A. F., & Samuels, M. P. (1997, November). Covert video recordings of life-threatening child abuse: Lessons for child protection. *Pediatrics, 100(5)*, 735–760.

237   *murder until proved otherwise*: Dyer, O. (2004, January 3). Meadow faces GMC over evidence given in child death cases. *British Medical Journal, 328(7430)*, 9.

238   *convictions have already been overturned*: UK Health Minister orders review of 285 cot death murders. (2004, January 20). *Medical News Today*; Sally Clark Doctor wins GMC Case. (2006, February 17). *BBC News*.

238   *unneeded and painful medical procedures*: Schreier, H. (1993). *Hurting for love: Munchausen by proxy syndrome* (p. 25). New York: Guilford Press.

Chapter Ten: The Kindness of Children

243   *brain-related functional problems*: Perry, B. D. (2002). Childhood experience and the expression of genetic potential: What childhood neglect tells us about nature and nurture. *Brain and Mind, 3*, 79–100; Perry, B. D. & Pollard, D. (1997). Altered brain development following global neglect in early childhood. *Society For Neuroscience*, [Proceedings from Annual Meeting] New Orleans.

Chapter Eleven: Healing Communities

262   *the number was just five*: Burguiere, A. & Klapisch-Zuber, C., et. al. (Eds.) (1996). A history of the family, volume I: Distant worlds, ancient worlds and A history of the family, volume II: The impact of modernity. Boston: Harvard University Press.

262   *26 percent of Americans live alone*: Morrow, J. A (2003, November 1). Place for one. American Demographics.

262   *had an episode of serious depression*: Klerman, G. L. & Weissman, M. M. (1989, April 21). Increasing rates of depression. Journal of the American Medical Association. 261(15), 2229–2235.

263   *factor of ten in recent decades*: Burke, K. C., Burke, J. D. Jr., Rae, D. S., & Regier, D. A. (1991, September). Comparing age at onset of major depression and other psychiatric disorders by birth cohorts in five US community populations. Archives of General Psychiatry, 48(9), 789–795.

266   *from a grandparent, can make*: Else, L. (2006, April 8). Meet the Alloparents. New Scientist.

270   *by the time she turns eighteen*: American Psychiatric Association. (1998). Psychiatric effects of media violence. APA Online.

Chapter Twelve: A Picture, Not a Label

285   *For example, a retrospective study in a representative sample of 9,282 adults*: McLaughlin, K. A., Green, J. G., Gruber, M. J., Sampson, N. A., Zaslavsky, A. M., & Kessler, R. C. (2010). Childhood adversities and adult psychopathology in the National Comorbidity Survey Replication (NCS-R) III: Associations with functional impairment related to DSM-IV disorders. *Psychological Medicine*, 40(5), 847–859. http://doi.org/10.1017/S0033291709991115

286   *As the former head of the National Institute of Mental Health, Tom Insel, once put it*: Szalavitz, M. Mental Health Researchers Reject Psychiatry's New Diagnostic 'Bible.' *TIME* online, May 7, 2013. Accessed 2/24/17 at http://healthland.time.com/2013/05/07/as-psychiatry-introduces-dsm-5-research-abandons-it/

286   *As Insel wrote*: Insel, T.R. Transforming Diagnosis. Blog of the National Institute on Mental Health. April 29, 2013. Accessed 2/24/17 at https://www.nimh.nih.gov/about/directors/thomas-insel/blog/2013/transforming-diagnosis.shtml

Chapter Commentary

306   *For every one dollar invested in high quality early childhood programs like preschool and support for new parents* Perry, B.D. & Jackson, A. (2014) Long and winding road: From neuroscience to policy, program and practice Insight: Victorian Council of Social Services Journal 9: 4-8; See also: https://heckmanequation.org/

310 *Changing the average level of activity in stress systems and their respon-siveness or reactivity*: Beeghly, Marjorie, Bruce D. Perry, and Edward Tronick. (2016) "Self-Regulatory Processes in Early Development." Oxford Handbooks Online. 2016-02-11. Oxford University Press. Accessed online, 3/1/2017 at http://www.oxfordhandbooks.com/view/10.1093/oxfordhb/9780199739134.001.0001/oxfordhb-9780199739134-e-3&gt

316 *The first ACE study, which looked at the current health of 17,000*: Felitti, Vincent J et al. Relationship of Childhood Abuse and Household Dysfunction to Many of the Leading Causes of Death in Adults. American Journal of Preventive Medicine, Volume 14, Issue 4, 245-258. See also: https://www.cdc.gov/violencepreven-tion/acestudy/about.html and www.acestudy.org

318 *In 1984, there were 102,100 children in "out of home" or substitute care—in other*: Quality Improvement Center for Adoption and Guardianship Support and Preservation. "Introduction To The Qic-Ag Permanency Continuum Framework," p.6. Accessed online 3/1/2017 at http://qic-ag.org/wp-content/uploads/2016/05/SFC-QI-CAG-00-Introduction1.pdf

321 *children in foster care has been so dramatic that the Government Account-ability Office has issued*: Kutz, G.D. "Testimony Before the Subcom-mittee on Federal Financial Management, Government Information, Federal Services, and International Security, Committee on Homeland Security and Governmental Affairs, U.S. Senate: Foster Children: HHS Guidance Could Help States Improve Oversight of Psychotropic Pre-scriptions." December 1, 2011. Accessed online 3/1/2017 at http://www.gao.gov/assets/590/586570.pdf

321 *an excellent example can be seen in the online series from the Mer-cury News by Karen de Sa)*: De Sa, K. "Drugging Our Kids." San Jose Mercury News, August 24, 2014. Accessed online on 3/1/2017 at http://extras.mercurynews.com/druggedkids/

321 *As Annette Jackson and I wrote in 2014*: Perry, B.D. & Jackson, A. (2014) Long and winding road: From neuroscience to policy, pro-gram and practice Insight: Victorian Council of Social Services Journal 9: 4-8

323 *became so pervasive that Joseph LeDoux*: LeDoux, J.E. "The Amyg-dala Is NOT the Brain's Fear Center." Psychology Today Blogs, 8/10/2015. Accessed 3/1/2017 at https://www.psychologytoday.com/blog/i-got-mind-tell-you/201508/the-amygdala-is-not-the-brains-fear-center

324 *In recent landmark cases, including two Supreme Court cases*: Gra-

ham V. Florida, 130 Supreme Court. 2011. Miller v. Alabama, 567 U.S. Supreme Court. 2013.

324 *The ChildTrauma Academy has been involved in educating*: Perry, B.D., Griffin, G., Davis, G., Perry, J.A. & Perry, R.D. (2017) The impact of neglect, trauma and maltreatment on neurodevelopment: Implications for the juvenile justice system in *The Wiley-Blackwell Handbook of Forensic Neuroscience* (Anthony R. Beech, Adam J. Carter, Ruth E. Mann & Pia Rotshtein Eds.) John Wiley & Sons Ltd (London) See also: Griffin, G., E.J. Germain, and R.G. Wilkerson. 2012. "Using a Trauma-Informed Approach in Juvenile Justice Institutions." Journal of Child and Adolescent Trauma 5: 271-283.

338 *a remarkably effective organization called A Home Within, founded by Dr. Toni Heineman*: Toni Heineman, June Madsen Clausen, Saralyn C. Ruff, Wendy Von Wiederhold, Psychoanalytic Social Work, 2012. For as long as it takes: Relationship-based play therapy for children in foster care. See also: Ruff, S. C., Aguilar, R., & Clausen, J. M. (2016). An exploratory study of mental health interventions with infants and young children in foster care. Journal of Family Social Work. doi:10.1 080/10522158.2016.1181128

344 *one common example is the "point and level" system often used in residential programs*: Mohr, W. K., A. Martin, J. N. Olson, A. J. Pumariega, and N. Branca. 2009. "Beyond Point and Level Systems: Moving Toward Child-centered Programming." American Journal of Orthopsychiatry 79: 8-18. Accessed December 29, 2014. doi: 10.1037/a0015375

346 *CPS has been around for over twenty years and incorporates the key principles we teach in the NMT*: Pollastri, A., Epstein, L., Heath, G., and Ablon, J., 2013. The Collaborative Problem Solving Approach: Outcomes Across Settings. Harvard Review of Psychiatry, v. 21, p. 188-195.

Index

BRUCE D. PERRY, MD, PhD, is the senior fellow of The ChildTrauma Academy, a not-for-profit organization based in Houston, TX, and adjunct professor in the Department of Psychiatry and Behavioral Sciences at the Feinberg School of Medicine at Northwestern University in Chicago.

MAIA SZALAVITZ is an award-winning journalist who specializes in neuroscience. With Dr. Perry, she also cowrote *Born for Love: Why Empathy Is Essential—And Endangered.* Her other books include *Unbroken Brain: A Revolutionary New Way of Understanding Addiction* and *Help at Any Cost: How the Troubled-Teen Industry Cons Parents and Hurts Kids.*

Maia Szalavitz photo © Ash Fox